SNOW CAMPING

by

JO ANN CREORE

Photographs
Mike Sweet and Jo Ann Creore

Illustrations
Doug Rhyason

To Mimi

Printed in Canada

First printed in 1992 5 4 3 2 1

The publisher:
Lone Pine Publishing
206, 10426-81 Avenue
Edmonton, Alberta, Canada
T6E 1X5

Lone Pine Publishing
202A - 1110 Seymour Street
Vancouver, B.C., Canada
V6B 3N3

Canadian Cataloguing in Publication Data
Creore, Jo Ann.
Snow camping

Includes bibliographical references and index.
ISBN 1-55105-011-0

1. Snow camping. I. Title.
GV198.9.C74 1992 796.54 C92-091802-6

Cover photo and photography: *Mike Sweet and Jo Ann Creore*
Editorial: *Lloyd Dick, Debby Shoctor*
Illustrations: *Doug Rhyson*
Cover and layout design: *Beata Kurpinski*
Printing: *DW Friesen, Altona, Manitoba, Canada, R0G 0B0*

The publisher gratefully acknowledges the assistance of the Federal Department of Communications, Alberta Culture and Multiculturalism, the Canada Council, and financial support provided by the Alberta Foundation for the Arts in the production of this book.

Contents

Acknowledgements

Many people have contributed to this book, from Rick Checkland, who first introduced me to the techniques of safe winter travel, to those who have been my companions on winter outings over the years. Special thanks are due to Claire Israelson, who offered many helpful suggestions for the chapter on avalanches; to Brenda and Jim MacArthur, who read and commented on an early version of the manuscript and who posed for a number of pictures; and to Lea Callebaut, who helped put together the final draft. The book would have been far less readable without the expertise and advice of my editor, Gary Whyte. No one has contributed more than my husband, Mike Sweet — he took many of the photographs and collaborated closely on the content of the book from the very beginning. Any errors or shortcomings are solely my responsibility.

Introduction

Barely two decades ago, backpackers who camped in the snow were considered odd by their friends and unworthy of notice by outdoor equipment manufacturers. Today the selection of winter backpacking gear is almost as great as it is for summer activities. Cross-country skis suitable for off-trail use, improved fibres for clothing and sleeping bags, lighter and stronger 4-season tents, and packs specifically designed for ski touring all help to make winter touring safe, convenient and comfortable. Even though sleeping in the snow may still seem an odd way to spend one's time, more and more people are discovering that winter camping is not only possible but also a lot of fun.

Snow camping can be enjoyed in North America from the Sierras to Maine, from New York to Alaska, and almost everywhere in Canada. The main exceptions are some mountain areas and the polar region, where weather and terrain are so brutal that your only satisfaction arises from winning the battle to survive, not from the pleasures of camping. The techniques outlined in this book will not take you to the North Pole. But they are suitable for all conditions that you are likely to encounter, whether your idea of winter backpacking is to snowshoe a local trail that you have hiked in summer or to wander an arctic landscape with no

heated lodges, no trail signs and no rescue service. As well, the knowledge gained here can be essential to survival or enjoyment no matter what winter activity you are engaged in — day touring on skis or snowshoes, snowmobiling, hunting, ice fishing, or simply chopping wood, shovelling snow or going for a walk on a cold day.

HOW TO USE THIS BOOK

Much of this book is about keeping warm. Winter clothing and shelter are designed to combat various types of heat loss, and must be selected carefully according to the external conditions you will face. Procedures you use while travelling and in camp will be determined mainly by the requirements and limitations of the human body operating in a cold environment.

Chapter One presents the basic principles of keeping warm and safe in the winter wilderness. Subsequent chapters are written with the assumption that you understand these initial concepts.

Chapters Two through Eight cover the equipment you need to enjoy snow camping in any region of North America — how to select and buy it, how to use and care for it. If you are new to winter camping, you should read these chapters carefully. More experienced, well-equipped readers may prefer to pick and choose among the topics which interest them.

The remaining chapters deal with techniques which will allow you to explore the winter world safely and enjoyably. These chapters complement, but do not replace, instruction in relevant skills and procedures which are themselves the subject of books and courses. In particular, it is the reader's responsibility to obtain competent instruction in first aid, CPR, skiing or snowshoeing and, where relevant, avalanche awareness, mountaineering and glacier travel.

RISK

Just as summer backpacking exposes the participant to certain hazards, so too does winter camping. The dangers of cold, isolation, avalanches, unbridged water crossings and wildlife can be minimized by intelligent application of the procedures described in this manual, but they can never be completely eliminated. Winter camping skills can't be learned entirely by just reading a book — they must be practiced, preferably with experienced guidance or in non-threatening conditions. Beginner and intermediate winter campers should seek knowledgeable companions, attempt trips that are within their capabilities, always let someone know where they are going and when they expect to return, and err on the side of caution.

1.

Entering the world of winter camping

WHY CAMP IN THE WINTER?

There's a dusting of snow above the golden larches near Lake Louise. Rimmed leaves refract the morning sunlight as we brush the frost from our tent and warm our hands over steaming mugs of tea. Winter is returning to the back country. For most people it is time to put away their camping gear. For Mike and me the season is just beginning.

In the Canadian Rockies, where snow lingers on the high trails until mid-July, summer is a brief interlude. Even in the lower 48 states, a backpacker who ventures forth only in warm weather may spend most of the year at home. Yet with surprisingly little difficulty, you can extend your backpacking season. How? By learning to camp in the snow.

Snow camping can be as simple as a weekend spent following animal tracks in a nearby park or as elaborate as a multi-week ski tour in Alaska or northern Canada. In many areas, the back-country traveller is less restricted in winter. With a thick blanket of snow on the ground, you can leave the trail and, using low-impact techniques, camp almost anywhere without damaging the terrain. In fact, once you realize that in winter the mosquitoes are dead, the bears are asleep and the mud and muskeg are frozen, you may actually feel a twinge of regret when the rivers once again begin to run and the land turns green.

GETTING STARTED

Are you ready to try winter camping?

If you backpack in the summer, are able to carry your home on your back, can establish and break camp and generally cope cheerfully with living outdoors, you have the basic skills needed for snow camping. If you have never backpacked, we suggest that you begin with day trips the first winter and develop your camping skills in warmer, less demanding conditions next summer.

Companions

What else do you need? At the very least, a partner. Solo winter travel can be immensely satisfying, but until you know how to deal with the risks involved, go with other people. Most authorities tell you never to go alone under any circumstances. Since some individualists, including myself, do it anyway, we have included a short section on solo touring later in the book.

A group of four is the safest minimum for wilderness outings (if there is an accident, two go for help while one stays with the victim), but if you and your partner are on your own, you can still develop your skills without endangering yourselves. You will need to be conservative in your destinations, at least at first. You should not, for example, attempt overnight trips in mountainous avalanche terrain, to remote areas, or in extreme cold without competent companions. There are, however, many rewarding tours that you can undertake with confidence. This book will help you make appropriate plans.

Instruction

If your community has an outdoor club, you may be able to take a course on winter camping from them. Clubs often schedule outings which allow beginners to learn from more experienced members. Or you may know people who backpack on skis or snowshoes and who would be willing to include you in their excursions.

It is wise to find out a little about the qualifications of anyone who wants to lead you into the winter wilderness, especially if the trip is more ambitious than you would try on your own. People may be very "experienced" in the sense that they have backpacked in winter for several years without mishap, but they may never have encountered situations which require real expertise. Don't be afraid to ask if your leader has training in first aid and CPR or has led a variety of trips, including some that are more challenging than the one you are planning. If your trip will be in the mountains, make **certain** that your leader is trained in avalanche awareness and rescue. Ask how the group will be organized, if any instruction will be offered and what safety procedures will be followed. A good leader will welcome such questions and will answer them fully.

Professional guides are used more commonly in Europe than in North America, but that is no reason to spurn their services. Guides have much to teach you and they can also ensure that your excursion is both safe and enjoyable. They sometimes operate back-country lodges and often sign on to lead ski camps or tours for outdoor clubs.

Skis or snowshoes?

Perhaps you don't ski very well, or not at all. Why not try snowshoes? They are ideally suited to flat terrain where trees and brush are tightly spaced and also have a place in the mountains. They are less expensive, require less training to use than skis and encourage you to enjoy nature at a slower pace.

Skiing is the most popular method of travelling on snow. The more proficient you are the more you will enjoy touring, but minimal technique will take you far. I made a ski ascent of Mount Logan, the highest peak in Canada, with nothing more sophisticated than a strong snowplow and the ability to traverse and kick turn. For winter backpacking, you need to be able to control your speed, stop, and avoid skiing into trees and over cliffs. Take some lessons, but remember that neither the free-striding nordic style nor the graceful telemark will necessarily help you carry a 20 kg (44 lb.) pack down a steep, icy trail.

Very few people ski elegantly with a heavy pack. The main objective is to stay on your feet, since putting yourself back together consumes as much energy as climbing a small hill. Mike and I have worn climbing skins on descents, taken off our skis and walked (permissible only if the track is hard or will not be used by other skiers), and occasionally sat down and slid. The back country is no place for pretensions.

Physical fitness

Your physical fitness is another factor in deciding what winter tours, if any, you should undertake. Exhaustion may be little more than an embarrassment in the summer, but in cold weather it can be deadly. You don't have to be a marathoner, but reasonable aerobic conditioning and enough strength to carry a fairly heavy pack are essential. In general, you require a higher level of fitness for a trip in winter than for the same itinerary in summer.

Start slowly

Finally, there is no need to leap directly into overnight winter camping. You can develop your skills, fitness and confidence on day trips. You can book a holiday at a back-country lodge where you ski every day with a leader, returning to warmth and a good meal in the evening. You can take your first backpacking trips to established shelters. As you become more at home in the winter wilderness, the prospect of sleeping in the snow, whether in a tent or snow cave, will seem less daunting.

BASIC CONSIDERATIONS: HOW HEAT IS LOST AND RETAINED

Snow camping is fun if you know how to deal with the special problems of winter. No problem looms larger, especially for the beginning camper, than keeping warm. In the back country, the primary source of heat is your own body. If you understand how the heat you generate is lost and how to prevent that loss, you can be comfortable in virtually any conditions. Ideally, of course, you will not tackle arctic temperatures until you are at ease with moderate ones — nothing dampens enthusiasm like a weekend of shivering.

Whatever the temperature, the principles of heat conservation are the same. Heat can be lost by radiation, evaporation, convection or conduction. In simpler terms: 1) Remember why birds fluff out their feathers when it's cold; 2) Stay dry; 3) Stay out of the wind; and 4) Don't sit in a snow bank.

Why birds fluff out their feathers (Heat loss by radiation)

When the winter sky is bright and clear at night, expect the temperature to drop. When clouds obscure the stars, the night will be warmer. Clouds prevent heat from radiating away and dispersing in the upper atmosphere by reflecting it back towards the earth. Radiative heat loss affects your body as well as the earth. Your clothing and shelter act like clouds to retain heat around you, sometimes by reflecting it back, but more often by forming an insulating barrier that heat cannot pass through easily.

The most effective insulation in the back country is based on small pockets of trapped air. The feathers of birds, especially when fluffed out, and the fur coats of animals create many air pockets next to their bodies. Our human skin is useless for this task, so we have to cover ourselves in something that will perform the same function. Animal hides and goose down work well, as do some synthetic fibres, multiple layers of clothing, and, so long as you don't come into direct contact with it, snow (snow is mostly air).

Those parts of the body where blood flows nearest the skin require especially good insulation. In the hands and feet, blood vessels respond constantly to temperature, dilating to increase blood flow and promote heat loss when the body is too hot, constricting to reduce blood flow and reduce heat loss when the body senses a chill. Restricting the flow of blood conserves warmth in the vital organs at the expense of the extremities, which rapidly grow numb with cold or even suffer frostbite.

Birds depend on their feathers for insulation.

The head and neck also contain many blood vessels close to the skin, but these never constrict. Up to half of your heat loss can occur from your head. Mountaineers have a saying, "If your feet are cold, put on your hat." This is excellent advice even if your head doesn't feel cold. To restore blood flow to cold hands you need to do more than put on an extra pair of mitts (although that will help). You really need to warm your whole body, and a crucial step in that process is stopping heat loss from your head. You can keep warm by putting insulation between your body — especially your head, neck, hands and feet — and the cold air.

Stay dry (Heat loss by evaporation)

When a nurse rubs alcohol on your skin prior to giving an injection, you feel instant cooling. That is because alcohol evaporates very rapidly from the surface of the skin, taking some heat with it. While hiking, you may have enjoyed the luxury of dipping your bandana in a stream and placing it on your head or neck. As the water evaporates it cools you.

What you welcome on a hot summer day can be dangerous in winter. While skiing, your body generates more heat than it needs and perspires to keep your core temperature from rising too high. If your clothing retains this perspiration, it will be there, next to your skin, when you take a rest stop. Now you are no longer producing excess heat, but the evaporation continues. Soon you are shivering, and the effect is not much different from having someone throw a pail of water on you.

Staying warm in the winter means staying dry. You must minimize perspiration by regulating your pace and adjusting your clothing to maintain the proper body temperature. You will always produce some sweat, of course, but you can reduce evaporative cooling by wearing the right kind of clothing next to your skin. (See Chapter Two for details.)

A second type of evaporative heat loss is more difficult to prevent. When the outside air is cold, it must be warmed in your breathing passages before it reaches your lungs. Warming the air lowers its relative humidity. The body therefore re-humidifies it virtually to 100% saturation, losing heat by evaporation in the process. The colder the air, the greater the evaporative heat loss. Wearing a scarf or face mask over your mouth and nose in extreme cold will warm the air a little before it enters the breathing passages.

Stay out of the wind (Heat loss by convection)

The weather report gives the current temperature as -7° C (20° F) with a wind speed of 24 kph (15 mph) and a windchill of -21° C (-6° F). What is this mysterious windchill that always seems to make the day colder than it really is?

When you first step outside on a calm winter day you may not feel the chill for a few moments. That is because the body warms a small layer of air around it. The tendency of warm air to rise eventually disperses this layer when the surrounding environment is cold. If the layer of warm air is carried away by air currents, however, in what is called convection, cooling is instantaneous, and efforts by the body to reheat the surrounding air result in rapid and drastic heat loss.

Wind is a major and very dangerous source of heat loss for the winter traveller. Combined with extreme cold it can cause near-instant frostbite on exposed flesh and defeat any type of insulation that is not shielded. You don't really need to consult fancy charts to understand windchill. For practical purposes, simply bear in mind two principles. First, a small increase in wind speed causes a large increase in heat loss. Second, the colder the temperature, the more dangerous is any amount of wind. A slight breeze that feels pleasant in temperatures near freezing can be life threatening at -30° C.

Since it is pretty hard to tour the back country without encountering wind, your clothing and shelter must provide a small windless area for you to live in. The closely woven fabrics used in tents and the outer layers of clothing offer effective protection, as do snow caves, igloos and back-country huts.

Another source of convection is the movement of your body through the air. That is why you sometimes get frostbite on your face on a fast downhill ski run even when there is no wind. The small movements you make inside your clothes or sleeping bag can also send heat drifting away through any opening. Since warm air rises, you can lose heat from an unfastened collar while the loose cuffs on your trousers draw in cold air.

Don't sit in a snow bank (Heat loss by conduction)

If you put ice on a sprain, the area rapidly becomes cold and numb. The same thing will happen to your body if you sit or lie on the snow. Direct contact with a cold surface will rob you of heat. Some materials conduct heat away from you more quickly than others, which is why the grips on ski poles are not made of metal (skin will freeze to metal instantly in extreme cold). Winter camping requires that you use specialized mattresses for sleeping and pay particular attention to protecting hands (which must hold all manner of cold objects) and feet (which have to stand in the snow).

Once you become adept at preventing the various kinds of heat loss, you will find camping in most winter conditions at least as pleasant as in summer. There are times, of course, when even polar bears would rather head south. If the weather deteriorates to that point, what you know about heat conservation will help keep you alive while you boost your morale with thoughts of the stories you will be able to tell when you return to civilization.

ENJOYING AND PRESERVING THE WINTER WORLD

Winter camping offers a freedom that is rare in our daily lives. When we leave the trail-head we assume full responsibility for our actions and decisions. We set our own goals, determine our own limits. There is great satisfaction in knowing that we can take care of ourselves in an unforgiving environment.

With our freedom comes a responsibility to respect both the fragility and the power of nature. We humans can no longer roam the land as simple predators, killing animals for food and clothing, using wood indiscriminately for fire and shelter, leaving our trash for nature to absorb. There are too many of us and too little wilderness. Nor can we expect society to cheerfully bear the cost of rescue when things go wrong. Lives are endangered and huge sums of money are spent each year dealing with disasters which back-country users bring on themselves. Every such accident encourages governments and property owners to restrict access and impose new regulations.

As more people enter the back country in winter, it is essential that they know how to stay out of trouble and how to leave the land at least as unspoiled as they found it. The goal of this book is to help you do just that. You can travel safely and without impact in the wildest, most remote places on earth if you have the right training, the right equipment and the sense to use both properly. You can come to grief on the tamest local trail if you behave recklessly. By tempering your ambitions with sound judgement you will help to keep the wilderness wild and open to all who seek adventure there.

A winter camp

The meadow is warm and inviting in the early March sun. Lhotse, my dog, looks at me expectantly, then wanders off to sniff at some shrubs. The sun is still high, but I cannot imagine a more beautiful campsite. I dump my pack in the snow, call Lhotse over to remove hers and we both have a good stretch. Several people pass by, bound for higher, more distant, destinations. I wave and shout a greeting, and they leave me to my solitude.

After putting up the tent, I spend a few hours carving telemark turns through the soft powder of the forest, with Lhotse in frantic pursuit. We return to camp as the sun disappears behind a mountain and the temperature plummets. I change to down clothing, and place a couple of chemical hand-warmers in my gloves. Dinner is a slow affair; in the cold, simple operations like putting the stove together and melting snow for water take a long time.
I savour the boiling hot soup and gorge on noodles and sauce.

As the thermometer heads towards -29° C, I stow the kitchen gear in a pit by the tent and retreat to my sleeping bag. Lhotse snuggles beside me — by morning she will occupy half of the mattress. I watch the stars through the open tent door, then fall asleep relaxed, renewed, in tune with myself and the world.

2.

Clothing

Snow falls early at Lake Louise. By Christmas the trails around the graceful old hotel on the lakeshore are deep in powder, and inexperienced guests on rental skis are heading into the back country. When they encounter Mike and me on the trail, they invariably ask, "Are you going camping?" Our day packs stuffed with clothing are a source of wonder. These same packs have provided timely aid to more than one skier who failed to dress for the Canadian climate.

A common error made by beginners is to dress for only one weather condition. A Lycra cross country ski suit, for example, is well-designed for gliding along a fast track, but if you must stop to repair a binding you risk hypothermia. A down jacket may keep you warm in the coldest weather but it will drench you in sweat if you try to ski in it.

Winter clothing must keep your skin dry, insulate you from the cold, vent excess heat and protect you against wind, snow or even rain. It must allow you freedom of movement, weigh as little as possible and yet be tough enough to withstand hard use. It must perform these functions in any weather and at any level of activity. No single garment can meet all of these requirements, which is why we always carry a pack even on a short day tour.

LAYERING

Winter comfort is achieved through a system of adjustable layering. Four types of layers combine to meet the body's need for insulation and protection against convective and evaporative heat loss. As your activity level and heat generation increase, you remove garments; when you slow down or begin to chill, you add garments. Layering applies to all parts of the body, not just the torso.

The inner layer

Perspiration is one of the body's chief cooling mechanisms. When we overheat we become wet with sweat. Even during sleep, moisture continually evaporates from the skin's surface, taking some heat with it. In winter, we need to encourage evaporation when we exercise but conserve heat when activity stops. The chief function of the inner layer of clothing is to deal with the moisture generated by the body. A secondary function is to provide a sheath of insulation next to the skin. No other layer contributes so much to your comfort for so little cost.

The inner layer keeps your skin dry by wicking away moisture. If this is the only layer you are wearing, as during periods of intense activity, perspiration will be wicked directly to the outside air where it will evaporate. When you wear additional layers of clothing, the perspiration you generate will be dispersed through those layers. When you stop to rest there should be little if any moisture next to your skin so that you will not be chilled by continuing evaporation.

The active middle layer

The function of this layer is to insulate while you are actively generating heat, as when skiing or digging a snow cave. Garments in this layer should also transport moisture wicked by the inner layer through to the outside air. Since the need for insulation varies with temperature, activity level and metabolism, the insulating garments must be adjustable. Two or three thin sweaters, for example, offer a wider range of temperature control than one heavy jacket. Excellent specialized, stylish clothing is on the market, but unless you face severe conditions, you can probably find much of what you need for this layer in your closet.

A complete inner layer suitable for all conditions.

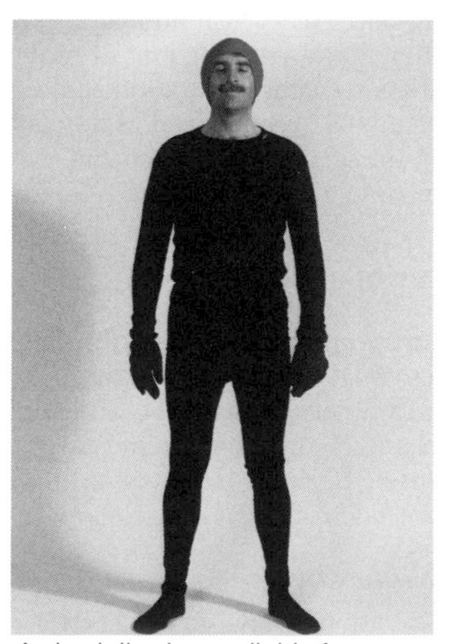

An insulating layer suitable for activity in extreme cold.

The shell layer

The shell layer protects against convective heat loss from wind. In wet snow or rain it must also keep the inner layers of clothing dry. At the same time, it must breathe so that perspiration does not soak your clothing from within. It must allow ventilation when you overheat. In very cold weather, the outer shell must be roomy enough to accommodate adequate insulation underneath.

The sedentary middle layer

Once you stop moving, your body's production of heat drops off rapidly. Any moisture in your clothing will continue to evaporate, adding to the chill. Throwing on an extra sweater may not be enough — you need down or some man-made equivalent which can trap large amounts of air and preserve every bit of warmth your body manages to generate. You will overheat seriously if you wear this layer for strenuous activity.

How the system works

One of my northern expeditions occurred during the time of the midnight sun. We often left base camp in mid-afternoon, skied, climbed and explored through the "night" and most of the next day until exhaustion

A waterproof-breathable shell layer that we use in the Canadian winter and arctic spring.

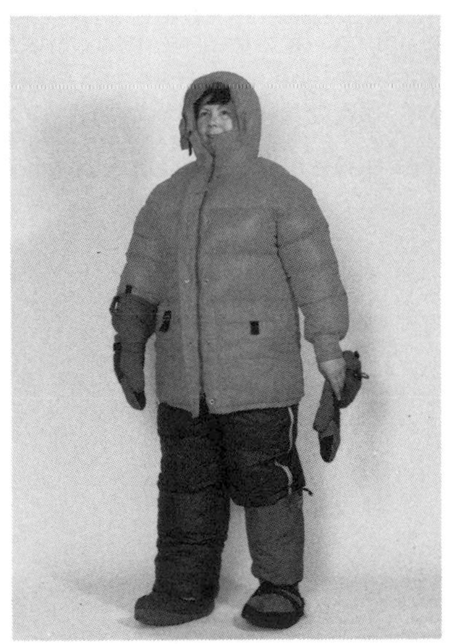

A sedentary insulating layer to wear in camp in severe cold.

overcame our desire to see what lay around the next corner. The temperature range during these trips was extreme. One minute we would be baking in the glare of a hot sun, wishing we had bathing suits, yet as soon as clouds obscured the sun, the wind would gust and the temperature drop well below freezing. We could have used a truckload of clothing to cope with the changing conditions, but we were limited by the need to travel light and fast. The layers we carried had to work well together, and we had to use them wisely.

Layering is more a principle than a specific set of garments. Control of body temperature begins with your intelligence rather than with your equipment. The goal is to remain warm and dry no matter what your level of activity, your metabolism or the outside conditions. Having the proper clothing will help you achieve that goal, but the best garments available will not cope with prolonged heavy sweating, incorrect pace or lack of common sense.

Small adjustments to the layers

When cold sets in, the body protects its major organs from heat loss by shutting down circulation to the extremities. The first sign you may have of a lowering of body temperature is cold feet or fingers. Your first priority is to prevent further chilling of the body. Since the head and neck are the areas of greatest heat loss, always add a layer to your head and cover up your neck regardless of whether or not you put on an extra sweater. Similarly, if you are too hot, remove head and neck gear. Open zippers in larger garments. Circulation increases to hands when you are overheated, so turning down mitt cuffs to expose wrists or removing the mitts altogether will help.

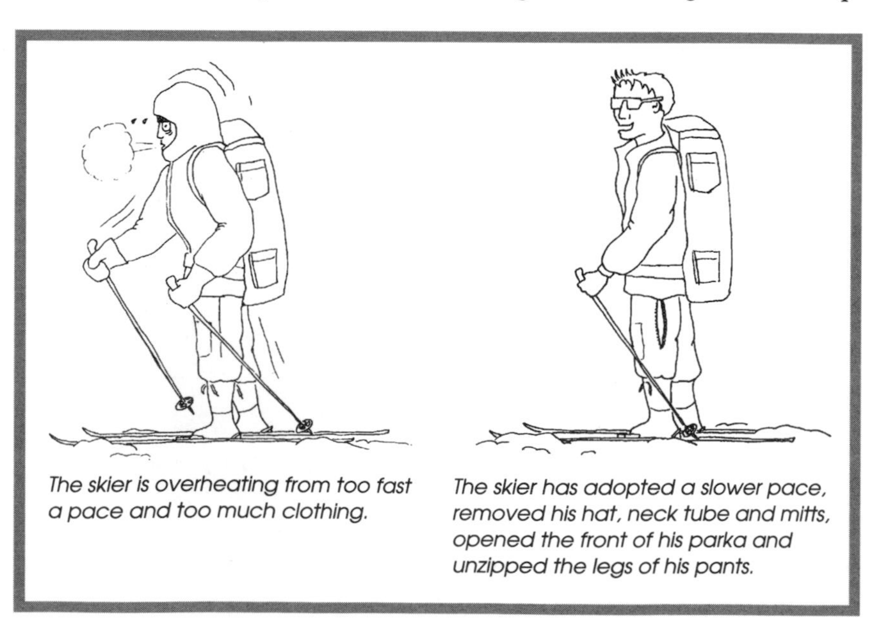

The skier is overheating from too fast a pace and too much clothing.

The skier has adopted a slower pace, removed his hat, neck tube and mitts, opened the front of his parka and unzipped the legs of his pants.

Major adjustments to the layers

If minor adjustments don't achieve the right temperature, you must remove or add large garments like a parka and sweater. Even though this requires a stop to get into the pack, overheating and chilling are serious problems that lead to dehydration, exhaustion and hypothermia. It is essential to stop as often as necessary. In particular, forget the idea that working up a sweat is a sign that you are getting a good physical workout, or that letting yourself shiver is a sign of toughness. What it mostly means is that you don't know what you are doing and are a potential liability to the rest of the party.

MATERIALS AND FABRICS

One outdoor store's recent catalogue contained such terms as: chlorofibre, fleece, lofted rib knit, pile, Versatech, Spandex, polyester, Supplex, microfibre nylon weave, polypropylene, Polartec, interlock, Lycra, Gore-Tex, Texolite insulation, Supermicroft, dryline fabric, and micro-porous polyurethane-coated. Pick up a different catalogue and you will find other terms, some generic, others trademarks. As a consumer, you need to know what properties are desirable in a particular garment and have some idea of how various materials and construction techniques affect those properties. There is no need to take an advanced course in textiles.

Until a few years ago, only natural fibres were available for outdoor garments. Although there are sound environmental reasons for using natural fibres, their tendency to absorb water is a disadvantage for the winter camper.

Cotton

Wet cotton not only has no insulating properties, it promotes heat loss from the body, making it unequaled for summer comfort but deadly in winter. Blue jeans, cotton t-shirts or sweat shirts, and corduroy knickers should all be avoided. If you feel that you must have cotton next to your skin, remember that wet cotton garments must be exchanged for dry ones as soon as your activity level drops or they will chill you. A garment that needs to be changed during the trip means yet another item in an already heavy load. The only area where cotton may be a good choice is on the feet. Some people cannot tolerate synthetic or wool inner socks — for them a thin cotton liner is acceptable.

Wool

At one time, wool was the primary material for back-country clothing. Today, you will see little of it in outdoor stores. Wool retains much of its insulating power when wet. Your perspiration-soaked underwear will keep you warm in camp but will feel clammy and heavy. Since wool dries very slowly, you are likely to be damp for most of the trip. Many people cannot wear wool next to their skin. For the middle layer, however, wool serves reasonably well, especially in loose-knit sweaters and hats, and it remains the best fabric for the insulating layer of socks.

Silk

Silk is used by a few manufacturers of outdoor underwear, either by itself or blended with wool. So long as it is dry it has a luxurious feel, but like wool and cotton it absorbs moisture. It also does not hold up well under the rough treatment of winter camping, making it particularly unsuitable for gloves and socks.

Down

Goose down is the warmest, lightest, most compressible and most expensive natural material used in outdoor clothing. Like the other natural materials we have mentioned, it absorbs water and must be protected from perspiration and external moisture at all times. It should be used exclusively for sedentary insulation.

Synthetics

For the inner layer, the materials of choice are synthetics such as polypropylene, chlorofibre and polyester, all of which may be treated or altered in various ways to improve performance. Because their fibres do not absorb moisture, these synthetics can wick perspiration from the skin to the outer layers of clothing or directly to the air.

The quality of the knitting, usually rib knit or interlock, affects how well the synthetic will fit, stretch and ventilate. Unless the garment hugs the body closely, it will not wick or insulate properly. Thinner fabrics ventilate better than thick ones. Fibres with a hollow core, or very thin fibres trap air for better insulation.

Early synthetic underwear absorbed body odour even more efficiently than it shed water. It was also known to shrink to doll-size or melt in automatic dryers and after a few wearings, pill and develop baggy knees, seat and elbows. Today you will find more durable, less odour-holding products that are relatively easy to care for. These often involve blends of materials which serve different functions, so that the same garment may wick on its inner side, absorb and evaporate on its outer side, and insulate as well.

For the middle layers, you will find a vast array of synthetic materials bearing different trademarks. The construction of the fabric — the way in which it traps air for insulation — is at least as important in this layer as the material from which the fabric is made. Fabrics which feel fuzzy, furry or rough (such as pile, fleece and loose knit) trap air better than silky or smooth ones. Pile is a mass of raised loops or tufts on one or both sides of the fabric. It can be deep or shallow. In the latter case the fabric is often called fleece, although this term is also applied to brushed fabrics. Tightly woven fabrics, with a few exceptions, provide less insulation but greater protection from the wind. Garments often combine a tight construction on one side with fuzz on the other.

Synthetic fibres such as Polarguard, Hollofil and Quallofil compete directly with down as super insulators for **the sedentary middle layer**. They are bulkier to pack than down but are less affected by moisture.

There is no question that Gore-Tex has revolutionized **the shell layer**, by combining for the first time the properties of being waterproof and breathable. Gore-Tex is a microporous membrane which keeps out water yet allows vapour to pass through. It must be bonded to other fabrics before it can be used in clothing. For several years Gore-Tex controlled the market. Today there are numerous imitators, many of which use a fabric coated with microporous polyurethane, but Gore-Tex still sets a high standard because of the strict control exercised on manufacturers using the product.

If you have worn waterproof-breathable garments in a summer downpour or if you tried them several years ago, you may be less than enthusiastic about their virtues. For winter, however, even an older, worn shell of Gore-Tex or similar material will work well to keep out snow and wind yet allow some evaporation of excess moisture to take place.

For non-believers, there are many windproof fabrics available that will serve the primary function of the shell layer — they prevent convective heat loss. They are lighter than Gore-Tex and the coated fabrics but are not as warm. If you wish, you can wear additional insulation under them. Be sure to carry waterproof garments as well, just in case.

BEFORE YOU GO SHOPPING

Fashion has expanded from the downhill ski resorts into the back country. New high-tech designs for outdoor wear appear on the market every year, and the scruffy backpacker in hand-me-downs is almost a museum piece. A few principles will help you avoid bankruptcy as you assemble a basic winter wardrobe:

- Keep it simple. Outdoor clothing should be easy to put on, take off and adjust.
- Look for versatility. A garment that can be worn in a variety of temperatures and conditions is better than one with a single use.
- Look for quality of workmanship. Seams that come apart and zippers that break are difficult to repair in the back country.
- Buy gear adequate for the conditions you will actually face, not the exotic expedition you hope to take some day.
- Evaluate the features on every garment as: **essential** for your purposes; **convenient** but not necessary; or **useless** for your kind of backpacking. You will save money by purchasing only essential features.

IN-DEPTH ANALYSIS OF CLOTHING NEEDS

Each part of the body has specific clothing requirements:

- The head requires continual adjustment of layers to control body temperature.
- The upper body requires easy adjustment of layers to cope with major changes in activity or outside conditions.
- The lower body requires some adjustment for temperature control and maximum convenience for attending to bodily functions.
- The hands must be protected while performing the many actions we demand of them and also require adjustment for temperature control.
- The feet require insulation from the cold, especially conductive heat loss. Footwear cannot easily be adjusted on the trail.

Head

Because the head and neck are so important in regulating body temperature, you may find it convenient to have a choice of fabrics and weight in hats. Thin, tightly-knit fabric offers some wind protection and takes up little room in pack or pocket. A light wool or synthetic stretchy knit hat ("toque" in Canada) is ideal for use on a cold day when you are working

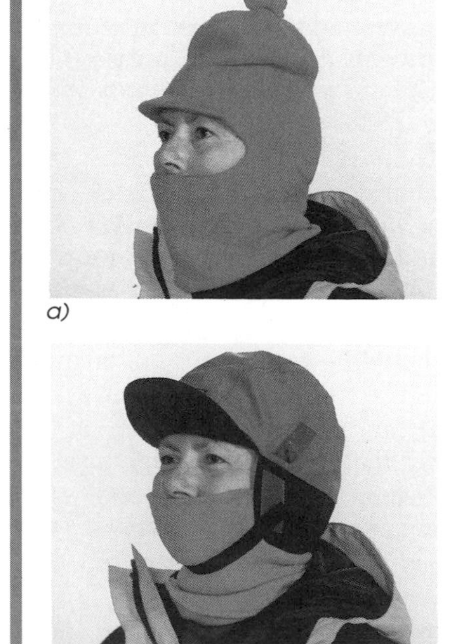

a)

b)

***a)** The versatile balaclava may be all you need to begin with. It can be folded up so that it covers only the top of the head, pulled down over the ears, extended to protect the neck, and then brought over the face to cover everything but the eyes. Balaclavas are available in natural and synthetic knits and synthetic pile, and in a variety of weights to suit different climates. A silk balaclava fits into any pocket and makes a good inner layer under a hat or in a sleeping bag. The main problem with these garments is their tendency either to stretch with use so that they are no longer snug to your face or to be so tight that you end up with the chin piece between your teeth.*

***b)** The functions of the balaclava can be split between two pieces: a hat for the head and ears, and a knit or fleece neck tube which can be pulled up over the lower half of the face.)*

hard and sweating but still need some protection for your head. Bulky loose-knit hats provide more insulation because of the air they trap, but little protection from the wind. Pile and fleece, if the exterior is tightly knit, offer both warmth and a little wind resistance.

Shell hats for extreme cold should protect the ears and as much of the neck, face and chin as possible. Since most winter shell parkas have hoods, you may omit the shell layer hat if you tour in moderate conditions where wind protection for the head is seldom needed. I like the added versatility of a separate shell hat, however, because hoods tend to be too hot in anything but a gale.

a)

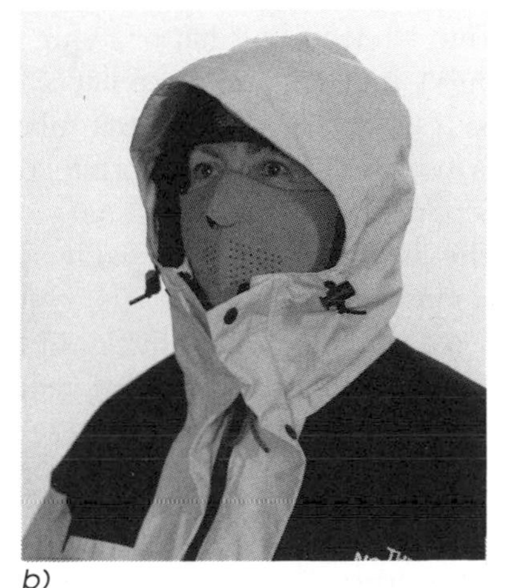

b)

c)

a) *The hood of a lightweight parka raised to shield head, face and neck.*

b) *For really extreme conditions, a neoprene face mask is about the only thing that will prevent frostbite. It also makes you feel warmer all over by blocking heat loss from the blood vessels in the face. Vents for nose and mouth allow you to breathe.*

c) *Sometimes when you stop along the trail you aren't chilled enough to put on a full down parka, yet you need a little extra protection for your head and neck. Most down and synthetic fill parkas have attached hoods. Consider a separate down hood that covers the neck and shoulders and can be carried in the top pocket of your pack for easy access.*

Winter backpackers may encounter extreme heat as well as cold. Sun and snow can turn a meadow or glacier into a reflective oven. For hot, sunny days a sun hat with a visor to shade the face is essential. I find that a baseball cap with mesh top works well, as do gardening hats. A strap to keep the hat on your head in the wind is desirable. Added sun protection can be provided by a cotton bandana that fits under the hat and shades the neck and ears.

Many people like to wear a head band over the ears and forehead. This doesn't contribute much warmth, but it keeps the hair and sweat out of your eyes and holds your glasses in place.

Selection of garments for the head, face and neck:

- Balaclavas in varying weights and materials
- Thin stretchy knit hat or toque
- Bulky knit, pile or fleece hat
- Knit or stretchy fleece neck tube
- Windproof shell hat with integral insulation
- Separate windproof shell hat
- The hood of your shell parka
- Neoprene face mask
- Separate down or synthetic fill hood
- The hood of your down or synthetic-fill parka
- Baseball or gardening hat with visor for sun
- Cotton bandana
- Head band

Upper body

You will need a full range of layers for the upper body because most of the major layering adjustments should be made here — changing sweaters is much easier than changing pants.

Synthetic **outdoor underwear** ranges from fabric so thin that you can read a well-lit page of print through it, to expedition weight, which is usually smooth on the outside with pile or fleece inside. Unless you face extreme cold or have a sedentary pursuit like ice fishing, you should opt for a fairly thin fabric, which copes better with sweat.

Desirable features of undershirts

- The undershirt should hug the body both to wick effectively and to provide a layer of insulation in the air pockets of the weave.
- The fabric must stretch to allow freedom of movement, yet return to its original shape to avoid baggy pouches which neither insulate nor wick.
- The shirt-tail should be long enough to keep your back covered when you bend forward.

- Long sleeves are best for winter use. Cuffs should stay in place when you put other garments on over them but must not grip so tightly that they constrict blood flow.
- A zippered neck vent, especially if combined with a snug-fitting high collar, allows maximum adjustment for temperature control, but some people find a high collar too hot. Buttons and snaps are okay in moderate climates but difficult to fasten in extreme cold.
- Pockets are useful since the undershirt is often the only garment worn on the upper torso while skiing. You may have to add your own, since few manufacturers provide them.

Although a garment's reaction to moisture is not a primary factor in choosing fabrics for **the middle insulating layer**, it should be considered. Perspiration will be wicked into middle garments by your underwear. If you are sweating heavily or you fall while skiing or a tree dumps a load of snow on you, your mid-layer may get wet. Most of the synthetic piles and fleeces marketed today for outdoor use do not absorb water and they dry very quickly. For serious winter use, synthetics are better than wool.

a)

b)

a) *A typical lightweight undershirt.*

b) *A polyester double-sided fleece sweater specifically designed to insulate during winter activities such as ski touring and ice climbing. The sweater is short, with a partially elasticized waistband to keep wind from entering. This length makes it suitable for use with a climbing harness. If you wear bib pants when skiing, the short waist will not leave your back exposed, and the sweater does not interfere with the hip belt of a pack. A longer sweater would be preferable if you wear waist-length pants.*

Useful features of sweaters for winter activity

- Full-length front zipper, making it easier to adjust for temperature control than a pullover style.
- Zipper backed by a flap to keep heat in and wind out.
- Zipper flap that extends slightly above the top of the zipper to protect the face from cold metal.
- High collar which covers the neck and lower part of the face when raised.
- Top of zipper trimmed smooth so as not to irritate the skin when the collar is raised.
- Cuffs elasticized for wind and snow protection.
- Zippers under the arms for ventilation.
- Several zippered pockets roomy enough to hold a compact camera and most of the small garments you will constantly put on and take off for temperature control, in addition to your hands if you need to warm them.
- Machine washable and dryable.
- Stitched and finished with an attention to detail that characterizes clothing suitable for the most extreme conditions, where failure of a seam or zipper could spell disaster.

Sweaters suitable for extreme conditions carry a hefty price tag. Since you probably won't want to tackle an arctic tour too soon, consider the alternatives below. Fleece and pile sweaters can be found in a wide range of weights and prices. Suitable wool sweaters can often be found in your normal wardrobe. In all cases pockets are a desirable feature, and two or three lighter garments are more versatile than a heavy one. High necks should be vented by a zipper or they will be too hot for strenuous activity.

Less expensive sweater alternatives

Lightweight:

- A stretchy (knit) wool or synthetic pullover.
- A stretch fleece pullover.
- A fleece or wool-knit vest.

Heavier:

- A deep-pile sweater with full front zip.
- A loose-knit wool or synthetic sweater, either pullover or front opening.
- A double-sided fleece sweater.

Avoid any garment with a large percentage of cotton, filled garments, and garments which combine insulation with an exterior wind shell. The latter do not breathe sufficiently to cope with heavy activity and are less versatile because you cannot separate the layers.

A good **shell parka** for winter should be made of a very rugged fabric. It will be stiff and heavy, but it will keep you warmer than a softer, thinner garment. As well, it will survive countless snags, crashes and abrasions.

Useful features for shell parkas

- Full-length front zipper for ventilation.
- Integral hood that cinches tight by means of a drawstring.
- High zippered collar and tailoring of hood to cover lower face and protect sides of face from wind.
- Shielded zipper and drawstring which cannot freeze to your face.
- Double draft flaps and snap or Velcro closures on front zipper for wind protection.
- Drawstring at waist to keep out wind.
- Cuffs reinforced and sealed with Velcro (elastic may get wet, snaps are awkward to close and may freeze).

a)

b)

c)

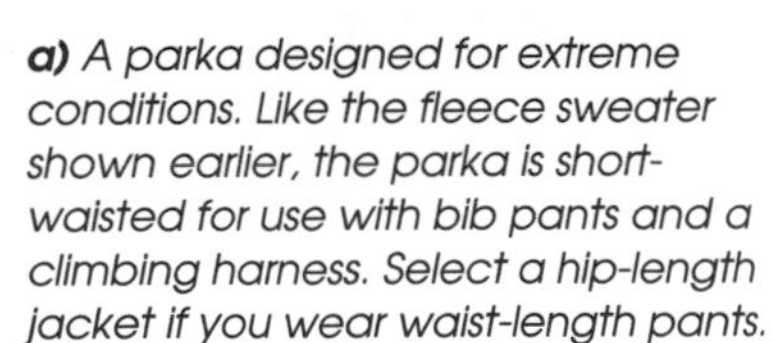

a) *A parka designed for extreme conditions. Like the fleece sweater shown earlier, the parka is short-waisted for use with bib pants and a climbing harness. Select a hip-length jacket if you wear waist-length pants.*

b, c) *The illustrated* ***down parka system*** *consists of a hooded parka and a down sweater. Both garments have sewn-through seams, but the seams on parka and sweater are in different places, so wind and cold cannot penetrate when both pieces are worn. We find the system too warm for most conditions, carrying only the outer parka in midwinter, switching to the sweater in spring.*

- A mesh lining and underarm zippers for ventilation.
- Large outside pockets with zippers and draft flaps.
- Internal breast pocket large enough to hold climbing skins.
- All seams taped to prevent leakage around thread holes.
- Shoulders and elbows reinforced to resist abrasion.

Many of the above features can be found on parkas which cost half as much as the one shown and are more than adequate for most winter use.

Avoid heavy parkas with a quilted or fill lining — they will be much too warm and allow no adjustment for ventilation. For the same reason we do not recommend anorak (pullover) shells, although a lightweight anorak windbreaker is acceptable in milder climates.

Desirable features of parkas for extreme cold

- Length to cover the hips.
- Hand-warmer pockets.
- Large cargo pockets.
- External draft flaps on zippers, with snaps, or preferably, Velcro closures for wind protection.
- Attached hood with drawstring and high collar to cover face and neck.
- Cuffs sealed by Velcro.
- Drawstrings at waist and below hips to keep out wind.
- An inside pocket large enough to hold a water bottle (handy while cooking on frosty nights).
- Top quality down fill, which has the best weight-to-insulation value, compresses easily, and lasts for years.

SYNTHETIC-FILL PARKAS

In very cold temperatures, snow is dry and your down parka will not absorb moisture from the outside (you can still soak it from within if you work up a sweat). If you camp in milder conditions, however, the snow will be wetter, and there is always the possibility of rain or mist. Synthetic fill will not absorb moisture—therefore damp synthetic fill is warmer than damp down. A synthetic-fill parka is also easier to dry in the field, making it attractive for longer expeditions. Neither type of fill provides much warmth when thoroughly wet. Down loses all its loft, and wet synthetic chills you through evaporation unless you have a non-breathable shell to put over it.

Synthetic fill is much cheaper than down and will keep you just as warm if you have room to carry it. Manufacturers' claims notwithstanding, parkas made with synthetic fill take up more room in your pack than down parkas with a similar insulating value. I would recommend synthetic fill if you camp in conditions which don't require a lot of insulation, if you camp in wet climes, or if your budget is limited and your pack roomy.

There are other economical alternatives to the down parka. You could buy a down jacket without hood and combine it with a separate hood, such as we discussed in the section on head gear. It is also possible to combine a light fill jacket with a fill vest to give extra warmth to the torso.

Avoid any fill with a lot of feathers. If you can't afford quality down, then synthetic fill is usually a better buy. Avoid as well any jacket with a heavy outer shell. These are often marketed to hunters but are much too bulky for winter backpacks. Also avoid waterproof-breathable fabrics in a parka. The garment will be less compressible, and the benefits do not match the added expense. You will have a shell parka, in any case, which should be large enough to wear over the fill parka.

Summary of clothing for the upper body

- Synthetic long-sleeved undershirt, preferably thin or medium weight.
- An assortment of sweaters, either synthetic or wool.
- Waterproof-breathable shell with hood, or a windproof shell and extra rain jacket.
- Down or synthetic-fill parka with hood.

Lower body

The outdoor practicum weekend for one winter camping course I taught coincided with a severe cold spell. Despite the temperature, our group was coping well and making good progress along the trail when we paused for a rest stop. As usual, the women disappeared into the bushes, and one failed to return. When I finally went after her, I was met by a furious denunciation of female anatomy and of my recommendations for clothing it. The woman had taken to heart my insistence on the value of multiple layers. She was wearing a shell layer of bib pants with a drop seat, mid-layer fleece bib pants with a crotch zipper, and inner pants with an elastic waist that had to be pulled down. She managed to get everything lowered to answer nature's call, but in order to put the outfit back together she had to strip off most of the clothing from her whole body.

Exposing your rear to an icy wind will never be a pleasant experience, but proper coordination of all layers on the lower body will at least shorten the ordeal. For women, who really have no option but to bare all, a well-matched opening system for garments is essential. There are three basic designs: a zipper under the crotch that extends far up both the front and back sides; a drop seat, which may be secured by buttons or Velcro in underwear, or by a rainbow-shaped zipper over the buttocks in a shell garment; and pants which simply pull down. The crotch and drop-seat openings are probably warmer, but pulling everything down at once is probably quicker. It is possible, though less efficient, to combine two different opening systems if you select carefully. For example, pull-down outer pants can be matched with either a crotch or drop-seat opening on inner layers. Pull-down inners work reasonably well with a drop-seat outer layer if the outer garment also has a front opening that extends to the waist, allowing you to grasp the waist band of the inner pants and pull them up. Putting three different systems together guarantees disaster.

The **inner layer** for the lower body, should be of a synthetic fibre. Because you may want to use a different weight of fabric for pants and shirt, separate pants are preferable to one-piece long johns. Elastic waistbands and exposed flies for men are more convenient than buttons, zippers or other fasteners. The pants should not bind in the crotch and should remain at your waist, not ride down when you bend over or raise a leg. Stretch synthetic briefs should be worn underneath. They are available for both men and women from Patagonia.

When I first began winter touring, everyone wore wool knickers over their underwear and carried light wind pants. Wool knickers, especially tweed, are warm, shed snow, allow full mobility and are fairly windproof. They are out of fashion at the moment, but if you can find them, they make a good second layer which seldom requires an outer shell. Lycra, which stretches but is not very warm, and corduroy, which is cold when wet, are not suitable for winter knickers, although a bit of Lycra added to wool improves the stretch of the garment. If you wear knickers, you will also have to find warm knee-length socks, which, like knickers, are somewhat out of fashion.

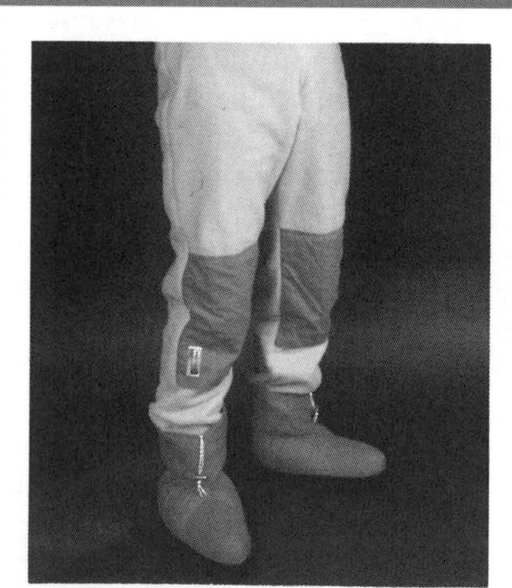

These insulating pants have full-leg zippers backed by fleece flaps, elasticized waistband and cuffs, a short front zipper and reinforced patches over the knees. Leg zippers allow you to put the pants on without removing your boots or skis. Insulating pants are also available in pile and wool.

Mike and I are wearing bib pants made of waterproof- breathable material.

Mike and I prefer to ski in Gore-Tex bib pants, which are wind- and waterproof and quite warm. We usually omit the middle insulating layer for the lower body and simply vary the weight of our underwear according to the temperature. For ice climbing, where one spends a lot of time sitting, and for skiing in extreme cold, however, we wear double-sided fleece pants.

Desirable features of shell-layer bib pants

- Full-leg zippers matched with a crotch or drop-seat zipper so that the pants can be put on or taken off without removing boots or skis. If your mid-layer fleece pants also have full-length side zips, you will be able to put them on under the bib pants without stripping, an excellent feature if you must make a long stop on a cold day.
- Joining point of leg and drop-seat zippers well below the level of the hip belt of your backpack, both to avoid discomfort and to allow easy access for ventilation.
- A front zipper, which even women will appreciate when they try to hoist and arrange their underwear after using the drop seat.
- Flaps to protect all zippers from wind.
- Small pockets on the thighs and a larger pocket on the chest.
- Patches to reinforce seat and knees. Ice climbers should look for additional reinforcement to protect the inner leg against crampons.
- Wide, adjustable suspenders that are comfortable under the shoulder straps of a pack.

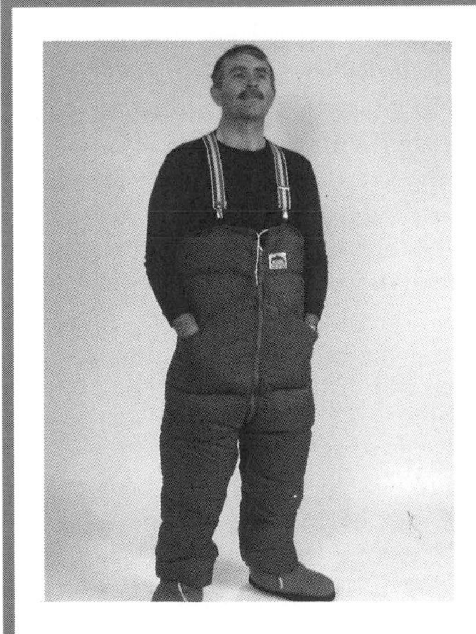

Down bib pants suitable for extreme cold. These are not baffled, but the legs zip together to form a half sleeping bag in an emergency or planned bivouac.

Shell pants come in more varieties than parkas because the requirements range from minimal to technical. If you wear adequate insulation underneath, any kind of wind shell will do for most purposes, although full-leg zippers are highly desirable. If you expect to wallow in wet snow, you want a waterproof fabric — waterproof and breathable if you plan to wear it constantly.

Avoid elastic waistbands on outer garments as they tend to ride down under pressure from your pack's hip belt. Rough fabrics hold the pack belt in place better than silky ones (nothing beats wool tweed), and also are safer if you fall on an icy slope. Side pockets on the hips are useless; the pack belt covers them. Small pockets on the front of the thighs are better.

If you have a good hip-length down or synthetic-fill parka and camp in moderate conditions, you don't really need **down pants**. If just a little more insulation is needed in camp, inexpensive ski warm-up pants, or fleece pants or even a set of expedition-weight underwear may suffice.

In severe conditions, fill pants can allow you to enjoy an evening of socializing rather than retreating to your sleeping bag as soon as the tent is up. Down or synthetic-fill pants should have full-length zippers so that you can get into them quickly. For arctic temperatures, make sure the zippers are protected by flaps. Pants with legs that zip together can be used as a half sleeping bag (or elephant's foot). Both waist-length and bib pants are available. Baffling in pants is very expensive because of the construction difficulties, but is well worth the cost at -40° C.

Clothing choices for the lower body

- Synthetic long underwear, weight determined by the amount of clothing worn over it, climate and activity level.
- Insulating pants: either knickers, which are designed to be an external layer, or fleece or pile trousers with a wind shell. The insulating layer under a shell may be omitted in most conditions.
- Shell pants: bib with a drop seat or crotch zipper, or waist-length. Windproof if worn over knickers, waterproof-breathable if worn over underwear or middle layer insulation. Alternatively you can wear a one-piece wind suit.
- Down or synthetic-fill pants: optional for moderate conditions, strongly recommended for extreme cold.

Hands

Hands are one of the first areas to suffer if your body loses heat. They are also a good place to shed layers if you are too hot. Because you grip or manipulate objects almost constantly during the day, your hands must be protected from conductive heat loss as well as from radiative and convective heat loss. Gloves and mittens take up little space in your pack or pockets, so don't be afraid to pack a lot of them.

I carry two or three pairs of synthetic **liner gloves** to be sure that one is always dry. Liner gloves are essential. In cold weather, they keep the skin of your fingers from sticking to or freezing from contact with ski bindings, cooking pots, stove, cameras and any other objects you must handle. In warm weather, they protect your hands from the blistering friction of ski pole grips and from sunburn.

We have yet to find a really good glove. If the fabric is thin enough to allow you to pick up small objects and do fine work, the finger tips will wear through after a few uses. If the glove is sturdy enough to survive a full season, you have to remove it to perform delicate operations. Gloves made of silk or the silver metallic fabrics are wonderful to work in but often don't survive even one trip. Avoid bulky knits which don't hug the skin properly. If you do much camping, you will probably go through several pairs a year, so there is opportunity to shop around.

Mitts are far warmer than gloves for the **middle layer**. Wool (especially boiled wool) and synthetic pile are equally satisfactory and can be found in a variety of weights to suit different conditions. Warmth is closely related to thickness. Unfortunately, the thicker the mitt, the more it restricts the functioning of your hand. Really bulky pile mitts are sometimes pre-shaped to the curvature of the fingers. About all they are good for, besides warmth, is holding a ski pole.

Mitts should cover the wrist. For warmth they must allow full freedom of movement for the fingers, without binding, yet keep empty, heat-robbing space to a minimum. If your liner gloves are themselves fairly thick, you may find that you need one size of mitt to wear over the liners

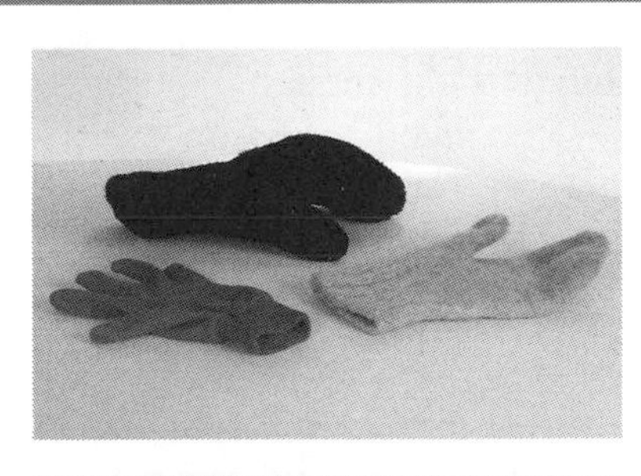

Heavy synthetic pile or wool mitts can be worn over liner gloves.

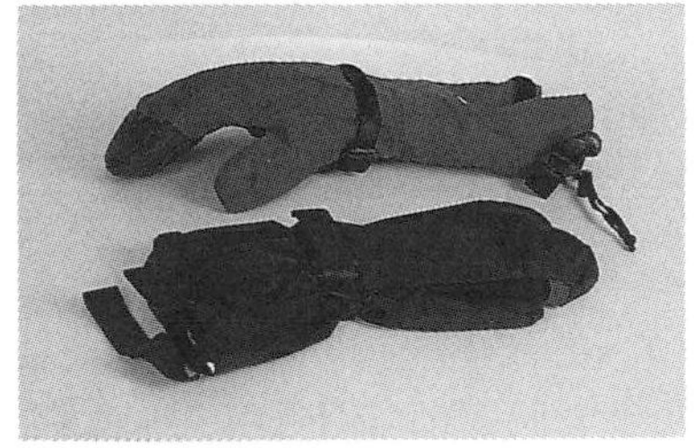

Gore-Tex shells which are worn over mitts and/or liner gloves.

and a smaller size to wear without the liners. Pay particular attention to the thumb, since this is usually the first area to bind.

For moderate conditions, you may prefer a mitt with an attached shell. These are more flexible than separate insulating and shell mitts, but not quite as warm. The insulating lining should pull inside out for drying.

Because your hands will spend a lot of time in contact with the snow, a **waterproof-breathable shell** is highly desirable, although windproof nylon will do if money is limited. Unless you tour in non-demanding conditions, outer mitts should extend onto the forearm, with closures at both the wrist and forearm to prevent snow and wind from entering, heat from escaping and frostbite to the wrist. Before you buy, try to do up the forearm closure with a mittened hand. Some mitts require the use of fingers to operate the closure. That's fine for the first hand, but what do you do for the other one? Remember that you will have your mitts on and off many times during the day, so they should be simple to operate.

Avoid leather, which rapidly becomes soaked in snow and is slow to dry. Down mitts are available. I have never found a use for them, since they are bulky, awkward, and the minute you grasp something, you lose the loft that provides all of the warmth in down. Use the pockets on your parka instead for rapid warming of hands. If your hands are really suffering during normal activities, that is a sign that you are not wearing enough insulation on your head and torso.

Summary of layers for the hands

- Synthetic liner gloves which fit well enough to allow you to pick up and manipulate small objects.
- Insulating mitts, either wool or synthetic. If they are to be worn over liner gloves, make sure that they are big enough.
- Waterproof-breathable shell mitts which extend to the forearm. These may be combined with an integral insulating layer for moderate conditions.

Feet

Feet lose heat primarily through conduction to the snow and from poor circulation, often caused either by a lowering of the body's core temperature (remember to put on your hat) or by tight boots and socks. If the air temperature is very cold, feet may also suffer radiative heat loss from inadequate insulation. Sweaty feet and wet boots or socks lead to evaporative heat loss. Remember also that wet skin blisters easily.

Mike and I prefer synthetic **liner socks** because of their wicking action. Some people cannot tolerate them and require cotton.

Wool generally out-performs synthetics for **heavy insulating socks**. You may have been told that you should wear two pairs of heavy socks, both for warmth and padding. If boots were readily available to fit all types of feet, this would be good advice. Since you may have to compromise on boot size (in order to avoid going barefoot), choose the weight and number of socks according to the space available. You must not bind the foot in any way or you risk frostbite. Extra warmth can be provided by insulated gaiters if your socks are not sufficient. At the other extreme, you cannot expect to stuff oversize boots with too many socks; they will bind and twist on each other, blister your feet and allow you no control over your boot when skiing.

If you suffer from very cold feet, you may want to consider **vapour barrier socks**. These are a waterproof shell worn over synthetic liner socks and under the insulating socks. The principle of a vapour barrier is simple—it completely prevents evaporative heat loss. But, vapour barrier socks do not seem to work for some people. Before you invest, try wearing a plastic bag on one foot. If the foot with the bag is noticeably more comfortable, then you probably will be happy with the socks.

Another product marketed for winter use is the battery-heated sock. I have reservations about depending on something that may fail, especially if it encourages you to wear otherwise inadequate foot gear. Murphy's law applies to winter backpacking — if a piece of equipment can fail it will do so in a raging storm, miles from shelter, and when you are exhausted. If you wear battery-heated socks, carry regular socks as backup and make certain that they fit inside your boots.

Ski and snowshoeing **boots** will be discussed in Chapter Four in conjunction with skis, snowshoes and bindings. No matter what type of ski boot you select, off-trail travel requires the use of **gaiters**. Gaiters come in different styles. Some are designed only to keep snow off socks and out of boots. They extend from the knee to just below the boot top.

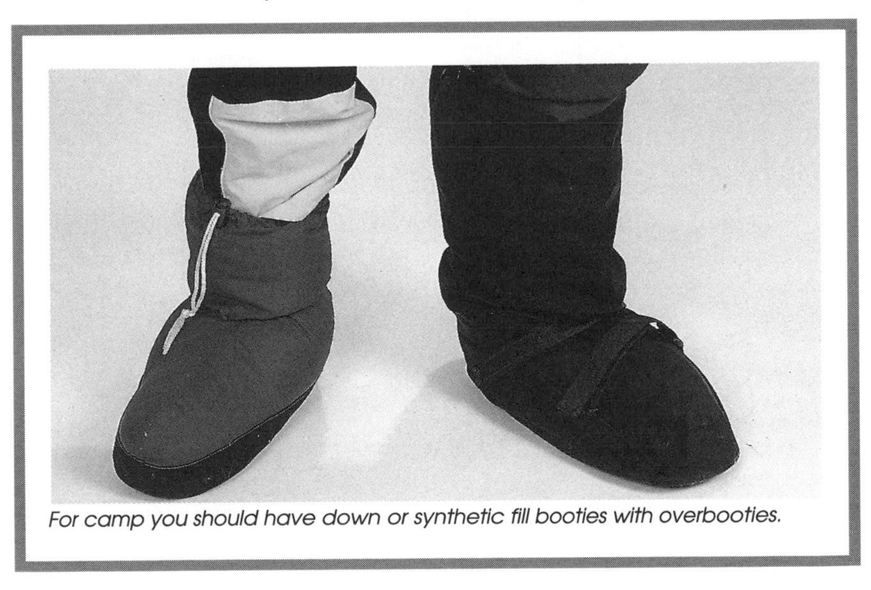

For camp you should have down or synthetic fill booties with overbooties.

Others, called supergaiters, cover the entire top surface of the boot to protect it from moisture. They have a rubber rand that seals tight to the welt. Some supergaiters have pockets of insulation over the top of the foot, where blood vessels are close to the skin, and around the calf to warm the blood going to the feet. You can easily add your own insulation to supergaiters . A waterproof-breathable fabric is best for gaiters since any moisture trapped in the boot leather can chill your feet during the day and will freeze overnight.

If you buy a full gaiter with rubber rand, be sure that it fits snugly. If the rand does not fit properly, it will ride up while you are skiing, allowing snow onto the boot. This can be prevented by attaching the rand to the welt with epoxy, but then you must live with a permanent meld. The rand should be slid back off the toe of the boot between trips to prevent it from deforming the boot. The use of a rand must be coordinated with your ski boots and binding to ensure that everything will fit together. (See Chapter Four.)

If you snowshoe and face extreme cold, you can use a complete **overboot**, which is both warmer and less trouble to fit than a supergaiter. You can buy warmer boots for snowshoeing than for skiing.

Once you take off your skis or snowshoes in camp, your feet will cool rapidly, both from conduction to the snow and evaporation of moisture built up inside. As soon as possible, you should put on **down or synthetic-fill booties**. Synthetic fill is cheaper and performs better in wet snow. If you wear double ski boots, buy the bootie to fit over the inner boot, both for extra warmth and firm support while walking around. Waterproof- breathable, **knee-length overbooties** will keep your

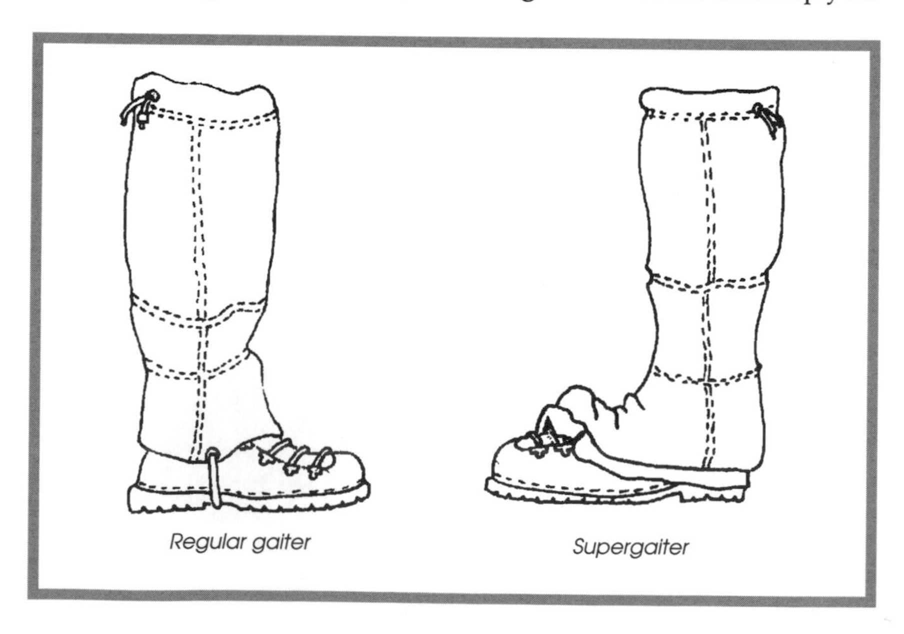

Regular gaiter *Supergaiter*

booties dry and on your feet in deep snow (booties have an annoying tendency to come off at the slightest pull). Booties and overbooties should have a layer of closed-cell foam insulation under the foot. The soles should be of a non-slip material (not leather or plastic) — sliding into the biffy is worse than embarrassing.

Recapping the choice of footwear:

- Liner socks, either synthetic or cotton.
- Wool or synthetic insulating socks.
- Vapour barrier socks.
- Boots (see Chapter Four).
- Gaiters for ski boots.
- Overboots for snowshoe boots.
- Down or synthetic fill booties for camp.
- Waterproof-breathable overbooties for camp.

VAPOUR BARRIER CLOTHING

We mentioned vapour barrier socks above, but in fact, vapour barrier clothing can be worn on the whole body to eliminate most evaporative heat loss. If you wear thin synthetic underwear under the vapour barrier to keep from feeling too wet, you will need surprisingly little insulation in outer garments. The minute you start to overheat you will be aware of the sweat build-up, a signal to slow your activity and adjust clothing. One advantage of a vapour barrier layer is that you need not worry about the breathability of outer layers. Standard rain gear, which is much cheaper than waterproof-breathable fabrics, can be worn. Vapour barriers are much too hot in temperatures near or above freezing, however.

HOW MUCH CLOTHING MUST I CARRY?

Beginning campers often wonder how much gear they need to pack to ensure that they will have enough layers. Until you gain experience it is better to take a little too much, but not so much that you can't carry it. Over the years I have found that the following system works well for me.

For head and hands I carry a variety of items. On a typical trip I would pack:

- Silk balaclava
- Thin stretchy knit hat
- Heavier synthetic hat
- Windproof shell hat with brim
- Neck tube
- Three pairs of liner gloves
- Two pairs of insulating mitts in different sizes

- Two pairs of windproof overmitts
- A pair of shelled pile mitts

Of course I don't wear everything all at once. Some items are for backup, others for making just the right adjustment for the conditions. For extreme cold or hot glaciers I would **add** appropriate items to the above rather than substitute. If you camp in moderate conditions, you could delete some of the heavier items.

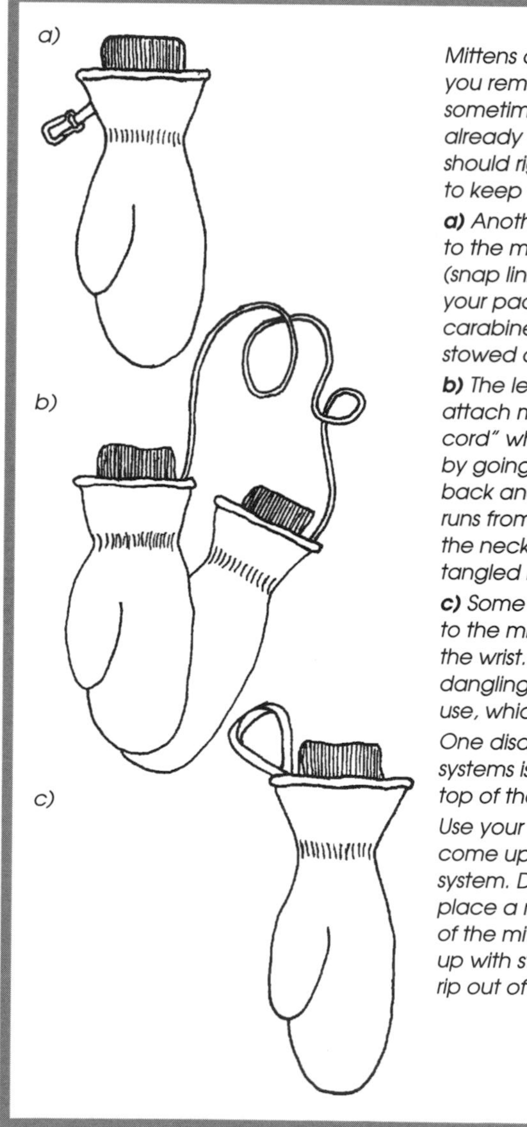

Mittens can easily blow away when you remove them, and are sometimes bulky to put in an already crowded pocket. You should rig some sort of attachment to keep them with you.

a) *Another method is to sew a loop to the mitt and put a small carabiner (snap link) on the shoulder strap of your pack. Snap the loops into the carabiner and the mitts are safely stowed out of the way.*

b) *The least satisfactory way to attach mittens to you is an "idiot cord" which joins both mittens either by going up one sleeve, across your back and down the other sleeve, or runs from the mitts to a loop around the neck. Invariably the cord gets tangled in other gear.*

c) *Some people sew an elastic loop to the mitt and slip the loop around the wrist. This leaves the mitt dangling from your arm when not in use, which can be awkward.*

One disadvantage to all of these systems is that snow can enter the top of the mitt.

Use your ingenuity and you may come up with a better attachment system. Do not, however, try to place a rivet directly into the fabric of the mitt. If the rivet isn't backed up with sturdy material, it will simply rip out of the fabric.

Beyond the head and hands, I don't carry multiple garments for the same function. Socks, boots, gaiters, underwear and my shell bib pants remain on my body all day. I carry one fleece sweater (its weight depending on climate), a shell parka, down parka, down booties and overbooties. If the weather is very cold, I add a down hood and down pants. If your feet sweat a lot or you plan to ford running water, you should carry extra insulating and liner socks. Many people carry spare underwear and sweaters, but if you minimize sweating during the day, you won't need to change garments; in an emergency, you still have your down clothing and a sleeping bag.

ADDITIONAL HINTS

- When buying clothing, check to see that the zippers are sturdy — either YKK or a brand of equal quality. Plastic and nylon zippers are not strong, and cheap metal zippers will freeze, jam or break.
- Make certain that zippers, belts, buttons and any other protruding or hard objects will not be subject to pressure from the hip belt or shoulder straps of your backpack. One of the reasons we prefer bib pants is their greater compatibility with a pack harness.
- Top-line clothing has ties attached to the zippers so you can grasp them with your bulkiest mittens. You can and should make your own ties if they are lacking. Use any cord narrow enough to fit the opening on the zipper pull and sturdy enough to yank on. The tie should be about five centimetres (two inches) long.
- Carry some small chemical warmers (the kind that you squeeze and knead to start the chemical action). Placed in a mitt or bootie, or next to the skin of your torso, they can provide rapid warming.
- Regularly check all seams and zippers so that you can make repairs at home rather than in the field. New garments are not immune to manufacturing mistakes, so check everything carefully before you use it the first time. Mitt linings seem particularly subject to sloppy manufacture. Pull them inside out and re-stitch as necessary.

3.
Sleeping Systems

SLEEPING BAGS

Before climbing Mount McKinley, I went to a local manufacturer of down sleeping bags and asked them to make me the warmest, lightest bag they could, regardless of cost (the weather on McKinley is about as bad as the planet produces). Fifteen years and countless happy nights later, I sold the bag for half the original price. It was still at least two-thirds as good as when I bought it.

A good sleeping bag is the most important purchase you will make. If you can't afford a four-season tent, your bag will keep you cozy in any kind of shelter. Knowing that you will sleep warm, you can remove some of that heavy extra clothing from your pack. If you buy quality down fill and take care of it, the bag will last a lifetime in moderate conditions and should give you at least ten years service in severe cold.

As you read promotional material from various manufacturers you may feel that only a molecular chemist with a strong background in sewing could fully appreciate what's being described. Let's sort through some of the issues

HOW DO YOU JUDGE THE WARMTH OF A SLEEPING BAG?

Not by the manufacturers' temperature ratings! What these tell you is how each bag relates to others made by the same manufacturer. A bag rated to 0° C (32° F) will have less insulating power than one rated to -10° C (14° F). No one can predict how warm a particular bag will be for **you.** You may find that a product from one company is warmer than a competitor's bag which is rated several degrees lower. It all depends on your metabolism, the conditions in which you use the bag and the reliability of a given manufacturer.

Sleeping bags don't generate heat — you do. Without the bag, however, the heat you produce would radiate away. The ability of a sleeping bag to conserve the warmth of your body comes mostly from its loft — the thickness of the trapped-air insulation it places between you and the cold air. Anything which reduces loft has no place in a winter system.

Features which affect the warmth of a bag

You may want to wear extra clothing when camping at temperatures near the bag's lower limit. The bag should be roomy (especially if you are one of those people who routinely crawl in wearing every garment available) but not so cavernous that you have a lot of wasted space to heat. The best way to test is to crawl in and see how it feels. The bag should not constrict your shoulders.

A hood that cinches tight around your face prevents heat loss from the head. I find the hoods of most bags very restrictive and prefer to use a separate hood that extends over my shoulders and that turns with me in the bag. This portable hood has the added advantage of being available anytime, such as during stops along the trail or sitting in camp. On bitterly cold nights, I pull the hood of the sleeping bag over the portable hood for extra warmth. Another useful feature is an inner collar on the bag which blocks convective heat loss at the neck when you turn over in the night.

A full-length two-way zipper allows you to use the bag in warmer conditions since you can ventilate your feet while keeping your torso covered (you can also walk around wearing the bag). Some couples like to buy bags that zip together. That's fine if you both need the same amount of insulation or can't bear to be apart, but most people are more comfortable in an individually regulated system.

It is possible to buy double bags. Used together, the inner and outer bags provide maximum warmth while either can be used by itself in spring or summer. You can create your own double system by adding an over-bag to your three-season bag. Double systems weigh more than single bags because each component has its own shell, lining and baffles.

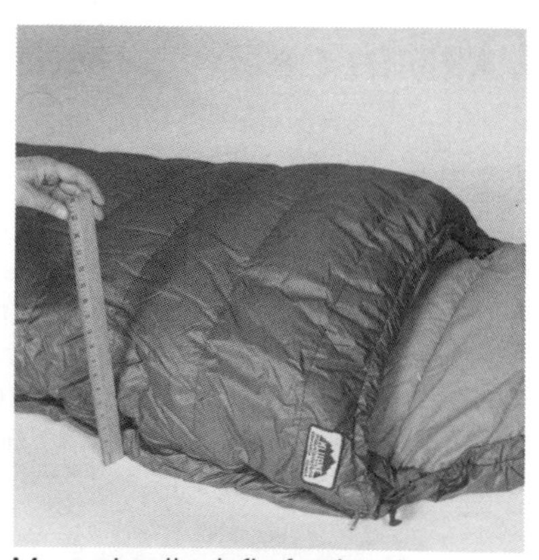

Measuring the loft of a sleeping bag. The down bag on the left has almost 10 inches (25 cm) of loft, suitable for arctic conditions (-40°). The synthetic fill bag on the right has about 4 inches (10 cm) of loft. It is a good three-season bag, suitable for temperatures slightly below freezing.

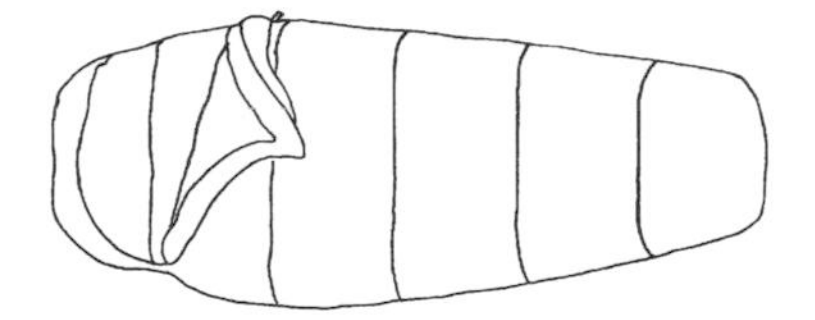

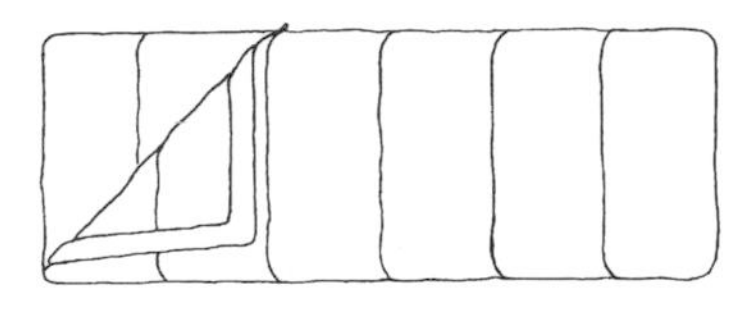

Bags come in two basic shapes: rectangular and mummy (wide at the shoulders, narrow at the foot). Rectangular bags are less claustrophobic but contain a lot of interior space for your body to warm up. Most winter bags are mummy-shaped.

Whichever shape of bag you choose, make sure that there is enough room at the foot to accommodate any items you have to stow there: boots, water bottle, camera, tomorrow's salami and cheese.

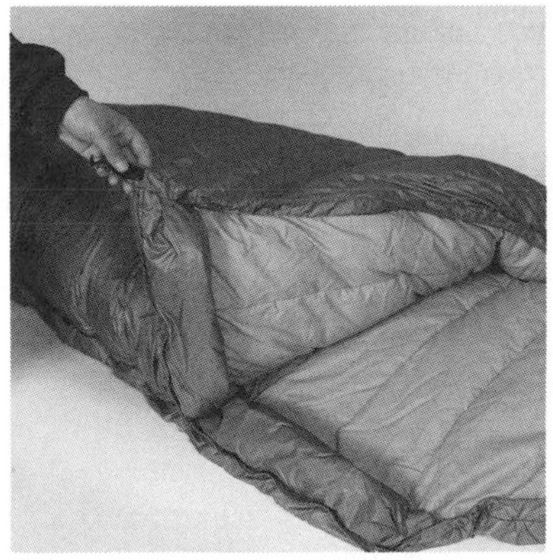

The zipper is another area where heat is lost. Good bags have draft flaps. On this arctic bag, there are draft flaps on both the upper and lower halves of the zipper.

The footbox should be shaped so as not to press on your feet.
The outer shell of the bag should be cut larger than the inner lining to avoid compressing the fill. This is called differential cut.

HOW WARM A BAG DO I NEED?

How warm a bag can you afford? Really warm bags are expensive. Really warm, lightweight bags are very expensive. A bag that is good to -40° C/F, however, can also be used at -5° C (23° F); the reverse requires either an incredible metabolism or more spare clothing than you want to carry.

So, should you purchase the warmest bag available? Probably not, unless you are planning an arctic expedition. Where and when do you expect to do your winter camping? If the temperature in the areas you visit seldom falls below -10° C (14° F), you may not want the extra bulk and weight of an arctic-class bag. Your metabolism is another important factor. Some people need all the insulation they can carry, others need surprisingly little. Only you can judge your physical requirements. Try to borrow or rent a bag for the first few outings if you are uncertain.

Our advice is to buy a bag that will keep **you** comfortable in the coldest conditions that you expect to face, even if only occasionally. Thus, if the normal nighttime low in the areas you frequent is -5° C (23° F), occasionally dipping to -18° C (0° F), then buy a bag that will handle the lower temperature. Alternatively, if you already own a good three-season bag and expect to ease gradually into winter camping with short trips, your best course may be to buy a less expensive over-bag and make a double system. This will give you time to assess your needs before investing in a single bag.

DOWN OR SYNTHETIC FILL?

The question of down versus synthetic fill has been debated for years, with no resolution in sight. Goose down has long been prized as a fill for sleeping bags because the plumules trap air efficiently, producing maximum loft with minimum weight. Down is rated according to how much loft one ounce will produce. Good quality down yields 550 cubic inches of loft per ounce, adequate for bags intended for moderate conditions. The better manufacturers use 650 or 700 fill in their winter bags, providing more warmth for the same weight. Always check the loft rating of the fill when buying a down bag.

The advantages of goose down are significant: it weighs less, is more compressible and lasts years longer than the best synthetic fibres. The disadvantages are also significant: the price is high, and down collapses into heavy clumps when wet. A sodden down bag is useless and almost impossible to dry in the field. Proponents of down tend to live in regions of dry snow, such as the Rockies.

It may seem strange that moisture should be a problem in winter, but in fact, the colder it is the more problems you may have. Condensation on the walls of your tent will fall on your bag. Ice will form on the outside of the bag near your mouth and nose from breathing. Your body emits perspiration constantly which may be trapped in the fill of the bag. You may spill the contents of your water bottle or, if you insist on cooking in the tent, your dinner. In a storm, spindrift can penetrate the tent. Wet snow is prevalent in some areas and can occur anywhere. It sometimes rains in February. And then there are those hapless souls who fall through thin ice and go for a winter swim with all their gear.

Synthetic fibres solve the moisture problem because they do not absorb water. If your bag gets soaked, wring it out, crawl in and it will still have enough loft to keep you alive (but certainly not comfortable). Since few fools actually go around dunking their bags, synthetic is prized by recreational campers because it outperforms down in humid conditions. Your body heat will usually dry a damp synthetic bag overnight.

Synthetic fill is much less expensive than goose down, although the better bags have design features that drive up the price. An argument frequently used against synthetic fibres is that they do not last as long as down. If you are planning to live in your bag for several months a year over the next ten years, this is a valid consideration. If you expect to do only a few short trips each season, your synthetic bag will give good value.

The main drawbacks of synthetic fill are bulk and weight. The North Face, a leading manufacturer of quality sleeping bags, lists the weight of their large size Tangerine Dream, a Polarguard bag rated to -30° F, as 6 lbs 9 oz, with a stuffed size of 13" x 24". Their warmest down bag, the Raging Inferno, rated to -35° F, weighs 5 lbs 14 oz, with a stuffed size of 12" x 20". These differences are significant when you consider the increased bulk and weight of everything else that you must carry.

A bewildering variety of fibres has appeared in the past decade, all designed to make down obsolete. Although some approach the weight-to-loft ratio of down, none has yet solved the problems of bulk and fibre breakdown. Short fibres, such as Quallofil and Hollofil, tend to flatten and separate into clumps and thin spots with normal use and washing. At the moment, Polarguard's continuous interlocking fibres seem to be the most durable and lend themselves to innovative constructional design in sleeping bags (although it is not necessarily best for clothing).

PURCHASING YOUR BAG

Regardless of which type of fill you select, buy from a manufacturer with a good reputation. If you are buying an expensive bag, make sure that you get a lifetime guarantee on workmanship and defects in material. Since your bag will be both a major investment and the key to happy snow camping you will want to shop carefully for it. Good bags are made by several large firms which market multiple outdoor lines throughout the continent and by a number of smaller companies specializing in sleeping bags and down gear. Ask advice from people who do a lot of **lightweight** winter camping. Hunters and snowmobilers seldom care how much their gear weighs. Stores which cater primarily to mountaineers, backpackers and ski tourers usually have someone who can help you. Never expect the staff in department stores, army surplus stores, or general sporting goods stores (such as those which cater to car campers) to know what kind of bag you need.

If you are isolated from expert advice, you will have to do your own research. Start by going through back issues of the leading backpacking and mountaineering magazines (I find *Backpacker*, *Climbing* and *Explore* to be particularly helpful). These regularly review products and they also carry manufacturers' ads. Write for the brochures, then phone the companies which impress you and discuss your needs. Use the prices of major manufacturers as a bench mark. The materials and workmanship needed for dependable winter bags are never cheap. If someone tries to sell you a $100 down bag for use at -22° C (-8° F), do your shopping elsewhere.

MATTRESSES

Whatever portion of your sleeping bag bears the weight of your body loses almost all of its loft and insulating capability. An effective mattress is as essential to a good night's sleep as your sleeping bag, for you can lose a lot of heat by conduction to the snow.

Two types of mattress are suitable for winter use: closed-cell foam and self-inflating, open-cell foam. Closed-cell foam pads are relatively cheap and light, if somewhat bulky. Choose one that is guaranteed to remain flexible at all temperatures. Buy the thickest that you think you can pack, or use two. Minimum thickness for winter is 15 mm (5/8 inch).

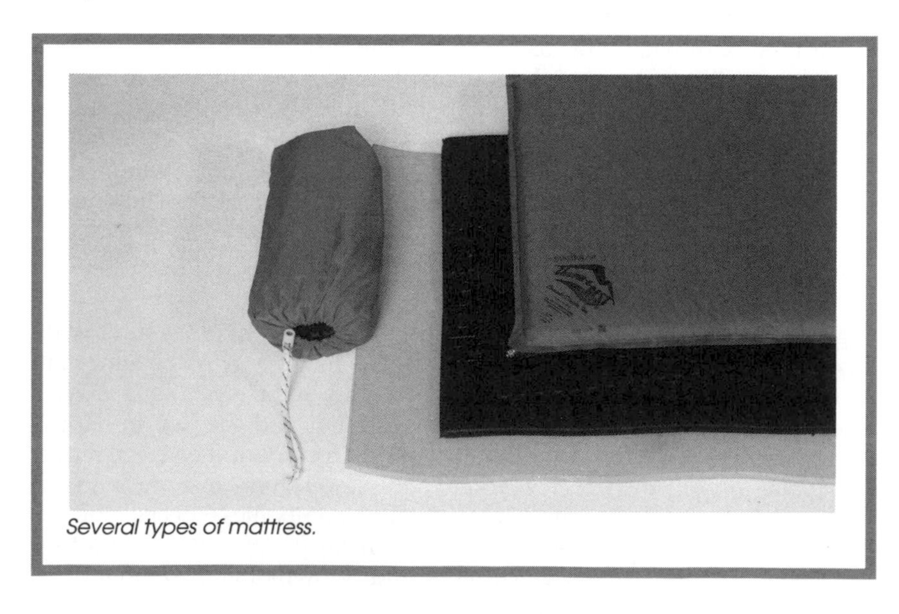

Several types of mattress.

Warmer, more comfortable and more compact than closed-cell foam, are the self-inflating, open-cell foam mattresses. They are also heavier, much more expensive and prone to springing leaks at awkward moments. The self-inflating feature works best in the summer. We always have to blow them up a bit in the winter. Make sure that the mattress you buy has a plastic valve. Your lips and tongue will stick painfully to cold metal.

The best system we have found so far consists of a torso-length, self-inflating foam mattress on top of a full-length, closed-cell foam pad.

TRICKS FOR SLEEPING WARM

Your head is the area of maximum heat loss and the area where it is easiest to make adjustments. Too warm? Uncover your head. Cold? Put on a cap, draw the bag's hood tight. Does your nose freeze? If you have a friend who knits, request a nose warmer for Christmas (a nose-shaped piece held in place by a band of elastic around your head). Also effective is a lightweight wool or synthetic cap that you pull down over your nose. Some people like to wear a balaclava, but I find that it ices up around my mouth. **Never** cover your nose and mouth with the sleeping bag — you will breathe incredible amounts of moisture into the fill.

Feet are another problem area, especially, it seems, for women. Down booties can be worn in the bag or you can place some clothing around your feet. Fill your water bottle with very hot water and put it in a sock at the bottom of the bag and you will enjoy its warmth for much of the night. Be sure to kick it away from you when it cools, or it will then

A morning ritual on a long trip: hanging the sleeping bags out to dry.

conduct heat away from your feet. Try putting a little extra insulation, such as a pack, under your feet. Chemical warmers inside your socks will also provide warmth for a few hours.

Always wear dry long underwear for sleeping. It will feel better against your skin than the nylon lining that most manufacturers use, will keep you warmer and will protect the bag from the oils in your skin. In extreme cold, most people put on extra clothing at bedtime. If some articles have become damp during the day you may want to take them to bed with you to dry. That's fine so long as you generate enough heat to dry both the clothing **and** the sleeping bag. If you can stand it, place the wet articles next to your skin. In extreme cold, sleeping with wet garments will lead to a build-up of moisture in the fill of your bag. Even so, if you are going to be out for only a day of so, a slightly damp bag at night may be less harrowing than garments which are rigid with ice in the morning.

Eat a sweet snack or hypothermia inhibitor (see Chapter Seven) just before retiring and keep both within reach to combat shivers in the wee hours.

KEEPING YOUR BAG DRY

On a one-night trip, this is seldom a problem. When you unpack at home you may be surprised at how damp your bag is. This is because the moisture that accumulated while you slept permeated the entire bag after you put it in the stuff sack. If your trip is an extended one, you must control this moisture. There are several steps you can take:

- **Hang the bag** on your skis or snowshoes as soon as you get up in the morning. By the time you have finished breakfast, the bag should be dry. Obviously the weather must cooperate, but I have managed to keep a down bag functional on month-long expeditions with this procedure.
- Buy a bag with a **waterproof-breathable outer shell**. Such a shell adds weight and a lot of cost but it effectively protects your bag from outside moisture and also increases its warmth. So long as the weather is not too cold, it will let the moisture from your body pass through harmlessly. At temperatures below about -15° C to-20° C (+5° F to -4° F), vapour from your perspiration may freeze to the inner surface of the shell, clogging the pores and trapping moisture in the fill.
- You can contain your perspiration with a **vapour barrier liner**. This is a waterproof, non-breathable sack used inside the sleeping bag. Most people have to try it once to get over their natural aversion to the idea. A vapour barrier liner feels warm almost the instant you get into it and can increase the warmth of a sleeping bag by several degrees. Although you might expect to become soaked with sweat,

your body will reduce its output of moisture as soon as it senses a certain level of surrounding humidity. These liners can actually reduce your fluid loss overnight. They are most effective at temperatures well below freezing, and thus complement the properties of waterproof-breathable shells.

You must wear only thin synthetic long underwear inside a vapour barrier liner. Anything else will be wet by morning. A friend of ours once crawled fully dressed into his vapour barrier liner in the hope of getting the earliest possible start on an ice climb the next day. When the alarm clock roused him, every garment he was wearing was soaked, and he had to wring the water out of his clothes before heading glumly back to the trail-head.

Mike and I discovered a further problem with vapour barrier liners the first time we used them. Because the liners are air tight, we slept blissfully unaware that our evening meal was causing some gastric turbulence. When we opened the tightly sealed liners next morning, the escaping vapours sent us scrambling, half-dressed, out the tent door in search of breathable air.

If your bag does not have a waterproof-breathable shell, you may want to use a vapour barrier both inside and outside the sleeping bag. This is the ultimate system since moisture cannot penetrate from any direction. Make certain that the exterior vapour barrier is large enough that it doesn't compress the fill of your sleeping bag. Never use an external vapour barrier without a well-sealed internal liner or your entire bag will become soaked.

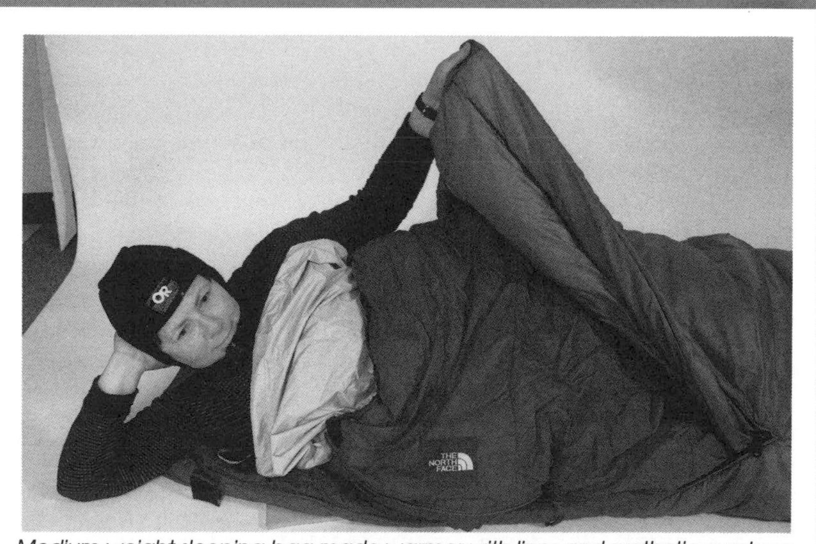

Medium weight sleeping bag made warmer with liner and synthetic overbag.

- Some people like to use a waterproof-breathable bag, called a **bivy bag** or bivouac sack, over their sleeping bag. This is especially necessary in a snow shelter or when sleeping in the open. The arrangement does not work particularly well in a tent where condensation tends to build up and freeze to the inner side of the bivy bag.
- Finally, you can protect your main bag with a **light synthetic over-bag**. Any condensation will accumulate on the outside of the easily dried over-bag.

STUFFING YOUR BAG

A winter bag will happily occupy all of your pack if you don't compress it. There are three main methods:

- Compress the bag by forcing it into the smallest stuff sack that will hold it. Start with the bottom of the sleeping bag and fill the stuff sack from the bottom up, being careful to use all available space as you proceed. This is much easier to do in your living room than in a cold tent, especially with a synthetic fill bag.
- Alternatively, use a larger stuff sack and then compress the filled sack with external straps.
- Some packs have a bottom compartment for holding the sleeping bag. This compartment should have a removable top in case the bag doesn't fit inside properly or you want to load the pack differently.

Always protect the bag with a waterproof cover — a plastic garbage bag works well.

STORING YOUR BAG

Dry your bag thoroughly after each trip. If it is not too damp it will air dry if left out of the stuff sack overnight. A wet down bag should be put in a large commercial dryer at very low heat. Some authorities advise adding tennis balls or a clean running shoe to the dryer to help break up the soggy clumps of down. Synthetic bags can be air or machine dried. Store your bag loosely in a large breathable sack, protected from sun or fluorescent light, moisture and high heat.

CARING FOR YOUR SLEEPING BAG

We know people who never wash their bags. Others believe that a bag should be cleansed periodically of body oils and perspiration, or at least of odour. Certainly clean fill insulates better than dirty, but washing can also affect loft, especially with synthetic fill. We lean to the wash-as-seldom-as-possible school, but recommend that you follow the manufacturer's instructions. Never dry-clean a quality down sleeping bag.

ALTERNATIVES FOR ULTRALIGHT CAMPING

Winter camping without a sleeping bag? Ask any mountaineer who has made a forced bivouac. Dougal Haston and Doug Scott spent a night on Mount Everest at 28,000 feet with little more than the clothes on their backs and emerged unscathed. But can you dispense with a sleeping bag and actually enjoy camping?

I decided to find out one frosty New Year's Eve. A planned trip had fallen through, and I was alone in Banff on a night that favours couples. Throwing some gear in my pack, I registered my intentions at the wardens' office and headed for the Tokumm Creek trail-head. The temperature was -30° C (-22° F) and dropping. I skied several kilometres by flashlight, dug a combination snow cave-trench under a fallen tree, placed a mattress inside, then put on all my down clothing and crawled in. It wasn't the warmest night I have spent but it was not unpleasant. With a few refinements, that equipment continues to serve me well on solo trips where weight is a serious problem.

Unless you camp regularly in sub-zero cold you may not have the necessary clothing for this system. You need a baffled down parka with hood, beefy down pants, preferably ones which convert to a half bag or elephant's foot (baffled if you can persuade someone to make them for you), down booties, expedition mitts or big pockets in your parka, and a light over-bag. Since you have to carry the clothing in any case for cooking and sitting around camp in arctic conditions, why not make it do double duty and sleep in it? A good metabolism, some tolerance for shivering and a cheery outlook are also very helpful.

4.

Skis, Boots and Snowshoes

Tangle Ridge, in Jasper National Park, has been the scene of more than one winter epic. The "trail" up makes you wish for cloven hooves, especially if you have a heavy pack. Most skiers try to find a gentler route through the trees for the descent. This is serious terrain — deep snow with variable crust; a slope angle that sometimes let you inspect the top branches of the tree immediately below you; and splendid isolation (there probably won't be another party along until the same time next year). Common sense dictates the use of heavy-duty mountaineering skis, and even with these I have never made a dignified exit from the ridge. The greatest humiliation was delivered not by the terrain, however, but by a friend who, on one trip, glided gracefully past me on the lightest, flimsiest skis imaginable. He arrived in the parking lot a full two hours ahead of the rest of the party, greeting the stragglers with the suggestion that when all else fails, we should learn how to ski.

My friend was tempting fate — I've seen too many people come to grief because their gear broke down and left them stranded in deep snow. When I go into the back country, I take skis and boots that will bring me home safely no matter what conditions I encounter. At the same time, there's something to be said for taking ski lessons.

SKIS

If you are an expert skier whose primary goal is to telemark or parallel steep slopes in the back country, you should select skis suited to the demands of your sport. How they perform on the flats with a heavy pack is secondary. If your interest is touring or if your off-trail experience is limited, you have different requirements. This section is intended for you.

Outdoor stores tend to stock skis appropriate to the locale. For example, if you live in a region where most trails are track set, and the terrain is not steep, you will not find the wide, metal-edged skis popular in the western mountains.

The people selling skis do not always provide the kind of advice you need. Even if they are highly knowledgeable they may not understand your particular requirements or be fully familiar with the latest models.

Nor will you receive much help from the evaluations of skis found in various magazines. Almost invariably, the ratings will tell you how well the ski glides on a track or handles off-trail descents by an expert skier in any kind of snow. Unfortunately, they say nothing about the ski's performance on the feet of a novice skier plodding along with an overnight pack or attempting a few turns on the slopes near camp.

Your choice of skis should be governed by the type of terrain you plan to travel and your skiing ability with a pack, both of which require time to assess. If you can find decent rental equipment, you should consider renting for the first few outings until you can judge your needs reliably. A second option is to buy used equipment while you look over what is available. Just about any ski that is sturdy enough for the terrain will get you started. You will then have time to talk to more experienced people and look at their gear.

Features of back-country skis

Width. In general, the wider the ski the more stable it is. Anything narrower than 48 mm, measured at the waist or binding area, will likely feel uncomfortable with a heavy pack even on an easy track. Consider 55 mm the minimum for mountain trails or for off-trail travel, although good skiers may be happy with less. If you are a poor skier and want to tour in the mountains, a ski with a waist over 65 mm (sometimes marketed as "fat" skis) will give you the most secure feeling.

Side-cut. This is the difference in width between the waist of the ski and the tip or shovel of the ski. The greater the side-cut, the easier the ski will be to turn. If you tour mainly in the flats or on a set track, side-cut is of minimal importance. If you plan to tackle open slopes, or would like to learn to telemark, look for a side-cut of about 10 mm or more.

Camber. This is the arch of the ski. If you track ski now you undoubtedly own double-cambered skis which are quite stiff and will make contact with the snow over their full length only with a vigorous kick. Most people plod with a pack rather than kick and glide. When you have heavy weight on your back, especially when going uphill, you want all parts of the ski to grip the snow firmly, not slide out from under you. Look for a single- or soft-camber ski if your touring will involve hilly or mountainous terrain.

Flex. In any ski shop you will see people grasping the tip of a ski and pulling the ski upwards or pushing down, supposedly to test the flex. Unless you know a lot about skis this ritual will tell you nothing. Ask for a ski with a relatively soft tip, especially if you will be touring off-trail, but avoid a ski that yields like a banana peel.

Length. The standard way to determine the proper length is to hold your hand above your head and buy a ski that comes to your wrist. Long skis are great for speed or a flat track, but they may be hard to turn and are very inconvenient on steep narrow trails. If you tour in flat terrain, use the standard test. For mountains, less confident skiers will be happier with a ski 5 cm to 10 cm shorter. Wide skis should always be chosen shorter. Most people opt for 170 cm or 180 cm.

Reinforced wood core or fibreglass-foam core. For rugged off-trail travel where a broken ski could have serious consequences, we use only reinforced wood core skis with a metal binding plate. In less demanding terrain, fibreglass-foam core skis from a reputable manufacturer are adequate. Some fibreglass-foam core skis also have a metal binding plate. Remember that in the back country, your equipment can never be too strong or too dependable.

Waxable or waxless skis. For a beginner, waxless skis will be somewhat less trouble if snow conditions vary a lot where you tour. In the Canadian Rockies, we usually carry only blue and purple wax plus climbing skins, so the advantage of a waxless ski is minimal. Don't expect experienced skiers to agree on this issue — both types of skis have staunch proponents. In general, however, you will find a much wider selection of skis among the waxables.

Base. This is the surface which you wax. A completely wooden ski with a pine tar base evokes pleasant visions of times past, but should be avoided for backpacking. Under certain conditions the base will absorb moisture. On a recent winter camping course, one participant who had such skis was unable to ski out because snow kept sticking to his bases, preventing glide and building an unstable platform underneath. The bases were too wet to accept his climbing skins, and he soon became exhausted from falling. Fortunately the track was solid enough for him to walk out. A variety of other bases are on the market and are generally satisfactory.

Edges. For mountain travel, skis should have metal edges. On flat terrain or set track, edges add weight and drag while conferring no advantage.

Ski Categories

Light touring, touring, back-country touring, telemark, fat, mountaineering, randonnée, alpine, etc.

Once upon a time, back-country skis fell into a few easily defined categories. Telemarking has become popular everywhere from downhill ski areas to slopes that I would hesitate to climb up with ice axe and crampons. As a result anufacturers have brought forth a rag-tag army of specialized equipment in search of your dollars. Fortunately, skis classed as light touring and touring, suitable for set tracks and rolling hills have changed little. But if you want to ski steeper terrain you will have to sort through a lot of promotional verbiage.

Any ski marketed for use primarily on packed slopes will likely not perform as well in the back country as one specifically designed for off-trail travel. A ski designed to handle "crud", "cement" and breakable crust may not be suited to a novice who won't be able to ski the stuff in any kind of gear. However, since skiing untracked slopes is one of the joys of back-country travel, you will certainly want to try it.

Ask for a ski that turns easily. If you are a mountaineer looking for skis to take you on the glaciers or well above tree line, you will find an alpine, randonnée or other wide ski easier to handle than a more narrow ski. New, lightweight, back-country alpine skis now weigh no more than heavy-duty mountaineering skis and have thus blurred the differences between alpine and cross-country equipment.

How to judge the demands of the terrain

We have used the terms mountains, hills and flats as if their meaning were self-evident. In fact, what a Floridian would consider hilly would qualify as flat in California, while westerners look at the eastern mountains and think "hills." A more useful way to assess the demands of the terrain where you ski is to think in terms not only of vertical contour but also of space, climate and isolation.

Vertical contour relates to the amount and steepness of up-and-down terrain you will face, as well as to elevation. You will find plenty of steep slopes in the east, but the mountains are lower and generally less rugged than the western ranges. In the west there will be lots of skiing above tree line and in Canada and Alaska, extensive glaciation. The more vertical the terrain, the stronger your skis and the better your skiing ability must be. You want sturdy skis that can hold a snowplow or sideslip and can survive repeated crash landings. Although metal edges are not as common in the eastern mountains as they are in the west, I have never regretted having them on my eastern tours.

Broad, open spaces are rare in the east, which explains why telemarking gained popularity first in the west. If you tour mainly on trails, you don't need to worry about flotation in powder or stability in crud — you want a good track ski. Glaciers and mountain slopes above tree line are subject to all sorts of wind and foul weather, and trails are non-existent there. Although I have seen good skiers manage a pack with narrow skis on glacial crud, back-country beginners should buy very sturdy skis with metal edges.

Climate is as important to ski selection as vertical contour. Mount McKinley is the highest point in North America and has about the worst climate. The New Hampshire mountains aren't very high at all, but their climate also rates as severe. Large parts of the arctic are flat. You need dependable gear for all three areas—if you break a ski or rip out a binding at -30° C, you have a major problem. As well, the warmest boots are wide, with thick soles, and require bindings that often won't fit on narrow, flimsy skis. We use sturdy mountaineering skis in the arctic and any place else where we expect severe weather.

To assess **isolation**, ask yourself what would happen if you needed help. Would someone likely pass by in a few minutes, a few hours, a few days, or would rescue consist of giving a decent burial to your bones years from now? An area that is crowded on a spring weekend may be deserted at -40°C. You may be only a few metres from a well-used trail, but if no one can see or hear you, you are isolated. The more isolated you are, the sturdier your skis should be.

SKI BOOTS AND BINDINGS

The advent of 50 mm bindings and "mated" boot-binding combinations means that boots and bindings can no longer be considered separately — these different types are incompatible. The best selection for back-country touring is found in the 75 mm width for both boots and bindings, but if you tour in non-demanding terrain you may welcome the light weight and convenience of 50 mm gear. Another option, for mountainous terrain, is the alpine touring outfit.

You must decide what features you want or need, determine what is available in your area, what you can afford, and perhaps be prepared to compromise. Touring in the arctic, where climate and terrain are severe and help is far away, demands warmer, sturdier and more dependable boots and bindings than weekend jaunts to your local state or provincial park (but remember that you can get frostbite anywhere).

Boots

Many people backpack these days in trail shoes that provide no ankle support, and you will see winter tourers wearing ski boots of a similar nature (most boots for 50 mm bindings are of this type). These boots are light, comfortable and allow freedom of movement. They also invite a severely twisted or broken ankle and are not nearly warm enough for extreme cold. Such boots have no place on an overnight mountain trip although they may be acceptable for day tours and for backpacking in very tame conditions and terrain.

Single leather boots that provides solid support above the ankles area good choice for steep terrain and cold climates. Lighter, more flexible leather is acceptable for less-demanding terrain, but the boot should still support the ankle firmly. The sole should be stiff for ski control (Vibram for walking, scrambling or climbing), and thick enough to insulate the foot. A stiff, well-padded upper, especially around the ankles, is necessary for telemarking and very helpful in any kind of off-trail snow or on a steep trail when you are carrying a heavy pack.

Sturdy, over-the-ankle boots designed for 50 mm bindings are beginning to appear on the market. Because of the way they meld to the binding they give good torsional rigidity for control without the weight of a thick sole. They unfortunately provide very little insulation to the sole of the foot, and the boot is poorly designed for walking. A major problem with this system is the way the bar on the front of the boot and the slot in the binding can ice up, making it impossible to lock the boot to the binding. Until improvements are made, such boots should be reserved for backpacking in non-demanding terrain and moderate climates.

Double leather boots are the warmest, heaviest and most expensive boots commonly used for ski touring. They are too warm and heavy for most purposes, but we use them whenever terrain and climate are severe. The heavy Vibram sole of the outer boot combined with the additional sole of the inner boot provides maximum protection against conductive heat loss to the snow. The inner boot can be removed at night and taken into your sleeping bag so that you put it on warm in the morning. Some double boots have interchangeable liners for different climates. If well

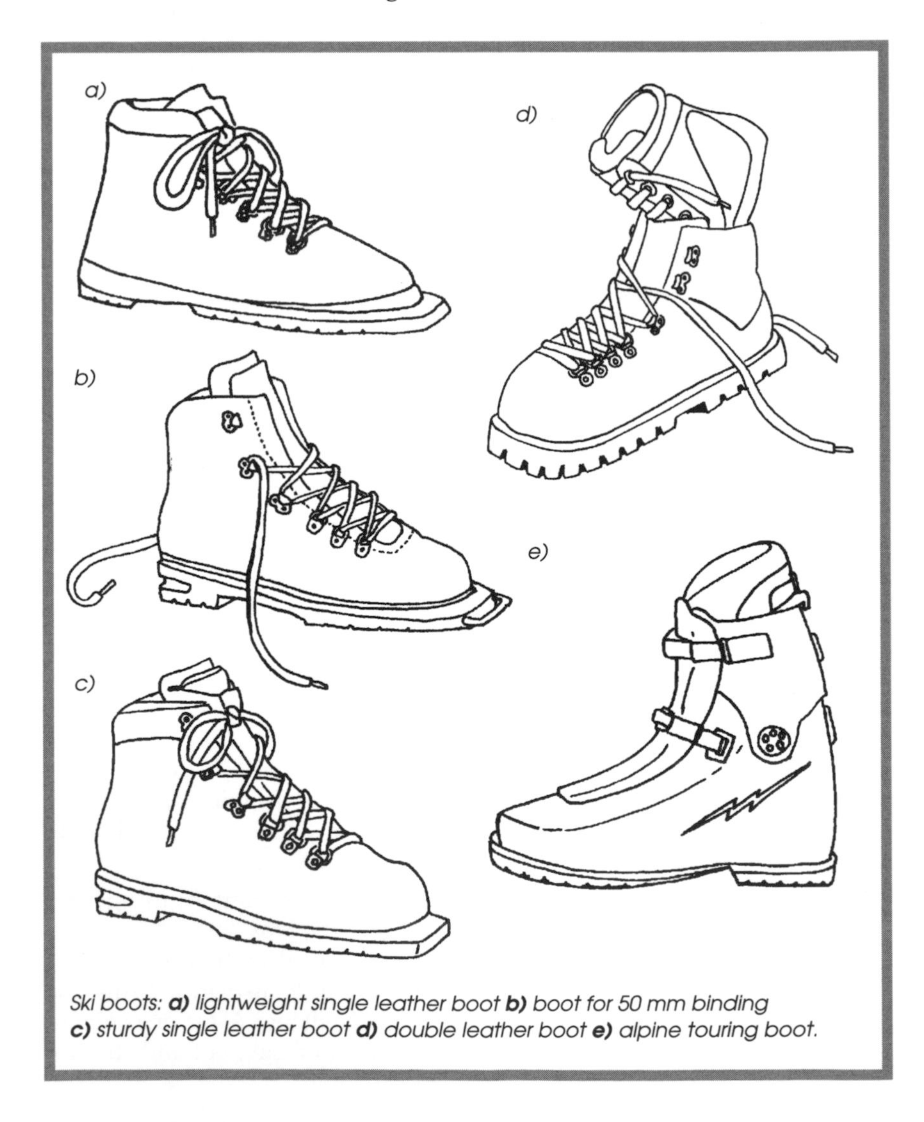

*Ski boots: **a)** lightweight single leather boot **b)** boot for 50 mm binding **c)** sturdy single leather boot **d)** double leather boot **e)** alpine touring boot.*

cared for, the outers will last for years and the inners can be replaced. The drawbacks of double boots include a weight significantly heavier than single boots, a cost that discourages stores from stocking very many (you may have trouble getting a good fit), and some loss of precise control over the ski, which worsens as the outer boot softens with use.

Alpine touring boots resemble downhill ski boots, but hold the foot at less of a forward angle.They allow some freedom of movement, have Vibram soles and cost a lot. They are designed for use with wide skis and alpine touring bindings. The majority of these boots are plastic and are not as warm as double leather boots. Their stiffness makes them unsuitable for prolonged flat travel. Some recent models are so light that I have gone back to using alpine gear after years of skiing only free-heel. The reason is the added control it affords with a heavy pack. Poor skiers will generally handle western mountains and glaciers better in alpine boots, but they may have trouble keeping up with people on lighter gear.

Shopping for your boots

Take a selection of socks with you when you shop for your boots, and don't go early in the morning when your feet are smaller than they will be later in the day. Winter boots must not bind your foot or toes in any way or you risk frostbite. They should have room for at least your liner socks and one pair of insulating socks. If you use an orthotic or insole, make sure it fits inside as well. Experiment with insulating socks of different weights. Try wearing two pairs (more will twist and create lumps). Walk around for at least a half hour to see if any hot spots develop. Never buy an uncomfortable boot with the thought of breaking it in. Even a boot that feels wonderful in the shop may be less satisfactory on the trail, but one that gives you a twinge in the store is guaranteed to become a torture chamber.

SKI BINDINGS

If your boot is designed for a 50 mm binding you have limited options. Not all 50 mm boots and bindings are compatible, so buy the binding when you buy the boot. Get the sturdiest one you can find because repair in the field will be difficult.

With a standard 75 mm ski boot you have a choice of three-pin, cable, cable plus three-pin, plate, plate plus three-pin, and plate plus cable, as well as a safety release for some bindings, and probably some new options by the time you read this. For non-demanding terrain, three-pin allows maximum freedom of movement. Select a reasonably sturdy binding, and if the bail is replaceable in the field, buy or order extra bails (not all shops keep them in stock).

The other binding types are designed for steep terrain and are largely a matter of personal preference. With a stiff boot, a three-pin binding will give you good control in most conditions, but if you use it a lot off-trail you may find the pin holes in the boot start to wear, or even that the toe of the boot will crack. Cables avoid this difficulty but restrict heel movement. A combination three-pin, cable binding gives you the best of both worlds — you three-pin uphill and add the cable for descent. In cold weather, however, you may not feel like fiddling with a cable at the top of the mountain. Plates give you the most control but can transfer a lot of force to your knees in a fall. Some cables and plates can also be used with hiking or climbing boots. Moderately effective safety release systems are available but do not begin to approach the dependability of downhill release mechanisms. They have some advantage if you are caught in an avalanche and need to get rid of your skis as quickly as possible.

Check that the binding fits both the boot and the ski. You don't want a binding that extends far over the sides of the ski or you will be catching on trees and rocks or losing your balance and toppling over sideways.

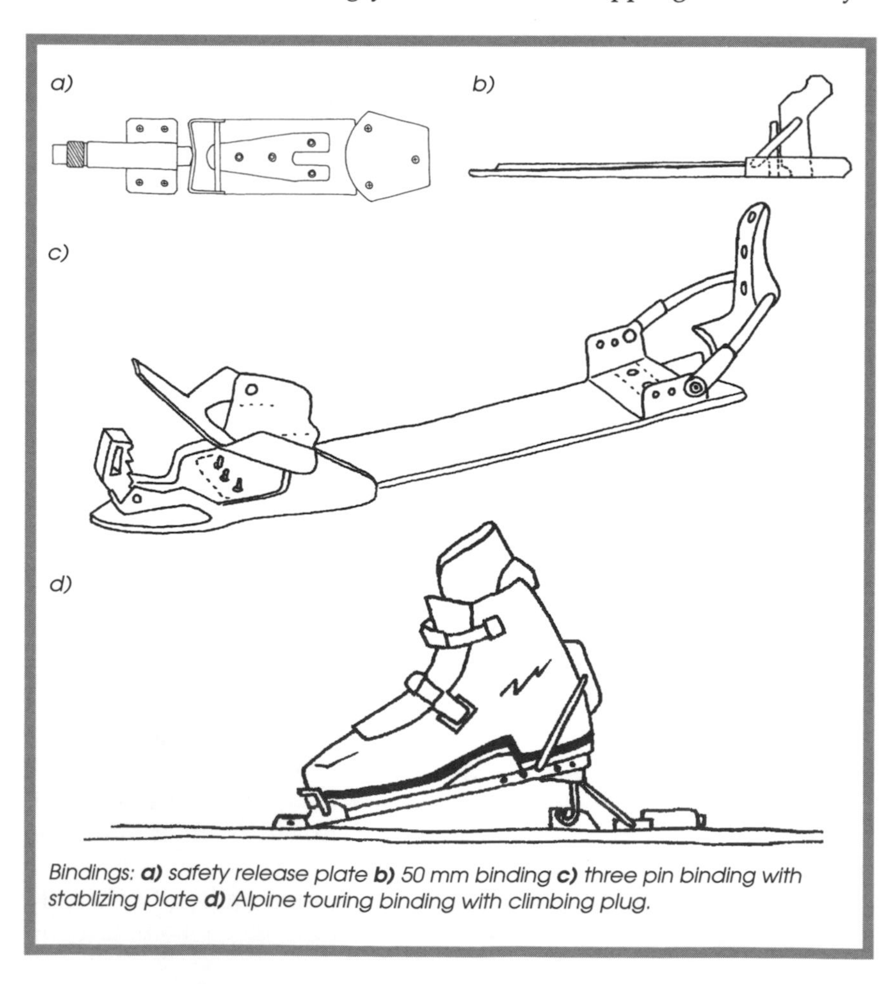

Bindings: ***a)*** *safety release plate* ***b)*** *50 mm binding* ***c)*** *three pin binding with stablizing plate* ***d)*** *Alpine touring binding with climbing plug.*

Some free-heel bindings are sturdy enough to use with alpine or wide skis, but many aren't. Double boots may be too large for some three-pins. If your gaiter has a rand (see Chapter Two), make sure there is room for it between the boot and the binding.

Alpine touring bindings are designed for use with alpine touring boots. They operate free-heel for touring and lock down the heel for descents. If you are willing to compromise the safety of the release mechanism you can also use climbing boots in some of them (a climbing boot may allow your foot and leg to twist without triggering the release). Because the Vibram sole of alpine touring boots may cause friction and delay the release, the safest bindings utilize a plate which performs the release independently of the boot sole.

FEATURES TO LOOK FOR ALPINE TOURING BINDINGS

- **Bombproof construction and a good reputation. Talk to skiers who have extensive experience with touring bindings, not just salespeople. Remember, the terrain where you take alpine gear is unforgiving.**
- **Reparable in the field.**
- **Easy switch between touring and descent modes, preferably without removing the ski.**
- **Climbing plugs for steep ascents, preferably workable with the ski pole (plugs are a device to raise the heel of the boot so that your foot remains nearly level when climbing).**

No matter what binding you select, always carry spares of whatever you need to repair or remount the binding in the field (bails, cables, screws, wire, strong tape, epoxy, steel wool for use with epoxy in screw holes, and appropriate tools). Buy the strongest, best quality binding you can find for back-country use. The extra weight and cost are minimal for the increased safety they bring.

POLES

Most fibreglass and metal poles marketed today are adequate for flat and hilly terrain. Metal is stronger than fibreglass. For track use, select a length that comes up to your armpit. The situation is a little more complicated in the mountains because long poles help while going uphill but short poles are better for descents. If you have to traverse a long steep slope, you will appreciate having one pole longer than the other. Poles which allow the length to be adjusted are very popular. The adjustment mechanism can freeze tight or refuse to grip, however, so if you believe that in the mountains "simpler is better," you should opt for a solid pole at whatever length suits you. In really steep terrain, you will be using climbing skins on the ascent, so long poles offer little advantage. Poles

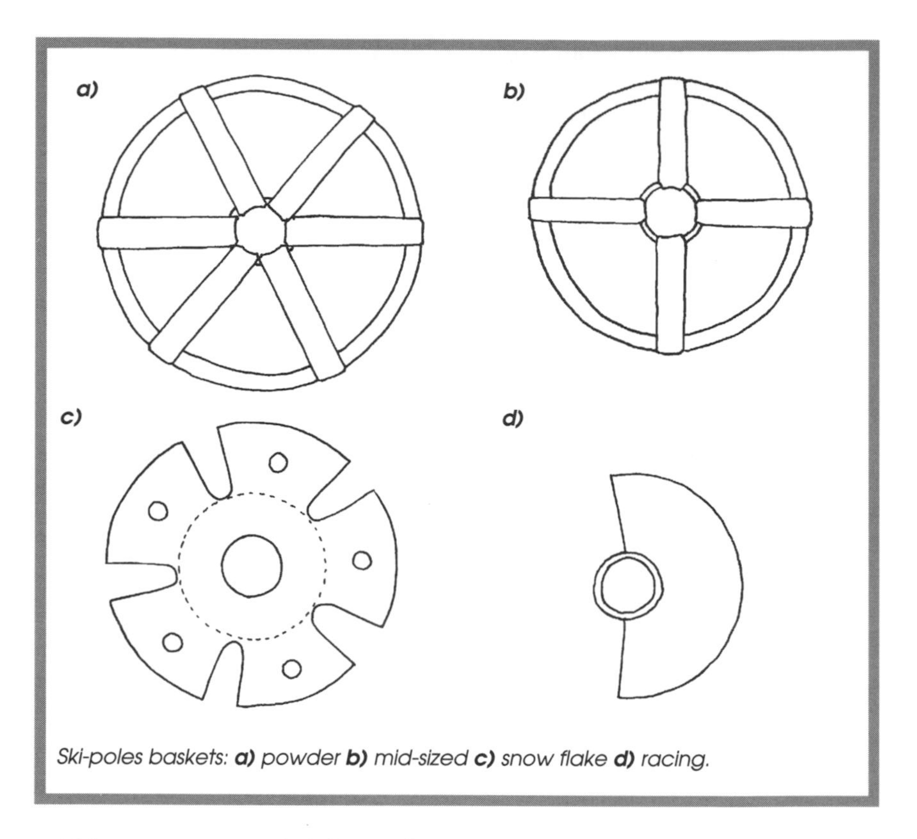

Ski-poles baskets: ***a)*** *powder* ***b)*** *mid-sized* ***c)*** *snow flake* ***d)*** *racing.*

which convert to avalanche probes are a wise precaution in the mountains since you may not always carry a separate probe.

Ski-pole baskets come in a variety of shapes and sizes. Large powder baskets support you best in deep, fluffy snow, but hang up easily on branches and pick up heavy snowballs in wet conditions. The small racing baskets won't give you the support you need when you and your pack start to topple over. Mid-sized baskets are best for most conditions. Those with an irregular rim, shaped like a snowflake, are less likely to get tangled in trees and bushes but catch easily in a climbing rope, an annoyance you don't need if you are skiing roped. Baskets with an unbroken outer rim and a cross of rubber in the middle are better for use with a rope but tend to hang up in the trees.

A few back-country ski poles have wrist straps that release from the pole under sufficient force. This is a feature that should be adopted by all manufacturers. If while skiing rapidly you entangle your ski pole in branches or brush, the force of your forward motion against the wrist strap can dislocate your shoulder. Always remove the straps from your wrists when descending a trail through the trees. Do the same when descending any steep slope, since a rigid ski pole can break your arm in a fall if you are attached to it.

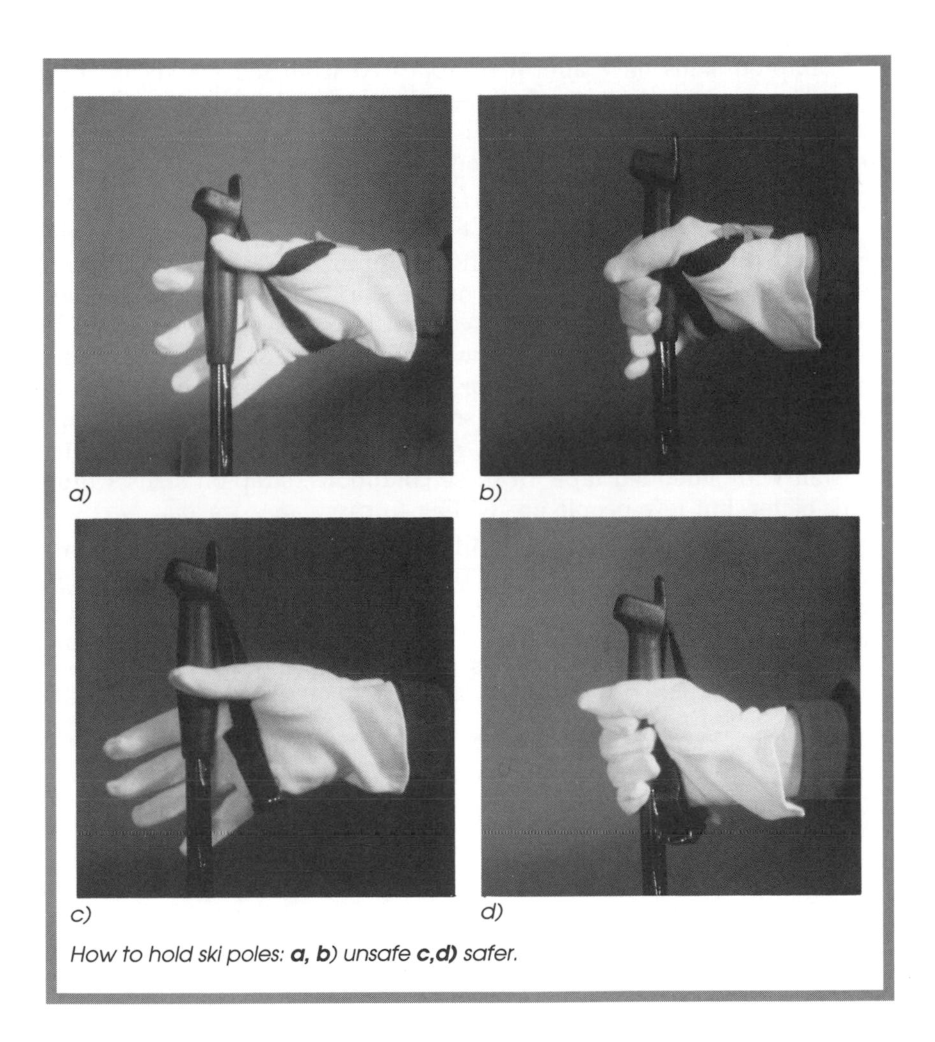
a) b) c) d)

*How to hold ski poles: **a, b**) unsafe **c,d)** safer.*

CLIMBING SKINS

If you ski anywhere but the western mountains, you probably rely on waxes to climb moderate inclines and use the herringbone technique when wax fails. You will find that trying to herringbone with a heavy pack is exhausting, as is having your skis continually slip backward when the wax fails to grip. If your trips will involve long stretches of even moderate uphill travel, you should invest in climbing skins.

Originally made from the skins of animals and strapped to skis with the hair pointing backwards, climbing skins today are made of mohair or synthetic plush. Mohair costs more, has the best glide and longest life if you don't abuse it. Nylon costs less, can take more abuse and perhaps climbs a little better when new. If you want to start an argument, ask a group of mountain skiers which is superior.

Strap-on skins have almost disappeared from the market because they allow snow to build up between the skin and the base of the ski. Today's skins adhere to the ski with a special glue which never transfers to the ski base and needs to be renewed only occasionally.

Skins will not stick to a wet surface, so make sure the base of the ski is dry. Try to keep snow off the glue. Hard ski waxes will not transfer to the glue, so if you are using nothing softer than purple wax, there is no need to clean the ski base before putting on the skin. Skins work better if they are not too cold, and they can be warmed briefly inside your jacket. In some conditions you may need to wrap duct tape (or other waterproof tape that works at low temperatures) around the tail and midpoints of the skis to keep the skins on. If the snow surface is sharp or icy, the tape will have to be replaced frequently. Keep checking it and try not to litter the trail with shredded tape. In these conditions, strap-on skins would work better, but few people are willing to carry an extra pair.

Skins are not designed for sliding downhill, but most ascending trails have some downhill sections. Today's skins glide smoothly enough (earlier versions tended to give a jerky ride), but they stop abruptly when the downward angle eases. To avoid being thrown forward by the rapid deceleration, keep one ski ahead of the other on descents.

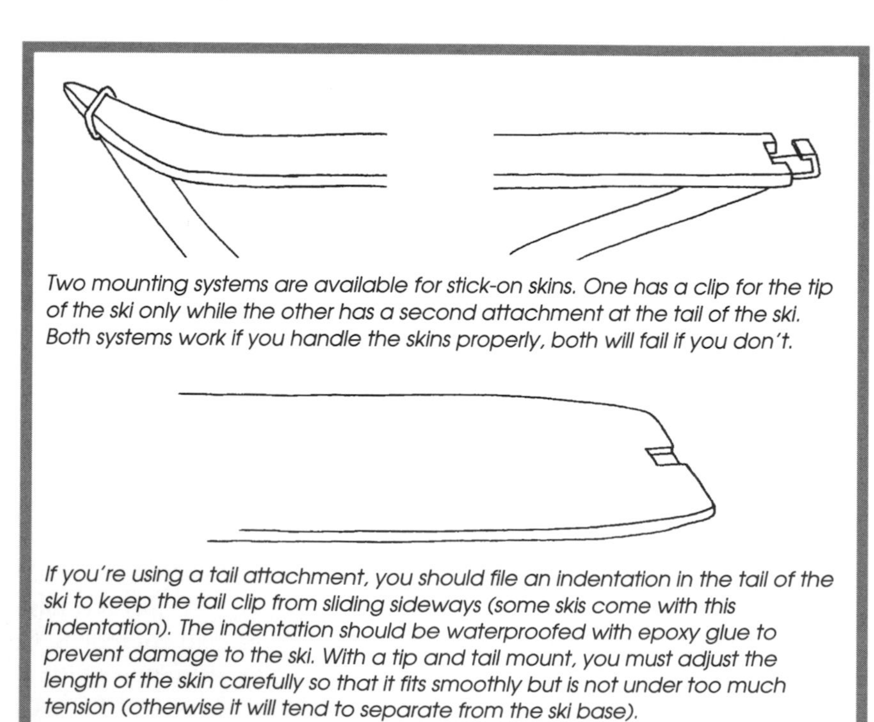

Two mounting systems are available for stick-on skins. One has a clip for the tip of the ski only while the other has a second attachment at the tail of the ski. Both systems work if you handle the skins properly, both will fail if you don't.

If you're using a tail attachment, you should file an indentation in the tail of the ski to keep the tail clip from sliding sideways (some skis come with this indentation). The indentation should be waterproofed with epoxy glue to prevent damage to the ski. With a tip and tail mount, you must adjust the length of the skin carefully so that it fits smoothly but is not under too much tension (otherwise it will tend to separate from the ski base).

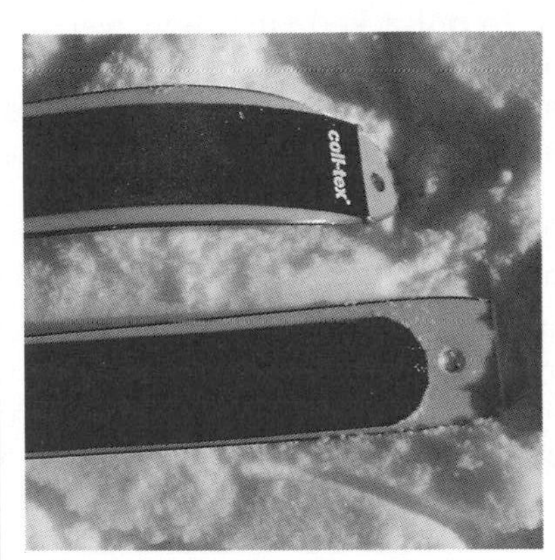

Skins come in different widths and should be almost as wide as the ski. If your mount has only a front attachment, trim the tail of the skin so that it ends about 5 cm (2 in.) from the tail of the ski. You do not want the skin to extend onto the portion of the ski tail that curves up. Round off the tail of the skin to avoid corners snagging in the snow and causing separation from the ski.

After use, dry the skins thoroughly before storing. In camp, they can be hung on a ski pole propped between skis to dry in the sun.
When you remove the skins from your skis, always fold them so that the glued surfaces are stuck together. You can either fold the tip and the tail towards the centre or place the tip and tail together and make one fold in the middle. Removing and folding skins in a high wind takes practice.

You should not make a practice of keeping skins on during long descents. Skinless skis are easier to control and provide a far better ride down. On wide slopes it is easy to traverse and kick turn if you are having trouble. On wide trails, use a snowplow or sideslip to control speed. These are basic techniques which you must master if you ski tour in steeper terrain. Nevertheless, when the trail is too narrow for standard braking moves and too long to sidestep, wearing skins may be the most practical way to avoid repeated and exhausting crashes.

Apply spray glue to the tails every few trips if there is no tail clip. Skins should be completely reglued about once a year, depending on how much you use them. Follow directions on the glue tube carefully and apply only very thin coats.

SNOWSHOES

Unfortunately for snowshoers, cross-country skiing has become so popular that many areas suitable for snowshoeing have been track set or have well-worn ski trails. If that track or trail provides the only passage to a destination, snowshoers will be about as welcome as snowmobilers (although skiers are not averse to having either one pack the snow **before** the ski track is set). If you have access to untracked land, however, and want a nature-oriented recreation or simply need a cheaper form of winter transportation than skis, consider snowshoes. Consider them as well if your feet are overly sensitive to cold because you can wear warmer boots than on skis. For that reason alone, snowshoes have a place in mountaineering, especially on mountains like McKinley and Logan where temperatures of -30° can occur even at the height of the climbing season.

The variety of frame shapes, materials and bindings for snowshoes will surprise you if you are a newcomer to the sport. Unless you live in an area where snowshoeing is very popular, you are unlikely to find knowledgeable salespeople in the stores, or even a very good selection of equipment. I would strongly recommend that you read *The Snowshoe Book*, by William Osgood and Leslie Hurley, for non-mountain touring, and *Snowshoeing*, by Gene Prater, for mountain touring, before purchasing anything. What follows are some general guidelines on what to look for.

The shape of the frame should be selected according to the terrain you will travel:

- **oval (bearpaw) for general use, especially in thick brush;**
- **long and narrow with a tail and upturned toe (Yukon) for deep snow;**
- **flat and wide with a long tail (beavertail) for mixed terrain and variable snow conditions;**
- **short and narrow, with upturned toe and a metal frame, for mountains.**

Traditionalists will enjoy snowshoes with wood frames and rawhide webbing. Rawhide webbing requires considerable upkeep and may attract animals that can reduce your shoes to shreds overnight. As well, you are restricted to relatively soft boots with no heel if you are to prevent the lacings from wearing through quickly. Rawhide is often replaced today with nylon and neoprene, but is still available and is unequaled for beauty.

Metal and synthetic snowshoes have appeared in recent years. Metal frames enclose a smaller, narrower webbing area than wood frames. They are especially suitable for mountaineering because of their strength and easy maintenance, but work well in any terrain. Hard Vibram soles will not damage them.

Synthetic snowshoes are very light weight and not suitable for rough use. Some skiers carry them for emergencies on long trips or for use in camp with down booties.

Bindings should also be suited to the terrain and activity. Simple bindings fashioned from a cord or rubber inner tube are easy to make and use but will not provide enough lateral stability for carrying a heavy pack and will be useless on hills or in extreme cold. For cold weather camping, select a binding that can be worked with mitts on — the fewer straps and buckles to be done up, the better. The binding should be designed to keep the foot from sliding forward when going downhill or backward when ascending. Metal snowshoes often have an integrated binding.

Traction devices or crampons are necessary unless the terrain is flat. Metal snowshoes usually come equipped with them. You may have to devise your own from instep or regular crampons if you have wooden snowshoes.

Boots for snowshoeing, as for skiing, should be selected for the climate in which you tour, but you have a much wider selection: trail shoes or moccasins (with rubber boots for wet snow), felt inners with waterproof outer boots, snowmobile boots, hiking or climbing boots (with a full overboot and insulated sole for the cold), army or K-boots.

For balance you need either a ski pole (or two) or an ice axe fitted with a ski basket. An ice axe is more practical for mountain touring. See Chapter Eight for a discussion of axes.

Learn how to repair your snowshoes in the field. Webbing can be replaced or mended, frames can be splinted, and an entire replacement shoe can sometimes be devised from the materials at hand. Metal-frame shoes are less subject to damage, but if they break down, knowing what to do is the difference between being stranded and getting out.

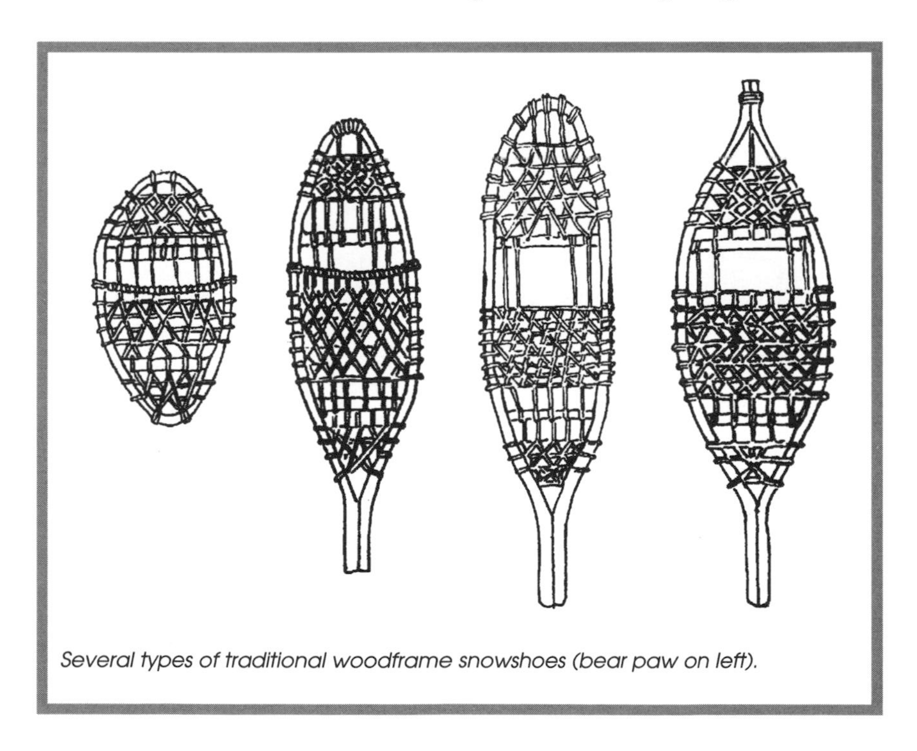

Several types of traditional woodframe snowshoes (bear paw on left).

5.
Packs, Sleds and Dogs

A large tea kettle simmered on the two-burner Coleman stove. As we put down our packs, a charming French couple invited us to share a hot drink and conversation. We weren't car camping — this was an isolated glacial lake on Baffin Island, north of the Arctic Circle, no place for rank amateurs. Our new friends were, in fact, far from being amateurs. They were equipped with the best equipment money can buy, and their spacious ($900) Kevlar sleds had ample room for luxuries.

PACKS

The main limitation to the amount of winter gear you can take with you is the fact that you have to carry all of it from the trail-head to wherever you set up camp. Your backpack must be light enough to lift and carry without exhausting you and it should be designed for the particular movements you will make. Sleds and dogs can help carry the load, but dogs are not permitted in many ski touring areas of North America, and sleds can be used only on certain types of terrain and in a limited variety of snow conditions.

External frame packs, which are favoured by many summer hikers, carry the load high and away from the body. It is impossible to ski well with such a distribution of weight. If your summer backpack is of this type, and you plan to ski rather than snowshoe, one of your first investments should be an internal frame pack that is large enough to hold the gear required for the area in which you are touring. Internal frame packs hug the body and move with you, especially the ones designed for skiing.

Adequate size

Your winter gear may not be much heavier than what you carry in summer, but it will certainly be bulkier. On a summer trail you can get away with strapping extra items just about anywhere. We've all seen hikers with a bedroll dangling precariously from the bottom of their pack, but you wouldn't want to attempt any serious off-trail travel with that kind of load. You can't expect to ski with it either.

Your physical size, weight and level of fitness determine how heavy a load you can safely carry (exhaustion must be avoided since it can lead to hypothermia) Pack weight is a more important factor than pack size. If a small woman can fit the harness to her torso, she can carry a huge pack loaded with sleeping bags and down parkas, items which weigh little but take up space. However, that same woman might be unable to carry 20 kg (44 lbs) in a much smaller-sized pack.

How large a pack do you need? You can answer that question only by answering some others: Where do you intend to tour? How long will your trips last? What sort of activities do you plan? How big and strong are you? Who else is available to help carry the load? What's the minimum amount of gear you have to carry, given your answers to the preceding questions?

In general, packs with a capacity of 4,000 to 5,000 cu. in. (65 to 80 litres) will be adequate for most weekend outings in moderate climates. Winter packs of 6,000 cu. in. (100 litres) are not uncommon, especially in severe climates. Some monster-sized packs, intended for expedition use, are much larger.

There are two schools of thought on pack size: get a large one so that you can throw things into it on a cold morning when you don't feel up to precision packing, or get a small one so that you will not be tempted to take more than you need. A large pack is great if you plan to go on more ambitious trips in the future, since packs are expensive, and it is better to have one for all purposes. On the other hand, big packs are heavy, and besides, you may never take that exotic expedition that requires more capacity. Both sides of the argument are valid.

Buy a pack large enough to hold everything you must carry. Sometimes, no pack is large enough, as here, on my climb of Mount McKinley.

If your ambitions are big and your purse small, I would recommend a larger pack. It can be cinched down to a compact size when not filled. If money is no problem, start with whatever is appropriate for the moment and add extra packs as your trips demand. The capacity of all packs can be increased with external pockets and properly located attachment straps.

Organization of the load

A winter pack should have, at most, two compartments in the main body: one at the bottom for the sleeping bag and another for everything else. If you select a pack with a bottom compartment, make sure that this compartment can be collapsed or folded out of the way for those times when you want to arrange your gear differently. Internal divisions waste space, add weight and seldom come in the right size and shape for your equipment.

A top-loading pack with a drawstring closure is best for winter backpacking. An extension collar at the top will offer storm protection and allow you to increase the pack's capacity. There should be a drawstring closure at the top of the collar as well as on the top of the pack body. The pack lid should be attached front and back with adjustable straps rather than sewn to the pack on one side, again to allow the load to extend above the main compartment.

Because some things will always be stowed out of reach in a single compartment that loads from the top, some packs have front zippers which allow access along the whole body. These zippers should be for extra access only and should be heavy duty and fully protected by storm flaps. If the entire closure system is zippered, your pack will have a more limited capacity, and you will also be dependent on a mechanical device that could fail. An alternative to front zipper entries is to provide large-capacity pockets on the front of the pack. Front pockets should not be used for heavy items, however, since these are better carried close to the body.

Compression straps on each side of the pack allow you to cinch the pack smaller. Depending on the length of these straps, gear ranging in diameter from tent poles to tents can be inserted under them. External side-pockets should be large enough to hold lunch, water and fuel bottles and anything else that you either will need during the day or don't want to store inside. They should also be detachable so that they can be left behind when your load is small. Pockets can be attached to the side compression straps, but be careful they do not interfere with arm motion. The sides of the pack should also have a pouch at the bottom to hold the lower end of any small item that could slip through the side straps, such as tent poles. This pouch should have a drainage hole for melting snow.

The lid should have a large-capacity zippered pocket for the myriad of small objects you will need on the trail (sun glasses, sun cream, spare mitts and hats, waxes, film, map, compass, etc.). A smaller pocket on the underside of the lid is handy for your wallet and keys.

One of the more convenient packs I have used has contoured hip pockets large enough for a water bottle, waxes, duct tape and climbing skins and, if you are flexible, these pockets are accessible without taking off the pack. Dana Design sells detachable pouches which hold small items, including a compact water bottle, in front of you. These pouches will fit any pack, not just those made by Dana. Some packs have small pockets in the padded hip belt. A feature I would like to see is a quick-release attachment on the hip belt for a padded camera pack or large insulated water bottle. Designs change every year, so be on the look-out for useful innovations.

Comfort

The above features relate to the pack's capacity. Equally important are the comfort features — how the pack fits, distributes the load, and moves with your body. I couldn't begin to describe all of the suspension systems and harness arrangements on the market. The object of this design ingenuity to is produce a pack that makes the weight of your load almost a part of your body. There should be no sore spots during the day or at the end of a hard trip. The pack should allow your arms to swing freely and should not affect your balance or mobility. It should adjust to loads and people of different sizes, shapes and weights. Given these requirements — which no pack fully meets — it is hardly surprising that most harness and suspension systems are pretty complex.

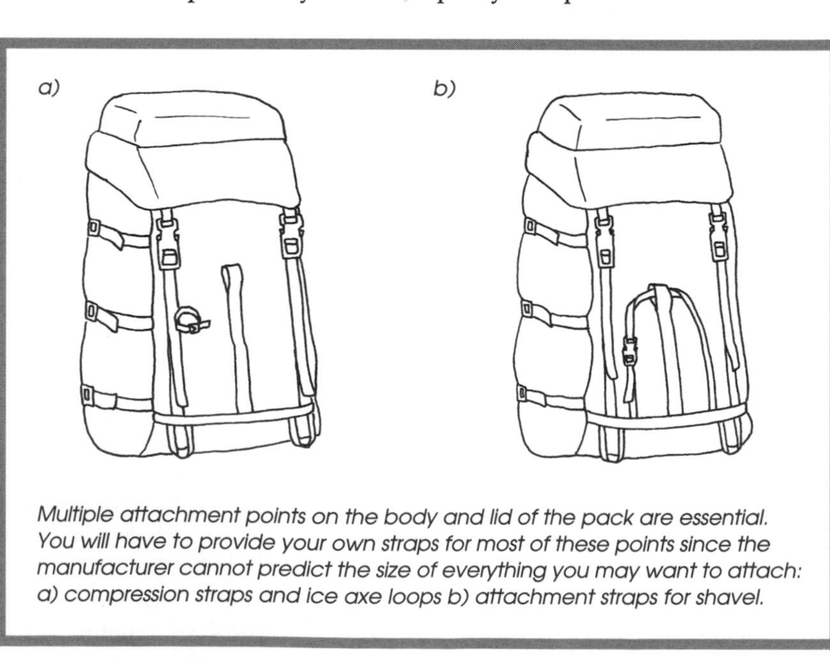

Multiple attachment points on the body and lid of the pack are essential. You will have to provide your own straps for most of these points since the manufacturer cannot predict the size of everything you may want to attach: a) compression straps and ice axe loops b) attachment straps for shavel.

Some typical comfort features:

- A well-padded hip belt, which will carry most of the weight. Don't stint on padding if you plan to carry heavy loads.
- Padded contoured shoulder straps. Not all of the load will be carried by the hip belt, and you may also want to change the distribution of weight between hips and shoulders during a long day. Proper contouring is important to allow free arm motion and to keep the straps from cutting off circulation to your arms or rubbing sores on your shoulders.
- Sternum or chest strap. If adjusted properly, this can take a significant amount of the load. Under certain conditions this strap can be dangerous. You will want to undo it when crossing rivers or avalanche slopes, or whenever the terrain is such that a fall could leave you hanging from your pack with the chest strap forced up against your throat.
- Stabilizer straps. The location and number will vary. Normally there will be straps going from the top of the internal pack frame to the shoulder straps. Stabilizers may also be located between the bottom of the pack and the hip belt, or descend from the middle of the pack to the belt or lower part of the frame. The purpose of stabilizers is to cinch the load closer to your body. Designs keep changing, so be prepared for different configurations.
- Contouring of pack and belt to hug the body. Avoid any pack that sits away from your body or moves independently of your torso.
- Torso adjustment. This allows a pack to be used by people with different measurements between shoulders and waist. There may be metal stays that can be bent to the shape of your back, interchangeable back frames and hip belts, and various levels for attaching the shoulder harness. Some packs claim to be adjustable enough to fit everyone. If that were the case, there would not be such an abundance of packs on the market.
- Back padding. One problem with internal frames is the tendency of poorly packed objects to protrude into your spine. Look for a good pad to cushion and separate the pack from your back.
- Special models for women. It took a long time for manufacturers to realize that women are not just small men. Their hips are larger, proportioned differently and do not move in the same way. Their shoulders do not usually have the same contours. Their centre of gravity is lower. Unfortunately, some of the packs advertised as women's models are still just smaller versions of the men's line. Only a few manufacturers offer expedition-size packs for females, but at least a start has been made. Since people don't come in standard models, the wider choice benefits everybody. I know men who prefer women's packs, and vice versa.

Dependability

Construction quality determines the dependability of your pack. If it comes apart in the back country, you simply have no way to carry your gear. Seams, zippers, hip belts, shoulder straps, lash points and the material of the pack body must not fail no matter how much you stress them. Zippers should be heavy-duty YKK or equivalent. Stress points should be bar tacked, double stitched, taped, riveted or reinforced with neoprene or leather as appropriate. The pack should have an unconditional warranty against manufacturing defects (small comfort if it fails in the back country, but at least it's an indication of the manufacturer's confidence in the product). Find out where the warranty will be honoured — if you have to send the pack to another continent for repairs, the guarantee won't be worth much to you.

Shopping for your pack

Mike and I own ten packs which we use regularly, with an even larger assortment cluttering the attic. We know our way around internal frames, but when we shop for a new pack we look for a knowledgeable salesperson to help us. Today's packs have such complex adjustments and differ so much from one another that trying to figure out how each works would be a waste of our time. At least one company has even produced a video to show customers how to custom-fit its packs. If you are not used to internal frames, you won't even know where or how to start when confronted with a store display of different models. If you can't find a competent salesperson, then at least try to have an experienced winter backpacker accompany you.

The store(s) where you shop should stock a variety of pack lines to ensure that they are not simply trying to unload whatever they have on the floor at the moment (the 1991 *Backpacker Magazine* Buyers' Guide issue lists 46 pack manufacturers for the U.S. alone). The salesperson should ask you enough questions to determine your general needs and then suggest packs which may meet them. It is essential that any packs you try on be properly adjusted to fit your body. Otherwise you will not be able to judge them accurately. Stuff the pack with climbing ropes or other heavy items and bulky clothing. You won't be able to simulate an actual load exactly, but try at least to have the pack full, including the lid pocket.

Test the pack in the shop. Raise your head to look upwards. Does the back of your head collide with the top of the pack? Bend forward, backward and sideways, tie your shoe laces, make quick movements in all directions. Does the pack disturb your balance? Wear the pack in the shop for a half hour or so (if the sales staff become impatient, do your shopping elsewhere). If the pack feels completely comfortable, has the desired features and checks out on quality of construction and warranty, find out if the store will allow you to return it if you encounter problems with it at home (obviously, they are not going to take it back if you use it on a trip).

At home, load the pack with your own gear. It may fit differently, or you may have underestimated the size you need.

PUTTING ON A LOADED PACK

When you put the pack on, you should follow a sequence of adjustments. This sequence should be followed every time you put on the pack, not just at the start of a trip:

- **Loosen all straps before you lift the pack.**
- **Position and tighten the hip belt first.**
- **Tighten the shoulder straps.**
- **Tighten the sternum strap.**
- **Now that the load-bearing parts of the pack are aligned, adjust the stabilizers.**

Wear the pack, fully loaded, around the house for at least an hour. Any discomfort you feel at this point will increase exponentially during an actual trip. Check that you know how to make every possible adjustment to the pack's harness, including torso length. Fine-tuning the fit can be tedious but it's well worth the effort. If adjustments don't solve all of the problems you are experiencing, return the pack to the shop.

If you follow the above advice, you should get a satisfactory pack on your first purchase. Unfortunately, no matter how carefully a pack is fitted in the shop or how comfortable it feels at home, the only true test is skiing with it for several hours, loaded with your own gear. For this reason, secondhand packs are readily available. Their only fault may be that they didn't quite fit the people who bought them. You may be able to buy a good used pack or sell your own costly mistake to someone else.

Loading the pack

It's easy to spot an inexperienced backpacker. A poorly balanced pack towers above the head. Every few strides, the hip belt is hitched up with the hands as the wearer struggles to ease discomfort. At stops, everything comes out on the snow as a water bottle or snack is retrieved from the very bottom. Until you have packed often enough to decide on the most convenient arrangement, you will undoubtedly spend time looking for things which aren't where you thought you put them. Having a general plan for packing will at least limit the search area for these items.

LOADING THE PACK FOR EFFICIENCY AND COMFORT

- Most of your gear should be pre-packed in stuff sacks to compress it.
- Leave some items loose to fill in spaces between the sacks.
- Sort your gear according to weight, fragility and need to access it on the trail.
- Women should pack heavy items as low as possible.
- If you are male, your sleeping bag should go in the bottom of the pack. Heavy items that you won't need until camp should be put in the middle. The heavier the items are, the closer they should be to your torso.
- Front access zippers allow you to bury a heavy repair/first aid kit at low- or mid-level and still get to it in an emergency.
- The top level is for items you will need frequently and which cannot be stored in pockets, like sweaters, down parka, lunch, water bottle (on a cold day it will freeze in a pocket). You should also put any fragile items on top or in pockets.
- Your foam mattress can be rolled up and strapped either under or on top of the lid if the pack does not have specific attachment straps for it.
- Fuel should never be stored in the body of the pack. If it spills you have a disaster.

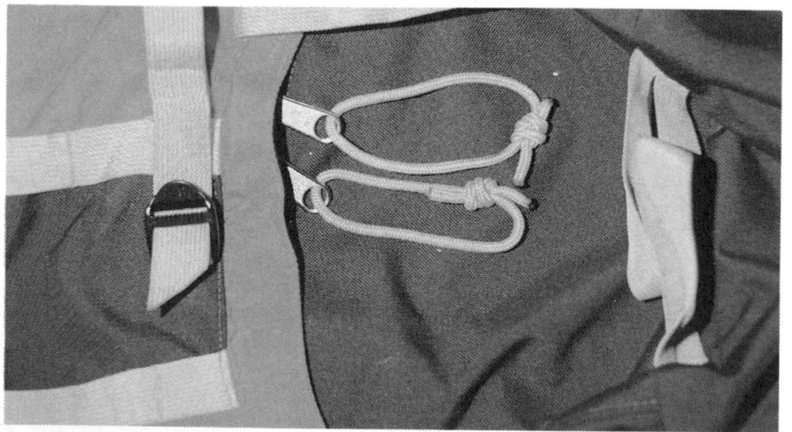

Before you take the pack on a trip, add ties, 5 cm (2 in.) long, to all zippers, so that you can work them with mitts on. Any straps that have to feed into buckles should be cut diagonally at the end. Square-cut straps often have to be coaxed through with fingers. Be sure to heat-seal the cut edge so that it won't fray.

If you put your camera in your pack, you aren't likely to use it (and if you don't use it you may as well leave it behind). Small cameras should be in a handy pocket of your clothing, wrapped in plastic to protect them from moisture and condensation. Larger models should be carried in a padded chest or waist pack, available in some outdoor stores and camera shops (use wide webbing for the waist belt).

With many internal frame packs you must be very careful not to place hard objects where they can jab your back. With any load that is close to the pack's capacity, you may have to try several arrangements before everything will fit. Try not to lash too many things to the outside of the pack. Heavy items go on the sides, either in pockets or under the compression straps, where they will be closer to your torso. Any load that extends above your head will snag low branches as you ski and may also be top-heavy.

SLEDS

On multi-day expeditions, a sled can make it possible to carry everything with you without ferrying loads or hurting your back. Sleds work best on well-packed snow or ice and where travel is mostly flat or straight up and down. Trying to traverse a steep slope with a 100 lb. sled dragging you downhill is an exercise for masochists. Unpacked snow may yield to a sled if it is fresh and fluffy but it will be almost impassable if heavy and settled. We use sleds on glaciers and in the arctic where the surface is usually wind blasted.

Children's plastic sled.

Kevlar sled.

A sled can be as cheap or expensive as you wish.Those which attach to the skier with solid poles give you the most control over the load — they will not, for example, ride up on the tails of your skis when going downhill. They limit your mobility somewhat and are expensive, but they are well worth the cost if you use sleds a lot. For the occasional expeditions where we need sleds, we prefer to rely on plastic children's models found in the toy section of a department store. They disintegrate after a few encounters with rocks and tip over with ridiculous ease, but they are cheap so we don't mind how much we bash them about. On Baffin Island, we dragged our "kids" sleds through gravel flats and boulder fields, and pushed them over the edge of icefalls, letting them find their own rapid way to the bottom. By the time the sleds fell apart, the expedition was over.

HOW TO MODIFY A CHILDREN'S SLED

- **Drill holes along the side rims for lashing down the load.**
- **Drill two holes on each side of the front rim and tie short cord loops through them. Use the outside holes for the rope that attaches the sled to the skier. The inner holes are for the brake.**
- **If the sled will be used on a glacier, drill a hole in the middle of the back rim and tie a short cord loop through it. This will be used to attach the sled to the climbing rope to prevent it from hitting you on the head if you fall into a crevasse.**

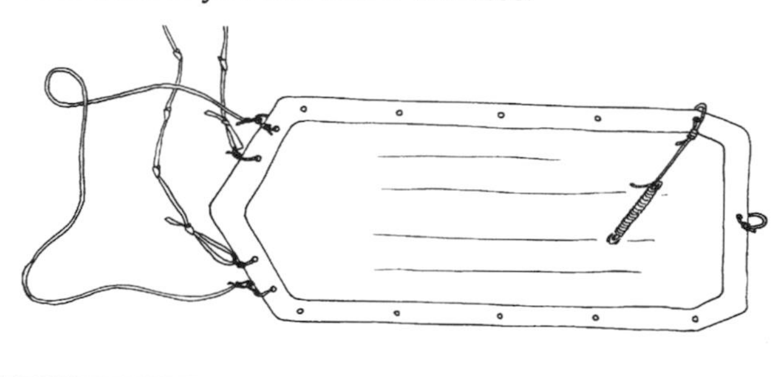

To build a brake, buy some one-inch nylon webbing about three and a half to four times as long as the sled. Fold it in half and make a knot in the middle. Make two or three other knots along each half of the webbing (the more knots, the more braking power), then attach both ends of the webbing to the holes at the front of the sled. When slipped underneath the loaded sled, the knots will create so much drag that you will be able to descend quite steep slopes under control. Flip the webbing on top of the sled for normal travel.

If the weight is not excessive, you may be able to tie your pack on the sled in such a way that you can put the whole load on your shoulders for difficult terrain.

DOGS

Dogs have acquired a bad reputation in the back country, thanks mainly to the thoughtlessness of their owners. Those of us who appreciate their companionship and tireless labour can only react with sorrow as more and more areas are closed to us. Our Alaskan Malamute can carry 11 kg (24 lbs). Hooked to a sled, she easily pulls three times that. We keep her out of set tracks, bury her droppings and make sure she doesn't bother other skiers. When someone's uncontrolled pet steals our lunch, digs holes or leaves "brown wax" in the track, dashes in front of us on downhill runs or barks hysterically, we understand why we no longer have the privilege of taking our dogs on many of our trips. This section is for those who tour in areas where dogs are still permitted.

One of our Keeshonds always runs between my legs when I snowplow. She can be brought safely down a busy trail. Sometimes, however, you have to leash the dog, either because the trail is too crowded or the park warden or ranger insists. As well, when the snow surface is hard, any dog is likely to chase deer and rabbits. Wildlife is already under severe stress in the winter. Never subject it to further discomfort, be it from your dog, your camera or your camping habits.

Running through snow is exhausting. Your dog should be full grown, fit and used to heavy exercise. Certain types of snow and ice can cut the dog's feet. Commercially made boots are available, but we have never found them to be very satisfactory. You can probably make better boots yourself. A dog that is not acclimatized to the cold has no place on an overnight camp-out even if it sleeps in the tent with you (and it probably will).

A trained dog makes life easier for you.

Every dog should at least pack its own food. Dog packs are available in some pet stores. The simplest design has saddlebags sized for small, medium and large dogs, with one strap across the chest and another under the belly to hold the bags in place. Such packs will slide off over the dog's head on a downhill run but are adequate for flat terrain. In the mountains you need one or two straps running from the chest collar to the belly and attached under the body to the saddle strap. Another strap should run from the saddle around the rear of the dog, under the tail. You may have to have such a pack custom made. The straps should have plastic or nylon fasteners that clip together. They will not freeze up in the snow nearly as badly as metal buckles. When you load the pack, make sure both sides are evenly weighted and that no sharp or protruding objects are next to the dog's body. The amount of weight that can be carried varies with the breed — ask your veterinarian. Accustom the dog to the pack before its first camping trip.

Northern working breeds can carry a pack and pull a sled at the same time (see *Canadian Geographic*, Feb/Mar 1990, for pictures of the harness used and an article about touring Baffin Island with dogs), but most family dogs should not try this. The plastic sled described in the previous section works equally well with dogs. The harness used for towing the sled can also be used to tow you on skis, an activity which is fun for both you and the dog (large breeds only).

A dog needs a firm track for either a pack or a sled. In deep snow, it will flounder even without a load. In camp, keep the dog tied up. Many dogs like to dig in the biffy and will eat human excrement. Resist the temptation to use the dog as a garburator for your excess food — it will

If you can't train your dog to tour leashed, at least when necessary, keep it out of the back country.

get diarrhea and become a thorough nuisance. You can, however, let the dog dispose of your dishwater if you don't use soap. A dog may resist drinking plain water in winter and become dehydrated. The scraps of food washed from the pots will make the water tasty for him.

Finally, if you want to take your dog winter camping, check that dogs are allowed in the area where you plan to camp and then obey the regulations. In that way you will help to preserve access for all dog lovers.

6.
Shelter

TENTS

Snow caves, igloos and bivy bags (a bivy bag or bivouac sack is a lightweight cover for a sleeping bag) offer adequate shelter in winter and they don't burden your back. So why do so many people still carry the extra weight of a tent? After you have completed your first snow dwelling you will understand why these structures are reserved mainly for base camps, where the effort of building them is offset by the comfort of the following days. I know campers who swear by caves, but I find them just too much work for one-night occupancy. Bivy sacks, in contrast, are no trouble at all, but they are not much fun in a storm. Besides, you can't sit up inside a bivy bag, and getting dressed while lying prone in a narrow bag is an ugly way to start a day.

Most people do not travel alone, and for the weight of two bivy bags you can have a small tent and the cozy feeling of a roof over your head. That, at least, is the theory. In practice, most of the two-person tents you

A four-season tent must be able to withstand the worst weather.

see in the winter weigh as much as five or ten bivy sacks and form a significant part of the pack load. Part of the reason is comfort, but another factor is cost. You can buy featherweight tents that have been tested on the world's highest mountains, but they are expensive and usually not very spacious.

If you normally camp in the desert or do your touring by bicycle, you probably own a one-season shelter and will have to invest in something sturdier for winter. Summer backpackers who hike in areas subject to heavy rain and wind should already own a good three-season tent. Most of these can withstand moderate winter conditions. In fact, tents which sometimes spring a leak in a downpour may perform better in snow. Unless your summer tent collapses in a strong breeze, it will get you started in winter camping. Remember, however, that people's tenting needs vary with climate, terrain, type of activity and tolerance for a heavy load or crowded quarters. Only you can decide which features are most important to you.

Four-season tents

Tents suitable for serious winter backpacking are classified as four-season or expedition tents by manufacturers. The lighter the tent relative to its strength and interior space, the more it will cost. For example, *Backpacker Magazine*, in its May 1991 evaluation of tents, listed the Bibler "Kiva", which weighs under six pounds and sleeps three to four, at $725 U.S. If you want a roomy tent for moderate cost, be prepared for extra weight.

Size. Larger tents are best for sitting out a spell of bad weather in comfort. Small tents are warmer but deposit more condensation on you and your gear. The arrangement of interior space is also important. Can a tall person sit up without brushing against the (usually frosty or wet) tent wall? Can two people sit up and get dressed at the same time? Where will the dog sleep? Is there a vestibule for cooking? Is there adequate ventilation (essential to prevent excessive build-up of condensation and also for cooking)?

Resistance to weather. Regardless of size, a winter tent should be easy to set up and anchor in the worst weather. The entrance, vents and seams should provide a tight seal against spindrift (fine particles of snow, driven before the wind, that can penetrate even a closed tent). The entrance(s) should be sheltered or designed so that you can come and go without filling the tent with blowing snow in a gale or with accumulated snow afterwards. Dual entrances are convenient, especially if your partner is cooking at one end, and they allow rapid escape in case he or she sets the tent on fire. Many tents flap wildly in the wind, but quieter ones are available — a feature that may be important to light sleepers.

Interior features. On a multi-day trip, small features can add a lot to comfort. There should be attachment points inside for lines to hang damp clothes on. Storage pockets along the walls hold small items that would otherwise get lost in the jumble of sleeping bags and clothing. A vestibule lets you store boots, packs and other gear out of the living area and also out of the weather.

Materials and construction. Most tents have a breathable canopy of ripstop nylon, with a waterproof floor and a separate fly. Single-wall tents in waterproof-breathable fabric are also available. The better manufacturers cut the fabric according to the direction of stress for added strength. Seams should be double stitched (lapfelled) and all points of stress reinforced. Seams in waterproof-breathable material should be taped or otherwise sealed to prevent leakage. Zippers should be made of sturdy metal which won't break or freeze.

Poles. These usually either feed through sleeves on the outside of the canopy or attach to the canopy with clips. The clips are easier to use but focus stress on isolated points rather than spreading it along a sleeve. Sleeves add weight if they are of solid fabric and are subject to puncture if they are made of lighter mesh. Both types of sleeves are found on good tents, however. Tent poles are normally of a tough grade of aluminum, although some high-tech fibres are also used. Too soft, and the poles bend out of shape; too brittle, and they break; too heavy a gauge, and they weigh too much.

Sectioned poles should be shock-corded, but standard shock cord loses its elasticity in the cold. Some manufacturers claim to use a material that avoids this difficulty, but we are not convinced by anything that we have seen so far. Elasticity can be restored by stretching and releasing the cord rapidly and repeatedly to warm it.

The fly should come as close to the ground as possible for winter use, to avoid spindrift, snow and wind coming in underneath.

Ease of setup. This feature is best appreciated when you make camp in a state of near exhaustion, after dark, in howling wind, at a temperature which forces you to keep your mitts on. If you and your partner can erect your shelter in those conditions without declaring war on each other, you have a good tent.

OBSTACLES TO EASY SET-UP

- **Poles and sleeves of different lengths, so that each pole must go in a specific sleeve;**
- **Complex pattern of non-continuous sleeves, so that a pole started along one sleeve track may inadvertently be switched to another;**
- **Sleeve ends which do not open easily to admit the pole;**
- **A pitch which is so taut that superhuman strength is needed to position the last pole or attach the last corner of the fly;**
- **Multiple tie-down points needed just to get the tent to stand up;**
- **Anything fiddly or complicated;**
- **Anything that requires the use of fingers rather than mitts.**

Types of tents

Internal versus external support. Tents fall into two broad categories: those which require guy lines to maintain their pitch, and those which are self-supporting (also known as free standing). Free-standing tents are popular. The pole configuration necessary to support the tent usually guarantees lots of shoulder room inside and a very taut pitch. Free-standers are great on ice or where the area is too rocky for tent pegs.

A free-standing tent can be set up anywhere, then moved to a prepared platform.

There are two disadvantages to free-standing tents. The extra poles and fabric needed for self-support add weight (except for the cross-pole design discussed below), and a tent that can be erected without being tied down is a balloon waiting to be carried away by the first gust of wind. We once participated in a tent chase on a remote glacier in British Columbia. It made great storytelling afterwards (ten people galloping madly after a cartwheeling VE 24), but at the time it could have had very serious consequences. Always hang on to your tent until it is staked down.

Tent design. When you first shop for a tent, the variety of floor plans and pole arrangements is bewildering. The basic patterns are pyramid, A-frame, hoop and dome, but mutations of these have given rise to a generation of hybrids.

Although basic shape affects ease of setup, interior living space and weight, it has little to do with ability to withstand winter conditions. **Pyramids** and **A-frames** are somewhat out of fashion, but two of the sturdiest winter tents ever made were the McKinley (a pyramid) and the North Face Mountain Tent (an A-frame). If you find either one in used but good condition, it would be the most economical way to acquire a four-season tent.

The easiest winter tents to set up have two **interior crossed poles**. With a larger tent, like the Bibler "Kiva", you crawl inside the collapsed canopy with the two poles, place the ends of the poles in the four corners so that they cross in the middle and position the poles correctly along the canopy with Velcro tabs. With a smaller tent, you do the corner placements from outside, then either crawl in or stand and put the open door of the tent over your head to work on the Velcro tabs from inside. These tents are free-standing.

Interior cross-pole tents have straight sides, giving more shoulder room, and are very quiet in the wind. Because the poles are inside the tent, there are no sleeves to feed through, saving weight, and no risk of puncturing or ripping a sleeve. If wind force becomes excessive, the Velcro tabs will give way before the poles break. The tent will collapse briefly, then spring back rather than break a pole or tear the fabric.

The only tents I have seen of this design are single wall using a waterproof-breathable fabric. In severe cold, water vapour will freeze to the inside of the canopy and destroy its breathability unless you can maintain a relatively warm interior temperature. Use a vapour barrier in your sleeping bag to cut down on the moisture being generated, and don't try to cook inside. The advantages of single-wall tents, in addition to ease of setup, are their performance in fierce winter weather and their light weight (about 2 kg or 4 lbs for a two-person model). The disadvantages are high cost, cramped space, poor ventilation and questionable performance in the rain (we consider our cross-poles to be one-season winter tents).

Next to cross-poles, **hoops** are the lightest weight winter tents. Three (occasionally two) hoops feed through sleeves on the tent body and fit into grommets at each end, producing a shape vaguely like that of a caterpillar. The tent must be pegged down at front and back to keep the hoops upright, and usually the fly requires side pegging. These tents are extremely stable and they shed snow well. Hoops allow plenty of shoulder room. Their main disadvantage is in not being free standing; the guy cords that keep the canopy and fly taut must be tightened from time to time, which can be difficult if they are frozen or buried in snow.

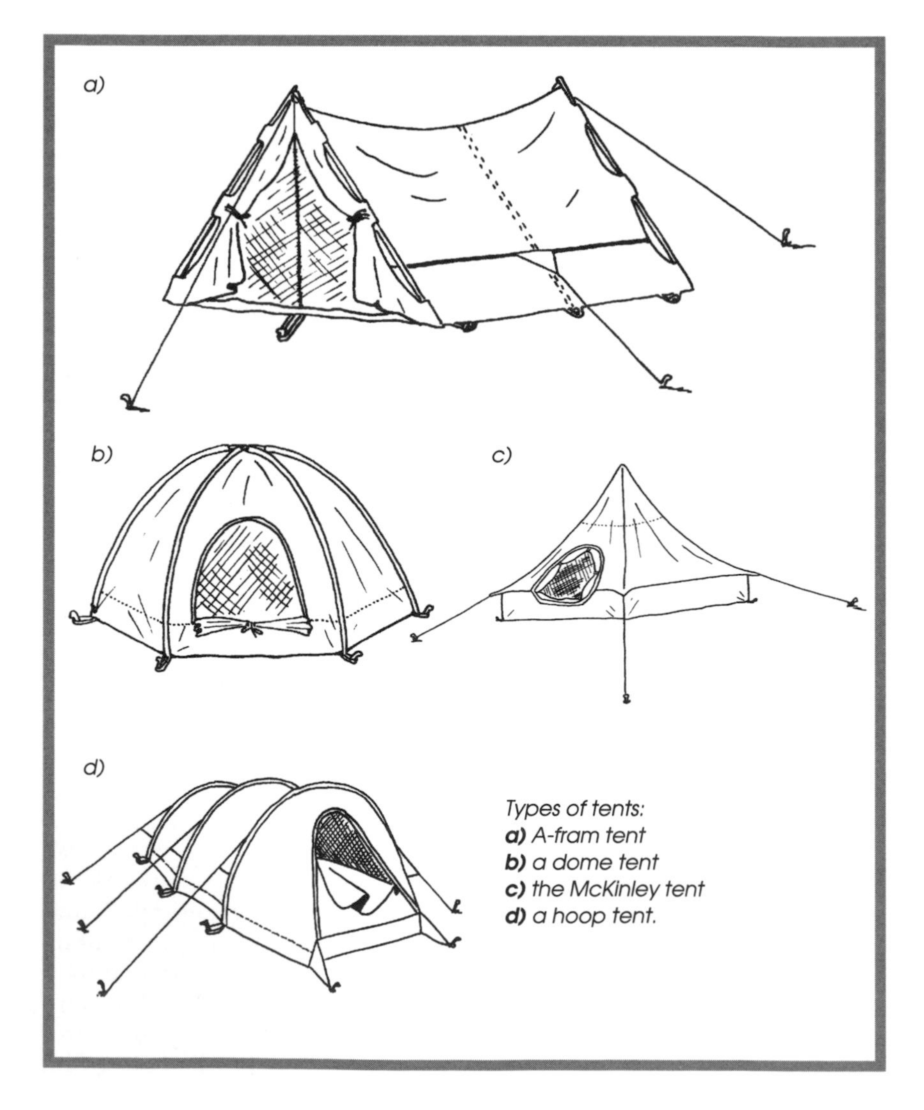

Types of tents:
***a)** A-fram tent*
***b)** a dome tent*
***c)** the McKinley tent*
***d)** a hoop tent.*

Domes provide spacious interiors and the convenience of being free-standing. If they are well made, they are very strong and stable no matter what direction the wind comes from. They are also heavy and somewhat complicated to set up.

A-frames are not widely marketed for winter use anymore, but the design is very stable and the cost usually moderate. Various combinations of poles may be added to make the tent free-standing and to improve shoulder room inside. **Pyramids** give campers the luxury of kneeling or even standing inside, with the resultant extra fabric adding to weight. They are complicated to set up and flap noisily in the slightest breeze, but, like domes, shed snow and can take the wind from any direction.

Do not feel limited to the pure designs listed above. Mixed configurations of poles perform well too. Most tents labelled four-season, no matter what their shape, will be adequate for average winter conditions. A few will withstand just about anything. If you decide at some time in the future to take on really wild weather, be guided by what mountaineers are using on Mount McKinley (now known as Denali) when you shop for your bombproof shelter.

Problems arise when, for the sake of economy, you want a tent that not only can handle heavy snow and howling winds but will also keep you dry in a three-day rain storm and cool on hot summer nights. Remember that the features you prize most in a summer tent (rain- and bug-proof, with gusty ventilation) are of little value in the winter and may be overlooked when you buy your winter shelter. True four-season tents exist. They perform equally well in all conditions and are durable enough for constant use. Our North Face VE 24, for example, goes car camping, sea kayaking and summer hiking in addition to being a mainstay of our arctic and mountaineering expeditions. When we bought the VE 24 many years ago, it had little competition for four-season honours. Today, there are enough serious competitors to make the choice very difficult.

Pitching a tent in winter

Rule number one: practice putting the tent up at home until you are thoroughly familiar with it. For an added challenge, try putting it up wearing mittens or in the dark.

At the end of a hard day of solo travel, my tent pitching routine can be devoid of frills. I whip out my little cross-pole, snap the two poles inside, set the tent on the nearest piece of level snow, ram my skis and ski poles into the stake-out loops on the corners, toss in my sleeping gear and then turn to other matters. The entire procedure can take as little as five minutes.

Most of the time, I devote a little more care to erecting my home, especially if I am not alone. The surface beneath the tent should be solid and level enough that people sleeping inside do not roll into each other. Therefore a platform must be constructed.

- **Select a good site** for your tent, preferably in an area away from snow-laden trees yet as sheltered from the wind as possible. If the terrain features high and low ground, try to locate the platform above a dip or gulley. The low area will serve as a sink hole for cold air while the tent will be warmer.
- **Mark out an area** larger than the tent and its guying anchors. You want to be able to walk around it without tripping over the guy lines. Use your shovel if the terrain is not level.
- **Prepare the platform** by packing it down with your skis. If you want to put up the tent immediately, pack the platform next with your boots, then again with your skis. After that, do not walk on the area designated for the tent, and walk on the rest of the platform as little as possible until it is firm enough to support you.

First, pack the platform with skis. Next, pack the platform with boots.

Tent laid out on platform.

If there is no hurry to erect the tent (perhaps you are going skiing or exploring for an hour or two), then skip the foot packing, make sure that the platform is as level as you want it and leave. By the time you return, the snow will have hardened enough to support the tent (it may even be firm enough to walk on, but check before plunging into it).

- **Erect the tent**. If you have a free-standing tent, you can set it up away from the platform, then move it onto the site. Otherwise, place the limp tent on the platform oriented so that the main entrance faces away from the wind. If severe winds are expected, however, place the entrance at 90° to the wind (otherwise, you will wake up to a tent full of spindrift). Follow the setup procedure for your tent.
- **Tie the tent down**. If there is much wind, make sure that you either peg down at least one corner (a ski makes a good temporary anchor) or assign someone to hang on to the tent while you are putting it up. Guy out the tent and fly as necessary to insure a taut pitch and to keep it from blowing away.
- **Protect the floor**. Cover the floor with your mattresses so that the weight and heat of people inside will not make craters in the snow underneath.

Tent pegs

The spindly pegs provided with summer tents won't work in snow, but a variety of other things will. Skis, poles, ice axes and shovels all provide good anchors, but may be needed for other activities. We prefer scooped out metal pegs with holes in them, although sturdy triangular nylon or plastic pegs will also do.

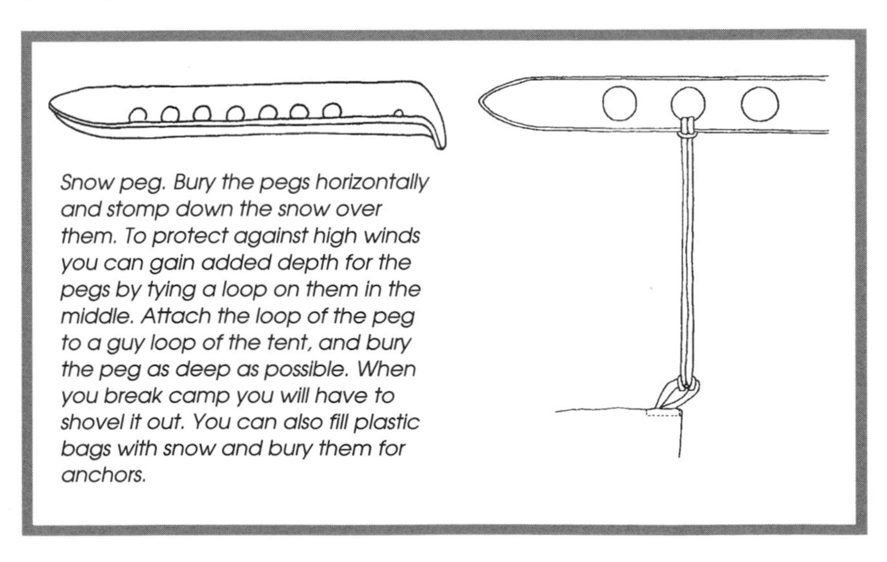

Snow peg. Bury the pegs horizontally and stomp down the snow over them. To protect against high winds you can gain added depth for the pegs by tying a loop on them in the middle. Attach the loop of the peg to a guy loop of the tent, and bury the peg as deep as possible. When you break camp you will have to shovel it out. You can also fill plastic bags with snow and bury them for anchors.

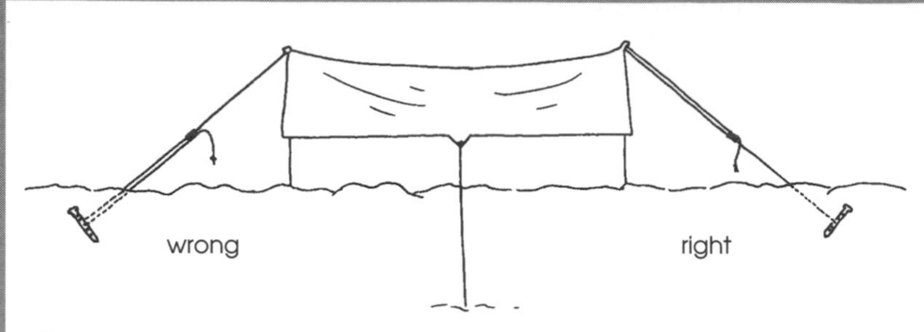

Sometimes you have to adjust the tension of the guy lines after the tent has been standing for several hours. This is difficult to do if the adjustable part of the cord has frozen into the snow. You can avoid this problem by attaching the adjustable end of the guy line to the tent rather than to the peg.

Dig a pit 30 cm to 50 cm (1 ft. to 2 ft.) deep at the door of the tent. You will be able to sit comfortably in the entrance to put on or remove boots. You can also lie in your sleeping bag and cook in the pit. If you have a vestibule, dig the pit inside it.

Above tree line, on glaciers and in other very exposed locations, you may want to surround your tent or camp with a wall of snow blocks. This will serve as a wind break to ease stress on tent poles and fabric, and reduce the amount of drifting (although in a bad storm you will still need to go out periodically to remove snow that is putting too much pressure on the tent). You may think that camping in such terrain involves more masochism than pleasure, but in fact some of the finest skiing and most scenic ski touring can be found in places subject to the wildest weather.

Tenting in wet conditions

At the opposite extreme to cold, dry conditions is camping in very wet snow or mud. A ground sheet may be necessary to keep water from penetrating the tent floor. Make sure that the edges of the ground sheet do not protrude beyond the floor of the tent, or you will end up with a pool underneath you. The fly must be pitched very taut to ensure complete separation from the canopy. Wet snow is heavy. If it forces the fly onto the canopy, water will start to drip into the tent. All seams must be perfectly sealed with seam-sealer. Check the condition of the seams regularly and renew the sealant, if necessary, before each trip.

BIVY BAGS

Weighing next to nothing, bivy bags provide a warm night's sleep for a single person. Many people carry them as an emergency shelter on day trips. A bivy bag should be waterproof on the bottom, waterproof-breathable on top, and should zip tight to keep out snow, spindrift and ice crystals. The zipper should have a close-fitting flap to protect it from wind and moisture. The bag should be wide enough for your mattress to fit inside. If you place the mattress **under** the bag you are sure to slide off in the middle of the night. One of our friends found this out the hard way when he made an emergency bivouac on a slope, awakening the next morning 15 feet below his mattress and boots.

Bivy bags are for people who like to lie in bed and look up at the stars, for photographers who want to take photos throughout the night (you can position a tripod over the top of the bag so that all you have to do is sit up and take your shot), and for those who must travel light. Don't try to use a vapour barrier liner unless you are in a tent or snow cave — how are you going to strip down to your underwear or dress in the morning if the weather is bad? Bivy bags are terrible on multi-day trips if you have to wait out a storm.

You will enjoy a bivy bag more if you can keep it off your face when it is closed. Deluxe models have a single hoop pole at the head, others use pleats and tucks.

SNOW SHELTERS

If you bury a pot of water 30 cm to 60 cm (1 ft. to 2 ft.) deep in the snow, it will not freeze, no matter how cold the air temperature (a point to remember if you have cans of pop or beer in camp). That is because snow is an excellent insulator. Its insulating properties can be used to keep humans as well as water (or beer) from freezing.

Building a snow shelter requires knowledge, a shovel and/or snow saw, and time. Snow caves and igloos are quiet and are warmer than tents because they are constructed with the living and sleeping quarters higher than the entrance so that cold air will not enter. They can be as spacious as time and imagination allow.

Snow caves

A cave is the ultimate emergency shelter. It can be built in almost any kind of snow, with any depth of snow greater than a few inches, above

An embankment is a good place to dig a snow cave.

Dig your entrance straight into the bank.

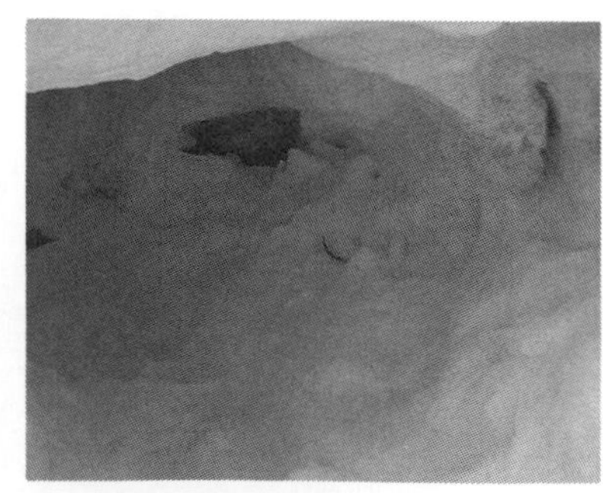

This tunnel had to turn left to avoid some bushes.

Inside a small cave.

or below the tree line. Truly horrific weather will destroy any tent. If you are caught in a sudden storm, its inherent warmth could save a life. For these reasons alone you should know how to dig a cave quickly and efficiently.

The easiest place to build a cave is on the lee side of a hill or embankment, perhaps just under a cornice, where the snow is at least 1 1/2 to 2 metres (yards) deep and there is a slope below you for dumping debris. **DO NOT USE SUCH A LOCATION IF THERE IS ANY DANGER OF AVALANCHE!** (see Chapter Eleven).

Building a snow cave

METHOD #1. Find a snowdrift or embankment that is taller than you are. If possible, place the entrance of your cave at right angles to the wind. Starting at the bottom, dig a tunnel straight in, about a metre (yard) wide and a little over a metre high. A second person should follow behind and clear out the snow as you dig. Continue to burrow like a

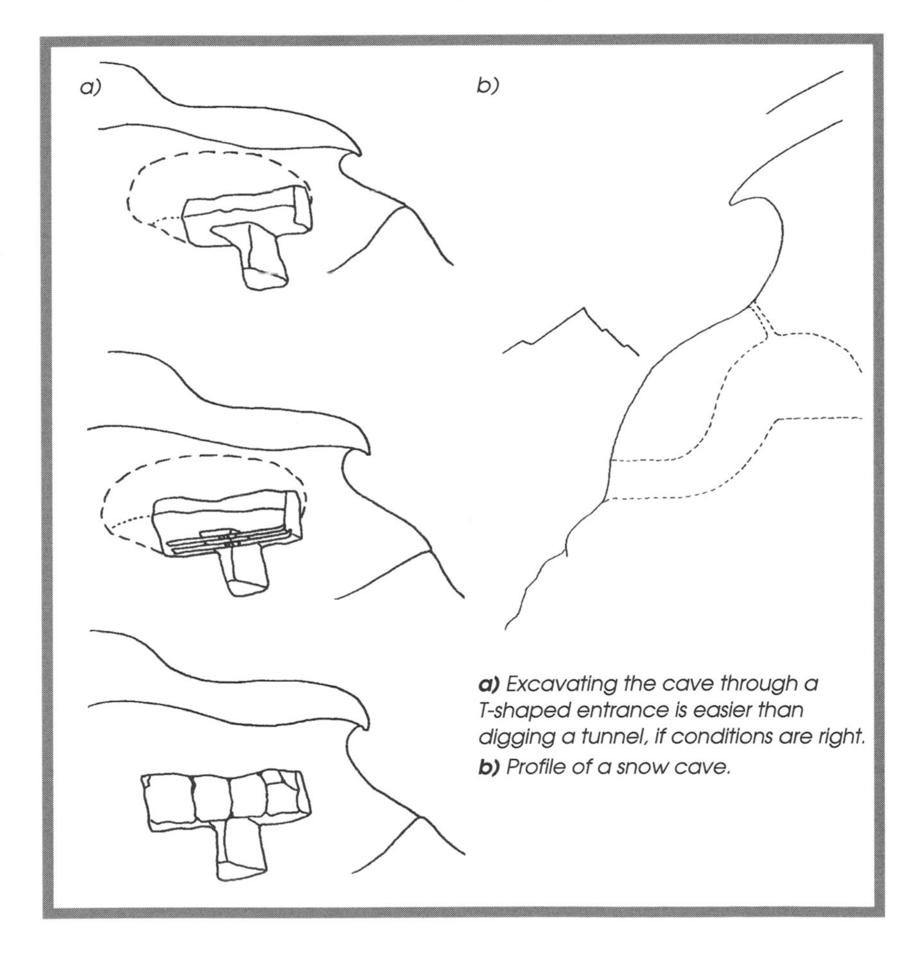

a) *Excavating the cave through a T-shaped entrance is easier than digging a tunnel, if conditions are right.*
b) *Profile of a snow cave.*

mole, slanting the tunnel upward and around any obstacles you may encounter (trees, boulders, bare earth, etc.).

Once you are in about a metre (yard) or so, widen the tunnel into a cave, digging upward. If the snow is deep enough you want to work in a standing position; at the very least you need to uncurl a bit by now. Fashion a sleeping platform above the level of the entrance to the cave and create any other furniture that appeals to you. The roof should be a dome shape for strength, 30 cm to 60 cm (1 ft. to 2 ft.) thick for insulation, and as smooth as possible to prevent drips. Punch a hole or two through the roof for ventilation, and your cave is ready for occupancy.

METHOD #2. If you have a large embankment or drift, and the snow is reasonably firm, a T-shaped entrance is easier to dig than a tunnel. Stand facing the snow bank. Clear off the loose snow to form a large T as tall as you are. Make the arms of the T as long as your skis and about 1/2 metre (2 ft.) high. Carefully cut one row of snow blocks, as big as you can handle, from the arms of the T and place them to one side.

Now dig out the vertical and horizontal sections of the T until you can stand inside the snow bank and have a snow wall at least 30 cm (1 ft.) thick. Face the bank and carve out your cave, using the arms of the T to dispose of snow debris. When you are satisfied with your home, place your skis across the horizontal part of the T and put the snow blocks that you cut earlier on top of them. Fill in the chinks with snow. You will use the opening under your skis as the entrance. Don't forget to punch a vent hole through the roof of your cave.

Sometimes you have to make a large pile of snow and dig your cave inside it.

When you don't have a snow bank for your cave

There may not be a convenient drift or embankment nearby for your cave. If the snow is deep enough, shovel down at least two metres (yards), making a pit big enough for you and your partner, then start digging your cave. Debris will have to be thrown up out of the pit.

If the snow is not deep enough, you will have to shovel a pile big enough to build a cave in. Pack the pile down with shovels as you build it, then leave it for a few minutes to harden. Fluffy powder snow will consolidate with this treatment, but depth hoar will not. You can recognize depth hoar easily — it refuses to consolidate when you step on it and if you try to make a snowball, it runs from your hands like sugar. Never allow depth hoar to be shovelled into your pile.

Place wands or sticks to a depth of 30 cm (1 ft.) at various places in the pile to help you judge the thickness of the roof as you dig from inside. Use your judgement as you hollow out your cave. If the snow seems unconsolidated, let it rest some more rather than risk having the pile collapse on top of you.

The worst place for a snow cave is on a flat glacier where the snow has compacted to an icy hardness. In my less rational days, I volunteered to lead a group on the Columbia Icefields to practice cave building. We made camp about three in the afternoon. At midnight, sounds of shovels and curses were still echoing across the glacier. Snow saws for cutting the hard snow would have saved us considerable grief. So would tents.

Cave digging is wet, exhausting work. A waterproof-breathable parka with hood, waterproof overmitts and a partner make construction more bearable. Switch places with your partner frequently to avoid working up too great a sweat. Depending on conditions, your architectural ambitions and your skill, the cave will take from one to several hours to build.

Life inside a cave tends to be damp, so many people use a bivy bag. If you cook inside, be sure to have adequate ventilation, including a vent hole right above the stove. Always take a shovel inside at night in case a storm blocks the entrance. If you plan on doing anything the next day, you should also take an alarm clock or arrange to have a tenting companion wake you. In the cave you may not know when the sun comes up, nor will you hear any outside sounds. You should also ensure that the entrance to the cave is clearly visible from the outside — you don't want to get lost while answering a call of nature at night!

Igloos

Most veteran winter campers have a "first igloo" story. The usual tale of woe involves a structure whose walls continue to spiral upwards without ever closing over the top. I slept in one of those in a howling storm on the Bow Glacier in the company of an unflappable Scotsman whose snores would have rattled the roof if we had had one. I have watched companions struggle for days to complete their ice palace while everyone else went skiing. In contrast, I have also been inside igloos large enough to seat twenty people and seen experts put smaller ones together in less than an hour.

Igloos are wonderful shelters, lighter and drier than caves and, if you know what you are doing, more pleasant to build. Just be sure to carry a tent until you have successfully built a few (reading a set of instructions, or even watching someone else does not count).

Cutting blocks for igloo.

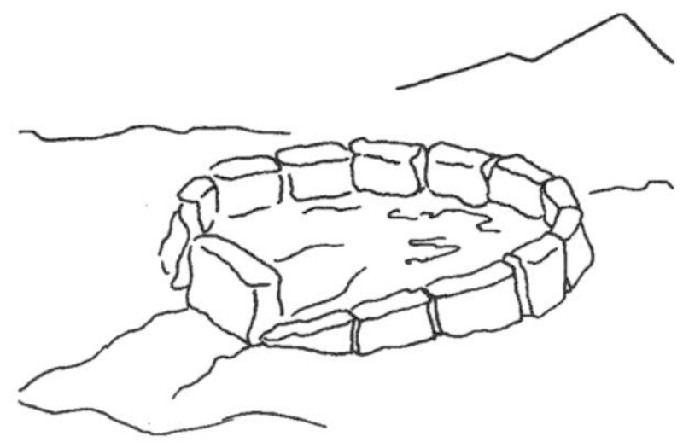

When the first circle is complete, taper the tops of the blocks so that they form a ramp on which to start the next layer. You want the igloo to grow as a spiral, with the rows tilting ever more steeply towards the centre.

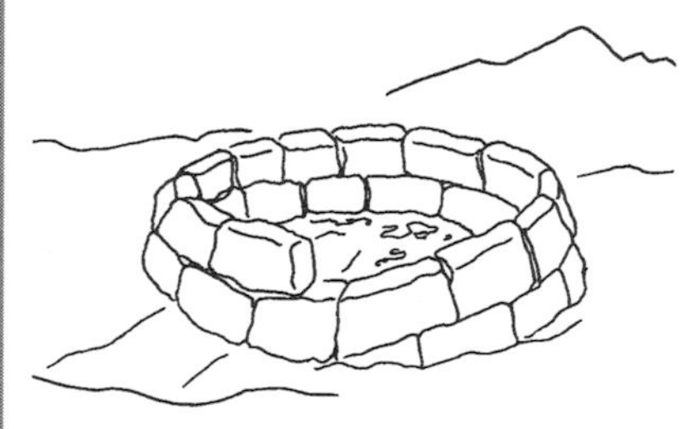

Position the second row of blocks so that they overlap the joints in the first row, always maintaining contact at the corners. As you progress through the second row, the angle of inward lean should increase to about 45°. Fill in the cracks with snow.

Continue layering and tilting blocks until the roof is complete. Now dig a trench from outside and cut out an entrance. You can roof the entrance tunnel if you still have the energy, but it can easily be blocked by a pack or tarp.

Unlike caves, igloos require consolidated snow that can be shaped into blocks firm enough to pick up and handle fairly roughly. Open areas where the snow is wind packed all winter are the best places to look. You may have to dig through a layer of new snow to find the hard pack underneath. Igloo building in soft snow is seldom worth the effort, but you can proceed as for a tent platform, packing the snow with skis and boots, and allowing it time to harden.

Draw a circle in the snow about two metres (6.5 ft.) in diameter (leave larger igloos for later). Using a snow saw (a specialized tool available in mountaineering shops), or a shovel, or carpenter's saw, cut blocks from inside the circle. This saves a lot of time since the floor is lowered and the walls raised with each layer of blocks. If the snow inside is not suitable or deep enough, you will have to quarry elsewhere.

The size of the blocks will vary with the consistency of the snow and how much you can lift or carry, but they should be about a third longer horizontally than vertically and about 15 cm (6 in.) thick. The bigger they are, the quicker your igloo will go up.

Place blocks on the outline until the circle is complete, tilting the blocks inward. They should make contact with each other only at the corners, so you should shave the sides into a slightly concave shape. This is important — too much pressure in the middle will weaken or even split the block, but pressure from the corners will compact and strengthen it. Further, if there are uneven points of contact, the blocks will not adhere to each other at the proper degree of inward tilt (that is, you won't have a roof). As you place each block, make sure that you have three points of solid contact, with the fourth corner ready to receive the next block. This method of shaping and placing blocks must be followed in subsequent rows.

As in a cave, the sleeping platform should be above the level of the entrance. Ventilation and light are no problem, since there will be plenty of chinks between the blocks. Take a shovel inside at night so that you can get out the entrance after a storm rather than having to knock down the walls.

Trenches

The twenty-minute snow shelter. No technique or special equipment is required. You can dig trenches with a cooking pot or a ski if necessary. If you need shelter for one in a hurry, a trench is the structure of choice.

Dig the trench just wide and deep enough to hold you (it should resemble a coffin). One or both ends should have a pit to draw cold air away from you. Cover the trench with 10 cm to 30 cm (4 in. to 12 in.) of snow supported in whatever manner you can devise — pine boughs will do in an emergency, but skis and poles covered by a tarp are better for the forest. Snow blocks set in an A-frame also make an excellent roof. A candle inside or a fire at one end add warmth. If this is an unplanned bivouac, use your pack for insulation under you, or cut more pine boughs.

Snow trench.

7. Food, Drink and Stoves

NUTRITION

My first mini-expedition was with friends who had little more experience than I had. We studied the literature on nutritional requirements for climbing and backpacking and dutifully worked out menus that provided 4,500 calories per person per day. Fortunately, squirrels ate some of our supplies, but on the last day we still had to pack out more than half the food that we had brought with us.

Today, having survived 17 days of instant mashed potatoes on Mount McKinley, 21 days of curried cabbage in the Himalayas and a climb of Huascaràn, in Peru, that featured chicken noodle soup at dawn, I know all too well that one person's nutritional convictions can be a dog's breakfast for the rest of the party. I also know that unless you are planning to walk to the North Pole, or participate in a lengthy high-altitude expedition, you can eat pretty much what you please on a trip and be none the worse for it. I have friends who travel for days on granola bars and cheddar cheese, others who stand outside in the worst weather and prepare gourmet menus.

There are two general requirements for winter meals: you need lots of fluid and you need complex carbohydrates to provide sustained warmth through the night and energy through the day. You can satisfy these requirements with a package of soup mix and some macaroni. The mashed potatoes on McKinley and chicken noodle soup on Huascaràn actually were good nutritional choices (curried cabbage is another matter).

Certainly on short trips you need not worry about getting the proper mix of vitamins, minerals, proteins and fats. Your food choices for winter camping should be governed by the weight of the product, its tolerance for freezing, ease and speed of preparation, taste, cost, and its ability to supply adequate hydration, warmth and energy to your body.

Portion size and calories

Few people will eat more than 500 mL (two cups) of main course for dinner, and many stop at half that amount. Until you know your appetite in a camp setting, it is better to underestimate the quantity of **cooked** food you will eat, although you must be certain that your food bag provides ample calories overall. You can supplement the cooked main course with desserts and items from lunch; this is far better than facing leftover macaroni and cheese at breakfast or having to carry it out. Of course, you will NEVER, EVER leave garbage behind. Resist, as well, the temptation to feed large amounts of leftovers to the dog. Unless this is its normal fare, it will get diarrhea and present a worse problem than the garbage.

Your major calorie requirements are best met with lunch items such as trail mix, hard cheese, sausage and candy — foods which provide 3.5 or more calories per gram (at least 100 calories per ounce). With a rich caloric intake on the trail, you can then plan a dinner menu of normal, appetizing food that includes lots of liquid. A moist main course based on pasta or rice will provide 350 to 600 calories in a 500 mL (2 cup) serving. You can increase the caloric value substantially by adding butter. With hot chocolate, sweetened drinks and dessert, you can easily consume 1,000 to 1,500 calories in the evening. Breakfast can be enriched by adding butter to hot cereal and eating the first sandwich of the day before breaking camp.

Let me emphasize, however, that people differ enormously in their calorie requirements for short trips. Mike, for example, has only about 12 per cent body fat. He needs frequent high calorie snacks to keep warm and maintain his strength. I don't have the nerve to measure my body fat, but I have enjoyed week-long solo trips on which I consumed little more than 1,200 calories per day. It is always advisable to overestimate your needs, however, especially if you carry the extra calories in a compact, ready-to-eat form such as trail mix. Once your body's energy supply is exhausted, food is the only practical way to restore it. There is also the possibility that your trip will be prolonged by bad weather or an accident, in which case you will need emergency rations.

LIQUIDS

You cannot carry or drink enough fluid on the trail to replace what you lose during the day. In very cold weather, you will lose a significant amount of moisture not only from perspiration but also from breathing. Cold air is dry. As you breathe, the air is first heated, drying it further, then humidified by your body before it reaches your lungs, resulting in fluid loss by evaporation. Once camp is established, your first priority should be rehydration. Drink enough to put out a normal volume of urine that is clear in colour. Infrequent urination and dark urine are signs of dehydration. Excessive amounts of tea or coffee, which are diuretics, can cause you to get up during the night, so you may want to emphasize fruit drinks and soup. Mike and I usually have tea, juice or non-alcoholic mulled wine as soon as we stop, then have soup for dinner, water with dinner, and hot chocolate and tea after dinner. We keep a water bottle handy at night in case we wake up thirsty.

Sources of complex carbohydrates

Pasta, noodles, potatoes, rice, legumes: these should be the main ingredients of your dinner, although there is no reason, other than habit, not to eat them for breakfast as well. Cereals, breads and trail mix are the more usual sources of carbohydrates during the day.

Whether or not you add meat to your meals is a matter of personal taste. You don't need the protein on a short trip. Freeze-dried meats tend to taste like cardboard, jerky is expensive, sausages often appear at lunch and are unwelcome again at dinner, cans are heavy, hard to use when frozen, and awkward to pack out. If you want extra protein at dinner, textured soya protein rehydrates fairly quickly and combines well with most dishes.

Use dehydrated foods to save weight

Water is heavy. If you pack canned foods, you carry a lot of water in addition to the can. It makes sense to take food in a dehydrated form and add water during cooking. Depending on the product, reconstitution can require anything from a few seconds to a few hours. In very cold weather, it is wise to select foods with short preparation times, both to save fuel and to avoid a long ordeal for the cook (remember that in such weather you will probably also have to spend a lot of time melting snow for water). In warmer climes, an extended dinner hour can be a high point of the day, so rehydration time is less relevant.

FOOD PREPARATION TIMES

Under 5 minutes

Instant soups
Instant mashed potatoes
Instant oriental noodles
Instant rice
Instant couscous
Instant hot drinks
Stuffing mixes
Some sauce mixes
Instant hot cereals
Instant freeze-dried dinners
Oat bran cereal

5 to 10 Minutes

Most soup mixes
Small macaroni
Noodles
Noodles-and-sauce mixes
Macaroni and cheese mixes
Some sauce mixes
Quick rice mixes
Some freeze-dried dinners
Quick oats and other cereals
Scrambled egg mixes
Popcorn
Mulled wine mixes
Instant puddings
Some freeze-dried dessert mixes

10 to 25 Minutes

Some soup mixes
Most pastas
Regular rice mixes
Quinoa (a high protein grain available in health food stores and some supermarkets)
Quick-cooking lentils
Some scalloped potato mixes
Some home-dried dishes (may require prior soaking)
Some freeze-dried dinners
Stewed dried fruits
Pancakes (unless you can operate several stoves and griddles simultaneously)
Biscuits, scones and other hot breads
Some freeze-dried dessert mixes
Cheesecake mixes

Cost

Freeze-dried foods are very expensive. Most people use them only on expeditions or extended trips where weight and space requirements are paramount. Supermarket shelves yield an excellent variety of inexpensive, carbohydrate-rich foods like pasta, rice and dehydrated potatoes, which can easily be made into main dishes with soup and sauce mixes. You can dress these foods up with a bit of parmesan cheese, seeds and nuts, good sausages, jerky or small cans of meat or fish. More expensive and heavier, but appealing to those who hate to cook, are foil pouches of things like beef stew, lasagna and Salisbury steak. You boil the pouch for five minutes or so, cut it open and enjoy what is essentially a canned dinner without the weight and bulk of a can. Toss in some oriental noodles and even the hungriest camper will be satisfied.

A home dehydrator allows you to prepare elaborate meals at home with the ingredients of your choice. Do not invest in one, however, unless you plan to use it regularly. You can buy a lot of food at the supermarket for the price of a good dehydrator. Many foods dehydrated at home require too much soaking time to be practical in winter, unless you are staying at a hut. Best bets are fruit leathers, dried fruits, jerky, sauces, and vegetable powders for soup.

Weight

The logbook at the Alpine Club of Canada hut in the Tonquin Valley, Alberta, has a long entry by a pair who skied in one Christmas pulling a sled containing a whole turkey and all the trimmings, including several bottles of wine. Their progress with this load was so slow (they also got lost) that they spent two extra nights on the trail. At their last bivouac they could actually see the warm, well-lit cabin across a deep valley. I have myself carried ice cream, canned cherries and a bottle of Grand Marnier to that same hut in order to enjoy Cherries Jubilee on New Year's Eve. Holiday follies aside, however, winter meals for the back country should weigh as little as possible.

Nuts, chocolate, dried fruits such as dates and figs, fatty foods (such as salami) and hard cheese, are all efficient calorie carriers for winter (30 grams or one ounce of peanuts, for example, has about 170 calories). Dehydrated complex carbohydrates, such as pasta, cereals and instant potatoes, provide fewer usable calories per gram because of the way they increase in volume when rehydrated, but they are essential items for most people. Jerky weighs little and has great flavour, but doesn't have much nutritional value in cold weather. Anything which is not dehydrated will be relatively heavy. This includes food prepared at home and then frozen, fresh fruits, vegetables and meats, food in foil pouches and cans. There is nothing wrong with heavy food if you don't mind carrying it. Extra weight has a cost, however, in loss of skiing pleasure, aching shoulders and exhaustion. You should pack frozen steaks or whole turkeys only if you really want to eat them, not because you are unaware of lighter alternatives.

Ease of preparation and cleanup

Preparation times are longer in winter because you don't work very efficiently in the cold. In addition, cooking times are longer in the mountains than at sea level because water boils at a lower temperature. The length of time required to bring water to a boil depends on how much water is involved, how hot your stove is, how well it and the pot are shielded from the weather, and whether you are starting with water or snow in the pot. If I were cooking a two course meal (soup and main dish) for myself alone, at -20° C (-4° F), starting from snow, I would expect the total mealtime preparation, including after-dinner hot chocolate and refilling my water bottles, to take at least one hour. I frequently spend two hours preparing elaborate meals for Mike and myself, which is a long time to stand around in the cold. I enjoy it and know how to stay warm, but I recommend that you stick to the simplest menus for your first trips.

Try to dirty no more than one pot, leaving a second pot clean for melting snow and boiling water. For example, instant soups and cereals can be made in your dinner cup. Your cup can also be used to mix sauces that will be added to pasta or rice. You will still have to cook the sauce with the pasta briefly, resulting in a bit of a mess. If you want to avoid a dirty pot, use foil pouches, adding pasta or noodles to the water while the pouch is heating (check that the pouch will not add dirt or other unwanted ingredients to the water). Drain the pasta, place in your cup and empty the foil pouch on top. You can avoid dirty dishes altogether by using instant freeze-dried dinners that reconstitute in their own package.

SAMPLE MENUS

BREAKFAST

No-cook breakfast (Hot water required.)

- Juice-flavour crystals (best if made with hot water on a cold morning).
- Instant hot cereal (oats, cream of wheat) or granola (good with hot water).
- Raisins, sugar and powdered milk for the cereal.
- Tea or instant coffee or instant hot chocolate.
- Hard or cream cheese (to provide sustained energy) with a roll or bagel.

Quick-cooking alternatives or additions

- Quick rolled oats, oat bran or similar cereal (add butter for extra energy).
- Scrambled egg mix.
- Noodle soup.

Base camp or lazy day breakfasts

- Pancakes and syrup.
- Hot breads prepared in a stove-top baker (available in outdoor stores).
- Bacon, sausage.

DINNER

No-cook hot dinner (Boiling water required, perfect for foul weather.)

- Instant soup.
- Instant mashed potatoes with butter, onion flakes and parmesan cheese or instant freeze-dried dinner or instant noodle dinner.

Quick one-dish dinners (Soup and main course are combined.)

- Package of oriental noodles with soup base. Small can of meat or fish to match flavour of soup base. Throw everything into boiling water, stir for two or three minutes, and eat. Serves one generously. Preparation time: under 5 minutes after the water boils.
- Package of soup mix (to make a litre (quart) of soup). One to one-and-a quarter cups of macaroni or other quick cooking pasta. One-quarter cup textured soya protein (optional). Grated parmesan cheese. Select a soup that is broth based, such as onion or vegetable. Cream of anything will stick in this recipe. Bring the soup to a boil, add pasta and soya protein, if using, and cook on medium heat until done. Top with cheese. Serves one giant appetite, two moderate eaters. Preparation time: about 15 minutes after the water boils.

Fairly quick two-course dinners in one pot (Soup is fixed first, then main course in same pot.).

- Instant soup (1 or 2 packets per person).
- Noodles and sauce mix with can of chicken, tuna or salmon,

or macaroni and cheese mix, or foil pouch of salisbury steak with instant noodles, or try one of my favourites: macaroni, soya protein, sun-dried tomatoes and Primavera sauce mix. Top with parmesan cheese.

Preparation time (cooking for 1 or 2): about 25 minutes after the water boils for the soup.

- Five-or-ten minute cooked soup with added pasta or quick rice.
- Instant mashed potatoes with canned corn beef or sausages. Heat vented can of meat in the water you are boiling for the potatoes.
- Or serve foil pouch cabbage rolls or beef stew, or a quick-cooking freeze dried dinner; these will stretch farther because of the pasta in the soup.

Preparation time (cooking for 1 or 2): about 25 minutes after water boils for the soup.

DESSERT

- Popcorn: You can buy foil containers with pop-up tops ready to use on your camp stove. For much less bulk, take small containers of popping corn and oil, or some powdered vegetable shortening (available from Harvest Foodworks in Canada), and pop the corn in your own pot.
- Dried fruit stewed in gelatin dessert mix (such as Jello).
- Fruitcake (ideal for extreme cold when you don't want to cook).
- Instant pudding mix, extra almonds optional. Pudding mixes are too heavy to be efficient for a long trip, but are fine for weekend tours. If the weather is too cold to make pudding, add more water and serve it as a hot drink.
- Cobblers and cake mixes designed for backpacking (not for extreme cold).

HOT DRINKS

- Hot chocolate mix.
- Mulled wine or hot cider mix (non-alcoholic).
- Powdered fruit drink mixes (some taste metallic when hot, so experiment).
- Gelatin dessert mix (Jello).
- Iced tea mix.
- Liquid (not frozen) concentrated juice (some of these reconstitute at a ratio of one to ten, making them practical for backpacking).
- Herb and regular teas.
- Instant coffee.
- Although alcohol should generally be avoided, there is no harm in adding a little flavouring to a hot drink just before crawling into the sleeping bag. You will feel a gentle surge of warmth which will be captured by the bag.

Food and drink on the trail

In much of the United States, trail food varies little from summer to winter. Sandwiches, tinned fish or meat, cheese, fruit, vegetables — the choice is virtually endless. Insulated by the pack, your food won't freeze. Indeed, the natural refrigeration of winter allows you to take items that don't travel well in summer. Leisurely lunch stops permit all sorts of elaborate picnics.

In northern latitudes, however, everything from your water bottle to salami can turn to a block of ice. A ten-minute stop may be the limit before cold starts to seep into your bones. Food must be easy to eat, high in energy, and tasty when frozen. Forget the oranges and celery sticks. Nuts, candies, dried fruit, hard cheeses, cured meats, peanut butter, granola bars, cookies, fruitcake—these are the snacks of the north. Trail mix (gorp) remains a favourite of many backpackers. The basic mix contains nuts, raisins and chocolate chips, but you can add sunflower seeds, coconut, banana chips, or anything else that appeals.

THE CANADIAN COLD BUSTER BAR

A recent addition to trail food has been developed by Dr. Larry Wang and associates at the University of Alberta. Called the Canadian Cold Buster Bar, it is a special formulation of common ingredients which tests show will delay the onset of hypothermia. Although you may not feel any warming effect after eating the bar, it allows you to work longer in a cold environment before your body's core temperature drops. The bar can be eaten as a normal snack instead of a candy bar and is especially useful if you begin to feel chilled. This hypothermia inhibitor was introduced commercially in Canada in December, 1991 and there are plans to market it in the United States.

LIQUIDS

The most important item in the winter lunch pack is your water bottle. Although I don't recommend it, some people never eat between breakfast and arrival at the campsite in the afternoon, but everyone has to drink. Many pages have been devoted in sports publications to the kinds of fluids which should be consumed during a day of strenuous activity. The average winter tourer needs only one instruction: carry whatever you find easiest to drink, especially when you are not thirsty. The sole exclusion is alcohol, which dilates the surface blood vessels, leading first to a delightful feeling of warmth followed by rapid chilling. Sugary drinks provide quick energy, at least to people who believe in them. Some products replace elements lost through perspiration. Caffeine beverages, like coffee and tea, are diuretics that can increase the body's fluid loss, but people who like sweetened tea in their bottle are seldom deterred by this information. Plain cold water is about the best thing you can drink because it is absorbed more quickly into the system than anything else. As a party leader, I would rather have you carry hot root beer, if that is what you want to drink, than some recommended beverage which will remain untouched all day.

Having settled on a liquid, your next problem is to keep it from solidifying in the cold. Various types of insulated bottles exist. Their efficiency in extreme cold seems directly proportional to their weight and the amount of space they take up in your pack. I prefer to rely on the same insulators that keep me warm in camp. A bottle of hot, sweetened tea placed in a down bootie, which can be wrapped in your down parka if necessary, will still contain liquid late in the day, no matter what the weather. Just make sure that your bottle is leak-proof. If in doubt, put it in a sealed plastic bag.

If you freeze your bottle you will have to thaw it in the field. When I was climbing Mount Logan, one member of our party had a metal bottle with a narrow mouth sealed with a rubber stopper. It froze one day and he tried to thaw it in boiling water. We were soon startled by an explosion from the kitchen, and our hapless companion emerged from a cloud of steam, the contents of his bottle dripping from his head and shoulders. Bottles for winter use should always have a wide mouth.

You can immerse the lid of a Nalgene bottle in hot water if the threads freeze shut (hitting the lid with a hard implement, may cause the bottle to leak). If the whole bottle is frozen, you will have to pour boiling water into it and gradually melt out the ice. This is extremely messy and unpleasant work which is likely to leave your mitts soaking wet. The best advice remains to keep the bottle warm at all costs.

Purifying water

The purity of running water in the backcountry, unfortunately, can no longer be guaranteed. Many summer backpackers now use filters, which are quick and don't impart a funny taste to the water. Use a filter in winter only if you tour in a moderate climate and the filter can be protected from freezing. The filter should remove any particles larger than 0.2 microns.

Boiling will purify water, although the amount of time needed depends on the pathological organisms to be destroyed. Five minutes is probably sufficient in most of North America. Twenty would be safer but is not practical for winter.

Iodine is an effective purifier, either in tablet form or in crystals, if you use it properly. It works **very** slowly in cold water; for best results bring the water to a boil, then add iodine and wait five minutes. You cannot, therefore, refill your bottle from an icy stream, put in iodine and expect to have a safe drink. Iodine gives a bad flavour to the water and some people have an adverse physical reaction to it.

Water obtained by melting snow is still reasonably safe in most of North America.

STOVES

The perfect winter stove has not been invented, but most of the ones on the market now are pretty good. As with other gear, you will have to decide which features are most important and accept less than ideal performance on the others.

You may be able to use your summer stove in the winter. Certainly if you camp in temperatures generally above -10° C (14° F) and do not have to rely on melting snow for water, you have a wide choice for cooking. If, however, -10° C is a warm day where you tour, or you expect to be in isolated locations, you need a stove which is impervious to cold, sturdy enough not to break in your pack and dependable in the field.

Fuel

The two major stove types for winter are those which use pressurized gas cartridges (propane, butane or a blend) and those which use a fuel tank with pressure pump for liquid fuels like white gas or kerosene.

Temperature affects your choice of fuel. For extreme cold, white gas (or naphtha, Coleman fuel, Blazo) is the primary choice in North America and is the cleanest burning. Unleaded auto gas and kerosene are also effective if the stove is designed to handle them. Optimus, Peak One (Coleman) and MSR make multi-fuel stoves. If the temperature is not far below freezing, propane will work, although the cartridges are very heavy. Blended fuel cartridges (propane and butane), which are much lighter, are readily available in Europe and are beginning to appear in North America. These work reasonably well, especially if you cook in a sheltered location, such as a tent or igloo. Butane is useless in extreme cold (although it burns very well above 20,000 ft). If the temperature is not much below freezing, however, especially if you plan to cook in a hut, tent or snow shelter, and you don't mind taking the cartridge to bed with you, butane is acceptable. Stoves using alcohol, wood or other solid fuel are best left for summer.

PLANNING TO TAKE THE STOVE OUT OF NORTH AMERICA?

White gas is hard to find in many places. Butane is common in Europe. Kerosene is the primary fuel in the third world. The MSR X-GK will digest just about any fluid that is combustible; consider it if you plan a world tour to out-of-the-way places.

If you camp in conditions where your life will depend on your stove, you need one which is field maintainable. This is not a minor point. Some of the best cold weather stoves available are made by Peak One (Coleman). They are easy to use, burn hot and are very tough, but if something goes wrong while you're on a glacier, you probably will not be able to fix it. In contrast, the only MSR stove I have ever seen put completely out of commission was one trampled by a herd of cows in Peru-just about any problem can be fixed in the field, even at -40° C. MSR liquid-fuel stoves are notorious for clogging up if not taken apart and cleaned **frequently**, however. Don't buy one if your idea of maintenance is to toss all your gear in a heap between trips.

Don't pay too much attention to the boiling times given by manufacturers. They usually refer to the number of minutes required to bring a litre or quart of room temperature water to a boil at sea level or in a laboratory. They give a reasonable idea of how the stove will work in a snow shelter or heated hut, but not in the wind at -20° C (-4° F). Some stoves will not boil water at all in these conditions. A good wind shield is essential in winter and it must be suited to your particular stove. Do not, for example, use the MSR wind screen, which is very effective, with another stove unless you know what you are doing. Too much heat reflected onto the fuel tank may cause an explosion. The MSR X-GK, with wind screen and heat exchanger, will boil water in any conditions the cook can tolerate.

If you plan to cook in your tent

Cooking in your tent is dangerous. You can burn up your tent and gear, or be suffocated by carbon monoxide. If you decide to cook inside anyway, exercise extreme caution.

You need a stove that does not flare up unexpectedly. Hanging butane stoves are probably the best, but investigate the design and the manufacturer's claims carefully. Gas cartridges can leak and some of them become unguided missiles if you try to remove them before they are empty.

The MSR heat exchanger wrapped around a pot, with the MSR X-GK stove in foreground.

The heat exchanger and the windscreen on the MSR stove protect the pot and concentrate the heat for more efficient cooking.

White gas is extremely volatile and dangerous to use in a tent. Kerosene is probably the safest liquid fuel, but is smelly, smoky and dirty. Never prime any liquid fuel stove in a tent.

As a general principle, all stoves should be lit outside the tent. In fact, it's not a bad idea to light them outside at all times, even if you're staying in a hut. At the very least, locate the fire extinguisher before people start cooking.

All stoves are lethal in unvented, closed spaces because of carbon monoxide. If cooking in a tent or snow cave, keep the stove near the entrance, under a vent if possible, and make sure that there is plenty of fresh air coming in.

Other factors to consider in selecting a winter stove

- **Burn time.** Having the stove run out of fuel while your pasta is cooking is annoying. The most convenient stoves are those which will run for a whole weekend on a single filling. MSR has the edge here because it uses a fuel bottle as its tank — the pump screws into the bottle replacing the cap. Bottles come in three sizes, the largest being 33 oz, enough to see two or three people through a long weekend even if they must melt snow. Figure at least one gas cartridge (regular, not mini-size) per day for two people if melting snow, and about 250 mL (1/2 pint) of white gas or kerosene per person per day.
- **The ability to simmer**. The MSR X-GK is an unrestrainable blowtorch, given to incinerating everything except water. The MSR Whisperlite is somewhat better, but gourmet cooks should look to Optimus, Peak One or any of the cartridge stoves for simmer control.
- **Durability** (as opposed to ease of repair). Close the case on an Optimus and you can use it for batting practice. If I were renting stoves or made a habit of dropping my pack off cliffs, this is the brand I would want.
- **Quiet operation**. No one carries on a conversation around an MSR X-GK. Most other stoves are reasonably quiet.
- **Stability**. Optimus has the edge, especially its 111 Hiker for large pots, followed by Peak One and the cartridge models. MSR burners sometimes flop out of position, melt through anything but asbestos and start to tilt in the snow almost as soon as you light them. Use a pad underneath (the bottom of a spring cake pan works well, as does a shovel), but you will still have to lift the stove and repack the snow underneath fairly often.
- **Ease of lighting**. Gas cartridges, if warm enough, are the easiest — simply turn the valve and light. All liquid fuel stoves have to be primed below freezing. Kerosene requires patience (some would say arcane ritual).

- **Safety**. No stove is so idiot-proof that you can't singe your face or burn down the tent with it. Safety comes from following the manufacturer's instructions to the letter, keeping the stove clean and well-maintained, and never allowing it to burn unattended, even for a few minutes. Any of the stoves currently marketed for winter use can be operated safely, and any of them can blow up if you are careless.

WORKING WITH WHITE GAS

Because it burns clean and hot, white gas is the most popular fuel for winter camping in North America. If you use it, you must be extremely careful at all times. On a cold day, white gas will cause instant severe frostbite if it contacts your skin. When filling your fuel chamber, set the stove or bottle on the ground with a felt-lined filtering funnel in the orifice (filtration is necessary to keep impurities from clogging the stove). Wear gloves and pour the fuel in slowly. Never perform this operation inside a hut or tent where spilled fuel can easily be set ablaze by a candle or lantern.

Priming your stove

Priming also requires caution. For some stoves, you must spread a priming paste on the generator, light it, wait until the paste is consumed, then turn on the fuel valve. The paste itself is relatively safe, but the fuel can flare as soon as it ignites. With other stoves, you must prime with white gas, pouring a little into a designated cup and lighting it. The gas will usually burn well for a few seconds, then die down. At this point you may be tempted to bend over the stove to see what is happening. DON'T! The gas will flare up as soon as it begins to vaporize, right into your face. Never put your face over any stove that is burning. You can inspect it safely and just as well from the side.

Insulating the stove from the cold

The fuel tanks of most stoves need insulation from the snow in order to function efficiently, since they rely on some heat pressurization of the air in the tank to provide fuel flow. If you don't insulate, you will spend more time pumping to keep the tank pressurized, and the stove will have reduced performance. You can use a closed-cell foam pad or a piece of styrofoam under the tank.

KITCHEN UTENSILS

The ultimate minimal kitchen set consists of a single pot with lid. You use it to melt snow, boil water, cook, eat and drink. One of our friends even cleans his pot by making tea in it. Winter cookware, dishes and procedures should be kept to a minimum.

A recent addition to cookware that is exceptionally useful for severe climates is the MSR heat exchanger. This is a metal wrapper with channels that attaches around the body of the pot and directs heat up along the sides. It reduces fuel consumption by about 25 per cent when melting snow or boiling water. It should not be used for cooking, however, because of the mess that results from boil-overs.

SUGGESTED KITCHEN SET FOR TWO PEOPLE

- **Two nested pots, one for water (1 or 1 1/2 litres or quarts) and one for cooking (2 litres). The smaller pot is not absolutely necessary but is very convenient. It can be kept clean if the weather is such that you don't feel like washing the cooking pot, and it provides added storage for water. You need at least one pot lid to conserve heat and fuel.**
- **Two 500 mL (2 cup) plastic measuring cups. A measuring cup can hold the liquidy meals you need, retains the heat of the food better than a plate, and doesn't conduct heat the way a metal dish would. It is also convenient for measuring and for filling water bottles.**
- **Two insulated or sturdy plastic mugs for drinks. Metal cups lose heat too rapidly, and metal can freeze to your tongue.**
- **Two Lexan spoons. To keep from losing the spoons in the snow, drill a hole in the handle of each one and tie it to the handle of the measuring cup with a long cord. Lexan will not freeze to your tongue as metal cutlery does.**
- **Two or three wide-mouth, non-metal water bottles. Wide-mouth bottles are much easier to fill than narrow necks.**

8.
Other Equipment

Every winter pack holds a number of small items that are important to the trip's success. The equipment listed below is grouped in three categories: required or strongly recommended for all trips, optional, and gear for special purposes.

REQUIRED OR STRONGLY RECOMMENDED FOR ALL TRIPS

Headlamp

Forget about flashlights. You can't ski, cook, put up a tent or change clothing very well with one hand, and drooling around a plastic object held between the teeth is uncouth. Buy a proper headlamp. Most of the ones available in backpacking stores work reasonably well, so look for the features you want.

For extreme cold I prefer a light that uses lithium batteries. These can be left outside overnight at -40° C and still work without a whimper. Lithium batteries last longer than alkaline and don't deteriorate on the store shelf. They cost a lot, die without warning or hope of resuscitation,

One model of headlamp.

and may not be available everywhere (they cannot be sent by air), but I wouldn't want anything else in January in the Canadian Rockies.

Alkaline batteries will also work in the cold if you offer them a little protection. Some lamps have a separate battery pack so that the batteries can be kept warm in a pocket. The wire running from the pack to the lamp invariably gets tangled in your gear and is vulnerable to being ripped out at the connections. If you can't get lithium batteries where you live, however, and your winter is severe, you may want to try this arrangement.

Sturdy construction is essential because any headlamp takes a lot of punishment. Look for simplicity of design as well. If you have to repair your lamp in the field you don't want to juggle springs or multiple parts. If you like to read lying down in the sleeping bag, look for a lamp that does not place the battery at the back of your head (very uncomfortable). Burn times vary greatly, but to be useful for the long dark evenings of winter, a lamp should give at least 8 hours on one set of batteries. Four D-cells will provide about 100 hours if you don't mind the weight.

Always carry spare batteries and bulbs. Remember, just about any lamp is capable of turning itself on in your pack. Either place duct tape over the switch or slide a piece of cardboard between the contacts.

Shovel

You can dig a snow cave with a pot, gouge out a biffy with your skis or level a tent platform by kicking at the snow, but why would you want to? Lightweight snow shovels are available in stores catering to moun-

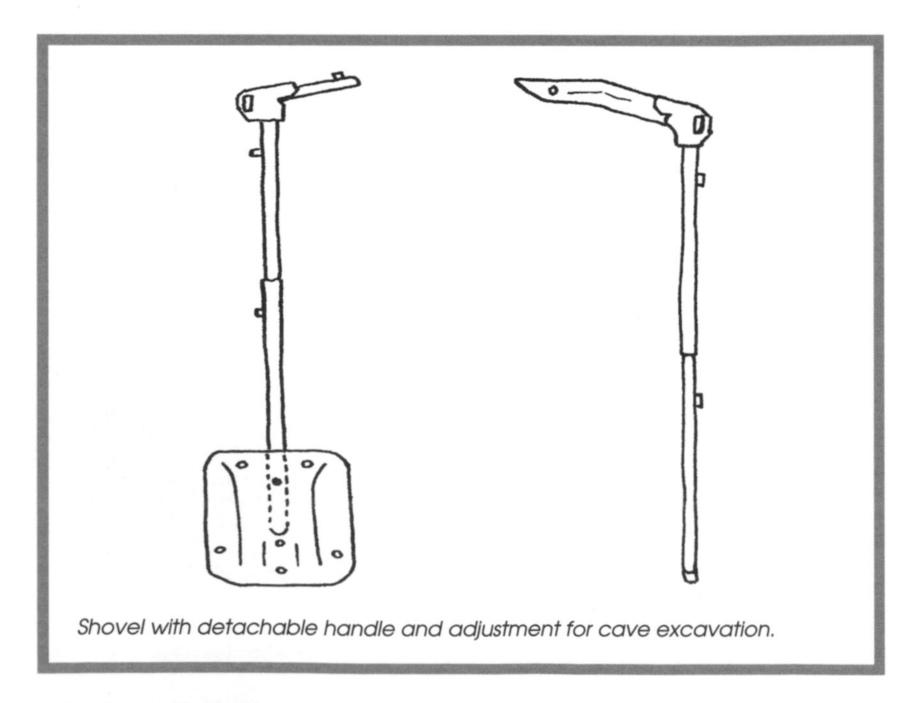

Shovel with detachable handle and adjustment for cave excavation.

taineers and winter backpackers. Blades may be made of metal, which works a bit better in hard snow, or Lexan or other synthetics, which seem less susceptible to breaking or deforming. Detached and telescoping handles, of either light wood or insulated metal, are easiest to pack. With a drill and releasable clamp you can make your own detached handle. If you plan a lot of snow caving, look for a shovel that allows you to mount the blade at right angles to the handle for carving out the roof of the cave.

In avalanche terrain, every member of the party should have a shovel, packed so that it is quickly accessible. If the shovel is mainly for camp use, then one for each tent or two for each caving party will be adequate.

Sun protection

Snow-blindness is the most immediate and painful consequence of inadequate eye protection. It strikes without warning, feels like sand under the eyelids and is so painful that it renders the victim virtually helpless. Even if you avoid snow blindness, long-term damage can result if you are habitually careless about your eyes. You must wear sun glasses which filter out all ultraviolet rays. Beware of lenses that reduce visible light but not UV transmission. These can actually harm your eyes by causing the pupil to enlarge and let in more of the harmful rays. For good measure, look for glasses that also filter infrared rays.

Above the tree line, glare and reflection from the unbroken snowscapes make polarized, non-reflecting lenses and side shields desirable. A hat with a brim also reduces glare.

Glass lenses must be impact resistant and shatterproof. Look for good ventilation and sturdy frames. In extreme cold, metal frames can be

Sun protection. On the left: brimmed hat, sunglasses with side shields; on the right: brimmed hat, bandana, sunglasses and zinc oxide on nose.

very uncomfortable on your face. A detachable nose shield offers good sun protection. Use a neck cord or other device to keep the glasses at least within reach if you crash.

The tint of the lens is a matter of personal preference. Some people prefer amber or rose for better perception of snow contours on cloudy days. Photographers will appreciate glasses which transmit natural colours. It is frustrating to shoot a scene which you think is bathed in beautiful light only to realize that the camera did not have the same warming filter that covered your eyes. For high altitude and glaciers, get the darkest lenses you can find.

I always carry a spare pair of sunglasses. In an emergency you can fashion cardboard into an eye shield with narrow slits to look through, or, if you wear prescription lenses, use tape to make side shields and to block all but a small opening on the lenses.

With skin cancer on the rise, sun protection for your skin is mandatory. After years of using a sun screen rated SPF 15, I have switched to a sun block of SPF 45. Many people like to put zinc oxide on their noses — a body part especially vulnerable to sun. Zinc oxide can be worn on the whole face, but it is a bit messy. Put the sun block on before you go out in the sun and keep renewing it as you sweat during the day. Snow reflects light onto your face from below, so protect the underside and inside of your nose, under your chin and behind your ears. The less skin you expose to the sun, the better. Keep the sun block warm and handy in a pocket and you will use it more often.

Repair kit

Although a party doesn't need more than one comprehensive kit, each person should carry some basic items, in case they become separated from the group.

PERSONAL REPAIR KIT

- **Spare cables or bails as required by your bindings**
- **Extra tip mount for your skins**
- **Duct tape**
- **Small screwdriver (the one on your Swiss army knife will do)**
- **Small vise grip or other tools as needed to adjust your binding or install a cable or bail**
- **Wire for temporary fixes**
- **Safety pins**
- **Cord**

On backpacking trips where retreat is short and easy even with broken equipment, personal kits may be sufficient. If getting back to civilization will be difficult or impossible without a field repair, you need a party kit. This kit should hold whatever is necessary to remount bindings, make broken skis or snowshoes functional, and repair packs and ski poles.

A TYPICAL GROUP REPAIR KIT FOR SKI TOURING

- **Good ratchet screwdriver**
- **Sturdy vise grip or clamp**
- **Needle-nose pliers**
- **Long screws with matching wing nuts for emergency binding mounts right through the skis**
- **Assortment of screws, buckles and bolts**
- **Quick epoxy glue**
- **Steel wool to glue into holes along with the screw**
- **Hole punch or awl**
- **Needles and heavy thread**
- **Large roll of duct tape**
- **Wire and cord**
- **Spare ski pole basket**
- **Ski tip**

Depending on the terrain and your gear, a different assortment may be more appropriate for you. Just don't make it too heavy — someone has to carry it.

First aid kit

First aid kits are as varied as the people who construct them. One experienced backpacking doctor I know carries only adhesive bandages, disinfectant and some morphine. He contends that he can improvise anything else he needs from the materials at hand. At the other extreme, I watched a trip leader in Peru open a kit the size of a small trunk and perform emergency surgery on a horse. The average party should avoid both extremes.

Knowledge is by far the most important part of your first aid kit. Know how to clear an airway, restore breathing and circulation (CPR) and control bleeding. Know how to treat shock, hypothermia and frostbite in the field (see Chapter Eleven) and how to stabilize neck and back injuries and suspected fractures. None of the above require fancy equipment but they all require some training. At a minimum, a back-country traveller, summer or winter, should take a course in first aid, preferably wilderness first aid, and CPR.

First aid requirements for a short trip

Experience will tell you what items are needed often enough to be a regular part of your kit. Usually these are treatments for minor problems which, if neglected, can ruin the outing: blisters, headache, stomach ache, diarrhea, small cuts or burns to fingers and hands. I always pack the following:

- Blister kit (moleskin, Second Skin, wide tape)
- Disinfectant swabs or towelettes
- Adhesive bandages
- Butterfly closures or Steristrips
- 4" x 4" sterile dressings
- Gauze,
- Scissors
- Tweezers
- Needle
- Pain and tummy soothers, some of which are prescription drugs
- Notebook and pencil for making notations in the event of an accident (essential).
- Thermometer

For trips into terrain where crash landings are likely, I expand our basic kit with one or two feminine sanitary napkins or diapers (to control bleeding) and some pantyhose (excellent for tying a dressing to the head or other awkward location).

Beyond these simple remedies there is plenty of scope to spend money and add weight:

- Wire splints
- Hypothermia thermometer
- Triangular bandage
- Tensor bandage (use only with extreme care in the cold because it may impair circulation)
- Large burn and surgical dressings
- Airway
- Inflatable splint
- Whatever pharmacological supplies your doctor will trust you with.

For expeditions, we pack a major kit with everything we could conceivably need that we know how to use.

Each trip participant should bring a blister kit, adhesive bandages, their normal pain and tummy remedies and their own prescription medications. Other items don't need to be duplicated and belong in the party kit. If you include in the party kit prescription drugs (especially powerful narcotic analgesics), make sure first, that everyone who might have access to them knows the contraindications to their use (carry a manual or sheet of instructions), and second, that you understand the legal ramifications of practicing back-country medicine. There is usually no problem among experienced wilderness backpackers, especially in remote locations where medical treatment is perhaps days away, but in populated or accessible areas it is often wiser, both legally and medically, not to play doctor.

Personal kit

The composition of your kit is highly personal. Don't forget the toilet paper and whatever hygiene supplies you need. If you wear contact lenses, try to keep them and their solutions from freezing. I used to wear a soft pouch around my neck at night for my contacts, while the solutions went into the sleeping bag. After years of poking at my eyes with frozen fingers each morning, I began using disposable lenses for backpacking. I find I don't have to remove them for the length of the trip, after which I go back to my regular lenses. If you wear contacts and will be doing a lot of winter camping, you may want to inquire about the disposable kind specifically for back-country use.

I have seen people shave and wash their hair on a glacier while others grow scruffy and stink. Soap and water are not very attractive at -20° C. Packaged moistened towelettes are a somewhat less painful alternative. To avoid conflict on a multi-day trip, let the cleanest person in the tent set the standard for the others.

Survival gear

About the only items I pack that are specifically for emergency survival are a separate package of matches in my pocket and a few candles. You should have food, clothing, shelter, first aid and repair supplies with you on any tour. External heat can be supplied by a lean-to and roaring fire, but there are other ways to keep warm. Very few people have the expertise to light a fire in severe winter conditions, especially when they are cold and tired. One candle inside a small snow shelter, however, produces significant warmth.

Throw some signal flares in your pack if you like. I sometimes carry them but have found that I use them mainly to convince martens that I am prepared to defend my camp.

Swiss Army knife or other multi-tool implement

The most useful features are screwdrivers of different sizes and types, two blades, can opener, scissors and awl or punch. If you can get pliers, bottle opener, magnifying glass, corkscrew and bottle opener without too much extra size or weight, these are also useful. Avoid monsters that are too large to carry in your pocket.

Whistle

This is the easiest way to signal for help or communicate with companions who are too far away to hear your voice. Plastic is better than metal for winter, but if you wear it around your neck it will always be warm as well as readily available.

Compass

If there is the slightest chance of missing a turn and getting lost on your tour, take a compass and map of the area. Many backpackers consider a compass obligatory on all trips, but since it is pretty hard to go astray in certain types of terrain (steep-sided valleys with only one entrance and exit) we sometimes leave ours at home.

The standard compasses used in the back country are made by Silva. There are a variety of models, and even though extra features mean extra cost, you will appreciate the convenience they offer.

COMPASS FEATURES

- **The rotating dial of the compass should mark the 360° of the circle in one or two degree increments. Larger increments will not give you readings which are precise enough for wilderness travel.**
- **Buy a compass with a large, transparent base plate which will allow you to see the grid lines on your map and make it easy to transfer a bearing to the map.**
- **The magnetic needle should float in liquid to keep it from vibrating excessively. Vibration affects accuracy. With a liquid-dampened needle, it is even possible (although difficult) to walk with the compass in your hand and follow a bearing.**
- **Unless you are very adept at calculating declination in your head, buy a compass that allows you to adjust for it. Declination is a measure of the difference between magnetic north, which naturally attracts the compass needle, and geographic north, which is the direction indicated by the grid lines on the map. Parts of North America have as much as 30° of declination, so that failure to adjust for it will almost certainly get you lost. (See Chapter Thirteen)**
- **For mountain use I prefer a compass with a mirror and clinometer. The mirror helps in establishing the precise bearing, can also be used as a signalling device and is a useful addition to the personal kit. A clinometer measures the angle of a slope, which is helpful in determining the avalanche hazard of that slope.**

Anyone can read direction from a compass. To use it with a map requires training. See Chapter Thirteen.

OPTIONAL EQUIPMENT

Camera Gear. Because of the overall weight and bulk of a winter pack, take a full-size SLR camera and lenses only if photography is a serious hobby. For most purposes, you can achieve excellent results with a small automatic camera that fits in your pocket. This will avoid the problems of cold batteries and having a separate pack and belt for the camera and lenses. Many of the newer pocket cameras have zoom and fill flash built in.

In a moderate winter climate you can use your summer camera with little difficulty. Just be careful when you bring it from the cold into a warm area. Condensation can work its way into the camera and cause damage. Place the camera in a sealed plastic bag before bringing it inside so that condensation will form on the bag rather than on the camera.

Extreme cold places severe demands on photographer, camera and film. Most cameras today depend on battery-supplied electricity to function. When the batteries get cold, the camera doesn't work properly. If you prefer SLR photography, and are facing daytime temperatures of -20° C (-4° F) or lower, I strongly recommend that you purchase a mechanical camera.

A mechanical camera is also a manual camera, however. You will have to focus and set exposure and shutter speed yourself, a difficult task when your fingers are clumsy with cold. If you don't feel comfortable with these tasks, either give your summer SLR the care it needs (sleeping with it, perhaps using a remote battery pack inside your clothing, changing the lubricants), or settle for a small aim-and-shoot camera.

Film becomes brittle when it gets cold, so handle it very gently. Advance and rewind the film slowly to prevent static electricity marks (these usually appear as a straight line across your slides or prints). Never handle a metal camera with bare hands in extreme cold — instant frostbite can result.

Winter light, or more precisely, snow, will fool the light meter of many cameras, causing them to underexpose. If you find that your winter photos are too dark or too blue, you can correct this by opening up the aperture by one or two stops.

If you have an auto-everything camera, you may not have a manual mode which allows you to set the aperture. You may still be able to outwit it, however. If the camera has a setting for under and over exposure (usually plus or minus EVA steps), set it to automatically overexpose by one to two full steps. If that is not possible, try setting the film speed to one or two speeds slower than the film that is actually in the camera.

If your camera won't allow either of these adjustments, see if it has an exposure lock. Aim the camera at nearby evergreens, rocks or people that have the same lighting as the scene you want to shoot. Lock the exposure, then re-focus, re-compose your picture and shoot.

Because of the brightness of snow, we recommend that you use films ranging from ASA 25 to 100, with an absolute upper maximum of ASA 200. You may find that your brand of slide film makes snow greyer, bluer or redder than it really is. New colour films appear regularly on the market, so experiment.

Skylight or UV filters should be used in winter. Polarizing filters also give nice effects. A 35 mm or 28 mm is probably best if you will be taking only one fixed focal length lens. In zooms, 35-to-105 or 35-to-135 lenses weigh less and are more compact than those that zoom to 200, although zooms seem to become smaller every year. Very light, collapsible tripods are available and useful for night shots or poorly lit day scenes. A light meter that stays warm in your pocket is also handy if the camera meter stops functioning.

One cold weather excursion with SLR camera, multiple lenses and all the trimmings will probably convince you that arctic temperatures and complicated photography are not very compatible.

Binoculars. Compact binoculars let you observe wildlife from a distance and inspect the route ahead or the slopes above for avalanche hazard.

Snow brush. A small brush for boots, clothing and tent floor will keep your living quarters dry.

Diary. Useful for recording trail and travel time information as well as your thoughts.

Frisbee. Great for the longer evenings of spring. Take the soft, floppy kind which won't break or take up much space in your pack.

Reading material, cards, small games. These help to pass time when waiting out a storm.

Alarm clock. The only way to ensure an early start.

Music source. A radio or tape player with tapes will help pass the time Use headphones, please!

GEAR FOR SPECIAL PURPOSES

Avalanche transceiver

Avalanche transceivers or beacons are small radio devices that transmit and receive a beeping signal. They are worn on the body and help to locate a person who is buried by an avalanche. Consider them required equipment in avalanche terrain.

Originally, Europe and North America manufactured beacons that operated on different frequencies. A standard has now been established at 457 kHz, but beacons using 2.275 kHz are still in use. Most new transceivers sold in North America are dual frequency.

Features of avalanche transceivers

Consider the following factors when deciding which beacon to buy (all of the ones commonly sold will work, but since they are expensive you may as well get the one best suited to you):

- Visual as well as auditory signal. Ortovox markets a transceiver that can be equipped with a visual indicator of signal strength. This is especially useful for people with even a slight hearing impairment and for anyone when the wind is howling.
- Emergency shift from receive to transmit. If a second avalanche

comes down while you are looking for victims of the first, you want your beacon to change instantly to transmit, so that rescuers can find **you**.

- Sturdy construction. Avalanches are natural occurrences of tremendous force, as life-threatening as tornados and much more common in the mountains. If you are caught in one, you want your transceiver to survive intact. If you are a rescuer you don't want wires pulling out or pieces falling off. Skadi makes a virtually indestructible transceiver that operates on rechargeable batteries. The beacon will operate up to a week safely on a single charge.

Remember, use of a transceiver must be practiced. See Chapter Twelve.

Avalanche probe

Once a victim's general location is established by a transceiver, probing is helpful in determining precisely where to dig. If the victim was not wearing a transceiver, probing is about the only chance you have for a live recovery. Probes are also useful on glaciers to determine the depth of the snow and identify hidden crevasses around your camp.

Ski poles that convert to probes are okay, but a real probe is better. Older models were fairly heavy and took time to assemble. Lightweight, shock-corded probes that snap together in an instant are now available. My own preference is that everyone should carry a probe in the mountains (you can't predict who or how many people will be buried), but a minimum of two or three per party is acceptable.

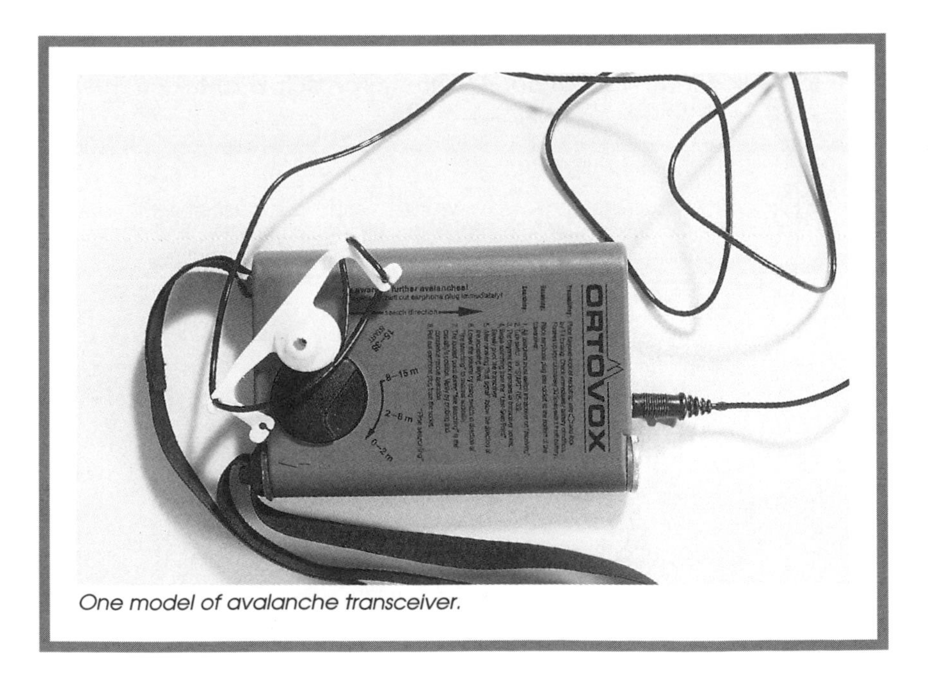

One model of avalanche transceiver.

Ice Axe

For the most part, terrain steep enough to require an ice axe is the domain of the mountaineer rather than the recreational camper. Even a short slope can produce an injury accident, however, if you hit rocks or trees or go over a cliff.

You can't really ski with an ice axe in one hand so skiers must depend on their metal edges to regain control in a fall (poles with a pick handle are available but are only for extreme terrain). A snowshoer, however, may find that an axe makes a good walking stick on steep slopes. Snowshoes are also less effective than skis for stopping a slide. When travelling roped on a crevassed glacier, snowshoers should always have an axe in hand to arrest a partner's fall. Once skis and snowshoes are left behind, an axe is a valuable safety feature when scrambling up small summits and exploring.

An ice axe for casual use should be the type sold for general mountaineering rather than for technical climbing. To get the right length for you, hold the head of the axe in your hand. With your arm hanging straight down, the axe should come about to your ankles. The shaft can be of wood or metal, although if you expect to get seriously into mountaineering or glacier travel, buy a metal axe for its greater strength. The head should be slightly curved. Sharply drooped heads are for steep, difficult climbing.

Self-arrest with an axe must be practiced until it is automatic. If you are disciplined, consult a mountaineering book that explains how to do it, then find a steep slope with a safe run-out. Practice arresting feet first, head first, forward, backward and somersaulting falls until you don't have to think about what to do. A better approach is to take a one- or

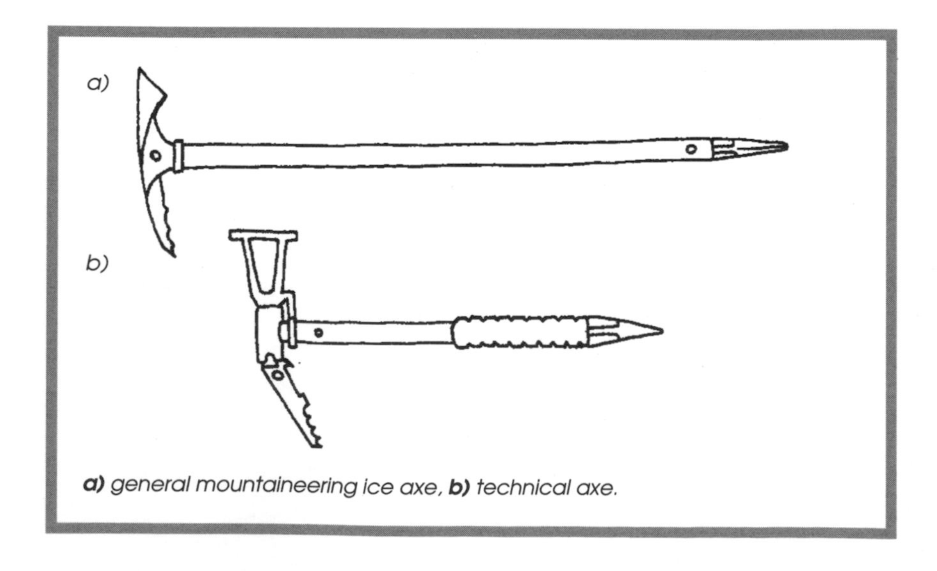

***a)** general mountaineering ice axe, **b)** technical axe.*

Harry McLean's Pu

111 St. Lawrence Street
Merrickville, Ontario K0G 1N0

"Good Beer - Good Cheer"
Always On Tap

YOU'RE PRETTY CUTE!

WANT TO GET
MARRIED & HAVE
SOME KIDS?!

I LOVE YOU
XOXO

two- day course in snow climbing, where the instructor will force you to do just that. If you can't be bothered to perfect the technique, don't bother buying an axe.

Crampons

These are spikes worn on boots to give traction on ice. Recreational backpackers don't scale icy cliffs, but you may encounter short stretches of terrain which are too slippery to negotiate easily. Instep crampons will probably be sufficient. If you buy regular mountaineering crampons, make sure they are flexible rather than rigid, and get the cheapest ones you can find, preferably secondhand.

Crampons are also available for skis. If you have a plate binding, the crampon fits on the plate and comes off the snow when you raise your heel, allowing the ski to slide forward. If the crampon attaches to the ski itself, it will create a lot of drag.

A word of warning: long slopes that require the use of any kind of crampon will be difficult to descend and can cause dangerous falls.

Altimeter

An altimeter is a barometer calibrated to the atmospheric pressure at different elevations. It is used to determine your elevation and, when matched with the contour or elevation lines of the map, can be very helpful in determining your exact location.

Since the altimeter is a barometer, its accuracy is affected by the weather. You will frequently notice, for example, that the altimeter reading changes overnight at your camp even though you have not moved. If the altimeter indicates that camp has risen 100 metres (330 ft), that is an indication of low pressure and possible bad weather. If camp loses 100 metres overnight, expect high pressure and improving weather. While it is nice to have the weather forecast, you won't be able to trust the altimeter's elevation readings unless you routinely reset it every time you come to a point of known elevation, such as a lake, pass, summit or cabin.

Cheap altimeters are useless for navigation and map work. If you want one, get the best you can afford. Altimeters are available in either metres or feet and differ in the highest elevations they will measure. Don't waste money on a model that will take you to the top of Mount Everest if Himalayan climbing is not in your future.

9.

Getting There

I heard the angry voices before I saw the skiers. The lead man was impatient to get over Maccarib Pass before dark. His wife was tired and worried about the third member of the party who was far behind, and the sight of my tent started a debate about making camp on the spot. When the third member arrived he was in the early stages of hypothermia, so while I tended to him, the other two set about erecting their tent. Unfortunately they had borrowed it from a friend and had never set it up before. A task that should have consumed at most ten minutes stretched to an hour of bickering and recriminations. Supper was prepared on my stove because the one they had rented didn't work. Next morning, cold and miserable, they packed up and headed for the trailhead without breakfast. This was the first time any of them had tried winter camping, and I was fairly certain it would be the last.

Your first experience with winter camping should be positive. You need to convince yourself that you can be warm and comfortable, can enjoy camping in the snow, and can return safely. You can ensure this by making proper preparations for your trip and by following good procedures on the trail.

PRELIMINARIES

Not only should you keep the first trips easy and simple, you should work up gradually to an actual camping tour. The more untried gear and skills on a trip, the greater the likelihood that something will not work, usually just at the moment when you need it urgently. Set up your tent at home. Cook something on your stove. Fit the skins to your skis and the gaiters to your boots. Learn to operate your ski bindings and adjustable ski poles. Make sure your pack fits properly. You may want to go car camping to get used to performing your camping routine in the cold.

Take courses from outdoor clubs and educational institutions or read relevant books and practice the skills you learn there.

Subjects to study

- Winter camping
- Avalanche awareness
- Orienteering

- Wilderness first aid and CPR
- Survival
- Anything to do with animal tracks, trees and fauna in your area
- Star watching (the winter sky can be spectacular)
- Snow and ice mountaineering
- Glacier travel
- Winter or nature photography
- Ski or snowshoe lessons

Use day tours to gain experience. For example, carry your stove on a day trip and make hot soup for lunch. Take out your map and compass and triangulate your position. Learn how to control body temperature at different levels of activity. Find out what clothing works for you.

Try to take your first overnight trip to a back-country cabin. If that is not possible, camp where a quick retreat to warmth is available, just in case the weather turns ugly, or your gear fails, or you can't keep warm for whatever reason. If your first trips will be in mountainous avalanche terrain or in a severe climate, you **must** go with people who know what they are doing because of the danger avalanches and extreme cold pose to the unwary. Your first camping trips should involve no more than a four-hour approach to the campsite and should not require advanced skiing or snowshoeing skills. Pick the most pleasant part of the winter for your initial excursions, when the sun gives some warmth and nighttime temperatures are milder. If you and your partner are on your own, pick an area where you will not be isolated from other campers or at least from day trippers.

A back-country cabin is a good destination for your first winter trip.

PLANNING THE TRIP

If you are going with an outdoor group, someone else will do the preliminary planning. If you are on your own, the responsibility falls on you and your companions. Your first task is to evaluate the group: what are the strengths and weaknesses, how much experience and knowledge do you each have, how fit is everyone, what are the individual preferences and personalities? Your objective must be reasonable for the entire group, not just the strongest or most vocal members.

Establish some organizational guidelines: is one person leading and making all of the decisions, or are you an informal group, or something in between? Learn as much as you can about the area by studying maps and trail guides and talking to others who have been there. Find out what regulations apply to winter backpackers. Make lists of gear and draw up a tentative schedule. Having a clear policy on late arrivals at the trail-head and on the consequences of failing to bring the required gear will reduce the likelihood of both, as well as make it easier for the party to enforce its safety regulations.

PRE-DEPARTURE ROUTINE

- **Find out what regulations apply in the area you plan to tour.**
- **Obtain all necessary permits and reservations.**
- **Check current conditions in the touring area, avalanche hazard (if relevant), weather forecast and road conditions.**
- **Check that all gear is in good condition.**
- **To save weight and space, repackage food in plastic bags (these can be reused on subsequent trips).**
- **Collect all the gear on your list and load it in your pack. If it won't fit, or the pack is too heavy, eliminate non-essential items.**
- **Tell someone where you are going and when to expect you back, as well as who to notify if you don't return.**

LAUNCHING THE TRIP

In an ideal world, the touring party arrives at the trail-head together, packs packed, boots on, ready to depart. Under a warm sun people chat about the trip, don packs and set off happily together on the trail.

Now the reality. One person has decided to sleep in his car at the trail-head and has barely begun to cook breakfast when others in the party drive up, ready to start down the trail. Another car arrives, its occupants having decided to organize their packs at the trail-head. There is no sign of a third group that is supposed to be going on the trip. The winter sun, not yet above the trees, will contribute no warmth for another hour or so. A strong wind is blowing. While some people are frantically stuffing gear in their packs, others are doing the parking lot trot, soon deciding to start down the trail, with promises to wait for the rest "as soon as they warm up." By the time everyone is finally under way no one is certain how many people are actually in the party, where they are or who is setting the pace. The group may arrive safe and sound at its destination, but only because nature sometimes allows fools to survive.

PARTIES AND PARTY MANAGEMENT

A party can range in size from a solitary individual to an army. Styles of party management can also vary, from dictatorship to anarchy. Whether you are a party of two or twenty, good party management is the one absolute essential for a safe and enjoyable winter trip. You want to arrive at the campsite well before dark, with everyone still warm, reasonably fresh and in good humour. There is no place in this scenario for lost skiers, exhausted stragglers, frostbitten toes or the innocent wanderer who thinks that other people will supply the gear he forgot to bring.

Most outdoor groups and all professional guides will offer structure and leadership to less experienced participants. If you do not have access to a winter outdoor club, or if you prefer to organize your own trips, the following pages will help you make important decisions. If you plan to let others do the leading, knowing a little about party management will make you a better participant.

AT THE TRAIL-HEAD

Evaluate the weather and trail conditions on the spot. If your trip is above tree line, you need visibility to navigate, so setting off in a storm may not be wise. If the temperature is -30° C (-22° F) with a wind blowing, do you really want to go skiing? If the snow is soft, the temperature warm, and you have streams or lakes to cross, will the snow bridges or ice be safe?

In general, the less experienced the party and the colder the climate where you tour, the more important it is that people arrive at the trail-head ready to go. Unless the temperature is balmy, boots should either be put on in a warm place before you reach the trail-head or be kept warm inside the car. If you forget, and find the boots iron-stiff with cold in the trunk, don't put them on until just before you leave. Your toes will still suffer but your body will begin to generate heat after a few minutes on the trail.

If the trail-head is bitterly cold, you may want to have an extra jacket that you can wear during final preparations and then leave in the car. You will appreciate not having to shiver as you do up your pack after adding your down parka to it.

You will probably want to check snow conditions at the trail-head before waxing your skis. A preliminary coat of hard wax can be applied ahead of time so that you may need only a touch of softer wax under the feet at the last minute. If you are using stick-on climbing skins, they should be kept warm in the car to make them easier to work with. Skins can also be warmed quickly by placing them inside your jacket in your armpit. Put them on the skis a little before departure time, then make a final check to see if they are sticking or need to be taped in place.

If you are ready before other people, you should note any party members who are slow to get organized and lend a hand. Someone should keep a tool kit handy to cope with last minute problems with bindings or skins. If there is a significant delay, everyone should put on warm clothing or get back in the cars while waiting. If you will be travelling in avalanche terrain (see Chapter Twelve), a designated person can conduct the beacon check in the parking lot while people are getting ready. Alternatively, you can ask the checker to move a short way down the trail and have each person ski by individually to check their signal. This method has the added advantage of forcing people to hurry up and leave. The goal is to get everyone in motion before anyone starts to shiver.

During the pre-departure routine, most people will become slightly chilled. Some will not have their packs perfectly loaded or their boots well laced, and many will be wearing too much clothing. The party should start off together down the trail as soon as everyone is able to move, no matter how disorganized. Keep going at a moderate pace until people feel warm, then stop to make adjustments. You will need to ski perhaps five minutes in warm weather, ten to twenty in cooler conditions. If people still feel cold after a half hour of travel, the pace is not fast enough, or they need to put on more clothing, or both.

ON THE TRAIL

Try to keep the first stop short, so that people do not lose the warmth they have just gained. As you set off again, certain principles of party movement need to be observed. No one should become exhausted, either from breaking trail or from struggling to keep up with the group. Care must be taken that no one gets too far ahead or behind and no one gets lost. The whole party should come together at regular intervals and before major decision points on the route.

A small party should travel close together at a pace that is comfortable for the slowest participant. If you find that pace too slow to keep you warm, put on more clothing. If you find it excruciatingly slow, put on more clothing and think about taking your next trip in faster company. Forcing weaker members of the group to move too quickly can lead them to exhaustion and hypothermia.

In good conditions, all participants should take turns setting the pace. It's fun and valuable experience. If a trail must be broken, stronger members should shoulder most of the burden, but weaker skiers will appreciate the nature of the trip more and will feel that they are contributing to the party if allowed to break trail for short stretches. In dangerous terrain, of course, the most competent person must lead.

Large parties almost inevitably string out along the trail. How such groups are organized depends upon the terrain, the weather and the overall experience and fitness of the participants. The worse the weather and conditions and the weaker the group, the closer you should stay together.

In safe terrain, the lead skier can keep track of everybody by making frequent short stops. If the entire group does not come into view within a couple of minutes, an experienced (or at least fit) individual should be assigned to bring up the rear. If, at rest stops, the stragglers do not arrive within five to ten minutes, a different form of organization is needed.

Any individual trailing the group by more than a few minutes is essentially a party of one. Unless that person is skilled, experienced and fully equipped for bivouac, and travelling conditions are safe, the straggler must be brought into the main group. Since the straggler is probably less fit than the others and incapable of a faster pace, it is the group which must make adjustments.

Only if their muscle is required for breaking trail should the fastest, strongest individuals be allowed to lead a large party of mixed abilities. These people are better employed at the end of the line, usually in pairs so that if the stragglers have problems, one person can stay behind to help while the other catches up to the main group with a message. In a party larger than ten, there should be strength and experience in the middle of the line as well. Macho types of either sex who complain about the slow pace should be given enough extra gear to carry to shut them up.

There are two circumstances in which a party should stay together no matter what the size. First, if all of the members are beginners. Shared ignorance may not keep you out of trouble, especially if all participants act like sheep, but it will probably increase safety somewhat and will certainly make you feel better if trouble occurs. The second circumstance involves situations of potential danger — avalanche terrain, bad storms, poor visibility, steep descents through trees, etc.

PACE

Pace is both a group and an individual matter. When a large party strings out along the trail, fast and fit individuals have a special responsibility not to get too far ahead of the rest of the group. Those in the middle will be able to travel pretty much at their own pace. The stragglers must do all they can to keep up with the group without exhausting themselves.

Let's take the middle of the line first -- those people who can set their own pace without worrying too much about the rest of the party. You should travel at a speed which you can maintain all day and which will keep you warm but not sweaty. On a beautiful spring day, under a blue sky and blazing sun, you can strip down to your underwear. Just be sure to apply and maintain a good sun block. As the temperature drops, the line between fast enough and too fast becomes finer. You should continually adjust hat, mitts, jacket, zippers and pace to maintain a comfortable temperature.

Those at the back of the line face a psychological as well as a physical problem. The rest of the group is ahead, waiting for you to catch up and probably getting cold. Those assigned to bring up the rear may be impatient (On well-run trips, these people understand that their job is to ensure that everyone has a safe and enjoyable time. If this is not the case, consider going with another group next time). However guilty and uncomfortable you feel about being slow, save your crash program of aerobic conditioning for another day. To push beyond your limits is to invite hypothermia and a crisis far worse than any annoyance caused by your slow pace. Concentrate on establishing a rhythm of breathing and striding. Set a pace that you can maintain all day, even if it seems like a crawl. If you begin to feel discouraged, divide the trip mentally into small segments so that you can have the satisfaction of achieving some intermediate goals. At the same time, be considerate of your fellow travellers. You may want to put away your camera, for example, so that others will not be further delayed by your photo stops.

Everyone should pay close attention to the least fit members. They may be embarrassed by their slowness and press too hard. Watch for excessive sweating, shortness of breath and signs of exhaustion such as staggering, unresponsiveness or frequent falls. Often, the best way to slow down unfit skiers who are pressing too hard is to put them right behind an experienced skier, who will adjust the pace to one that is comfortable for them and force the whole group, or at least a sub-group, to go at this pace. You may want to reassess your goals for the day and stop earlier (the nice thing about winter is that you can camp almost anywhere).

The unfit are not the only potential problems for a party. Every inexperienced winter tourer must be watched closely. Poor skiers can tire very quickly. Some people feel that maintaining a moderate pace or even stopping to adjust clothing or replenish fluids is a sign of weakness. Such individuals may overextend and exhaust themselves. People who are normally very fit may develop aches, pains and shaky limbs under the stress of winter travel. They may deny their symptoms and push on regardless or panic and assume the worst.

Nor are trip leaders immune to the perils of winter, especially if they feel that all responsibility rests with them. They may ignore signs of frostbite or overexertion in themselves while tending to the needs of the party. The competent winter party is a cooperative unit, each member responsible not only for doing his or her best but also for looking out for signs of trouble in everyone else.

REST STOPS

Prior agreement about the frequency, length and, if possible, location of group rest stops will avoid misunderstandings, such as the "lost" member who felt so fine he decided to ski all the way to the campsite without telling anyone. Slower members will take comfort in knowing that they will see their friends at least during scheduled breaks. Groups should keep in mind that few things are more discouraging for a straggler than to finally catch up at a rest stop only to see everyone pack up and leave. If the party is so spread out along the trail that leaders reach the rest area too far in advance of the stragglers, a change of pace and more frequent stops may be necessary.

Stops should be used efficiently. If at some point it will be necessary to change from wax to climbing skins, or vice versa, a rest stop should be planned for this location. Major junctions in the trail also make good stops, so that no one goes astray. In general, participants should expect regular rest stops no more than one to two hours apart. They should be asked to schedule as many activities as possible for these stops, rather than making frequent intermediate pauses and falling behind the group.

One problem that individuals should always attend to immediately, however, is blisters. That small "hot spot" on your foot can quickly become an angry open sore that at best will ruin your trip and at worst can disable you or lead to frostbite. It's never pleasant to sit down in a cold wind and remove boots and socks, but it's better than the alternative. Don't wait for a group stop. Get off the trail and reach for your first aid kit.

Lunch stop on a hot sunny day. All you need is sun protection.

Rest stop on a cold sunny day. The skier is bundled up in a down parka over a fleece sweater with the collar raised, plus wool hat and gloves. Sun protection is still needed.

In warm weather, leisurely lunches and frequent pauses will occur naturally. At -30° C, it is tempting to keep moving rather than stop and risk a chill. This temptation must be resisted. In cold weather, fluids have to be replaced often to avoid loss of energy and chilling from dehydration. All participants must be checked at regular intervals for signs of frostbite, hypothermia or exhaustion.

Rest stops can be very uncomfortable in cold weather. The heat you generate while moving causes you to sweat, even if only a little. When you stop, this sweat will evaporate and chill you. Therefore, the minute you stop you must put on extra clothing, even if you feel too hot. I always reach first for a hat or down hood. Then, depending on the outside temperature, I put on either a sweater or a down parka, plus a wind breaker if necessary.

The purpose of the stop is to replenish fluids, stoke up on energy-producing snacks, adjust clothing or equipment and tend to nature's call. Rest is, or should be, the least important part of the stop, since you will have been travelling at a comfortable pace all along. Even if you aren't thirsty or hungry, force yourself to drink and eat. Our bodies betray us by sending contradictory signals when we are dehydrated or blood sugar is low. The wise winter traveller determines in advance how much water and food should be consumed on the trail, and then consumes that amount no matter what.

Food and drink on the trail

Assuming that you drank enough fluids at breakfast, you can support a day of moderate activity with a litre or quart of water. Allow at least twice that if the day is very long, very strenuous, very cold or at high altitude. Feeding should be a near constant activity. Save the fancy ingredients for warm days. In cold weather you need foods which can be shoved in the mouth without removing your mitts.

The colder the outside air, the shorter your stop. When it's -25° C (-13° F) I'm happy with several five-minute breaks during the day, sometimes not even removing the pack, and with no long pause for lunch. Under a warm sun, however, it's nice to take off your skis, pull out a stove to brew tea or soup, make gourmet sandwiches, then lean back and close your eyes. Once you begin to feel a chill, it's time to get back on the trail. In cold weather, always check each other for signs of frostbite on cheeks and nose both during the stop and for a few minutes after you start skiing.

HANDLING YOUR PACK ON THE TRAIL

Even expert skiers feel awkward the first time they try to ski with a heavy pack. When you change speed or direction, the pack will try to continue its original line. Slow down too rapidly, and you will do a face plant in the snow. Lean back a little, and the pack dumps you on your buns. The myriad of adjustments you make with your body to maintain balance on skis become infinitely more difficult. You can be skiing along a perfectly flat track and suddenly fall over sideways.

Take note of how much trouble you have hoisting your pack in the parking lot. As the day progresses, the task will become harder. Keep this in mind as you wrestle the temptation to let it all hang out on an inviting powder slope, or to schuss a steep part of the trail instead of sidestepping down it. Of course, if your pack is of moderate weight and you are in good condition, falls are all part of the fun. If putting on the pack drains your energy, be conservative. There will be time to bomb the slopes pack-free once you arrive at your destination.

FALLS

If you fall, try to avoid the head-first tumble. The weight of your pack will drive your face into the snow. If your skis cross behind you and a tip digs in, you will be helpless until someone arrives to untangle you. Keeping one foot well ahead of the other in a telemark or modified telemark position as you descend a slope will help avoid this catastrophe.

If you do find yourself toppling head first, resist the temptation to break your fall with your arms, especially on hard-packed snow. What you are more likely to break with this manoeuvre is an arm. Try to roll and take the fall partially on your back.

The "chicken" fall – bailing out to the side to avoid worse trouble ahead – is no disgrace when you're carrying a pack. It will usually leave you in a good position to get up again. Do not, however, bail out into the base of a tree. The snow here may be unconsolidated, making it almost impossible for you to get out of the hole. People have suffocated in these holes.

Results of a head-first tumble with heavy pack. The weight of the pack drives the skier's face into the snow. He may require help to get up.

Always ski in control. This is good advice at any time, but essential for touring with a heavy pack. When you are several miles from the trailhead, broken skis and pack belts can be almost as disabling as sprains and broken bones. If you become disabled, you put the rest of the party in jeopardy.

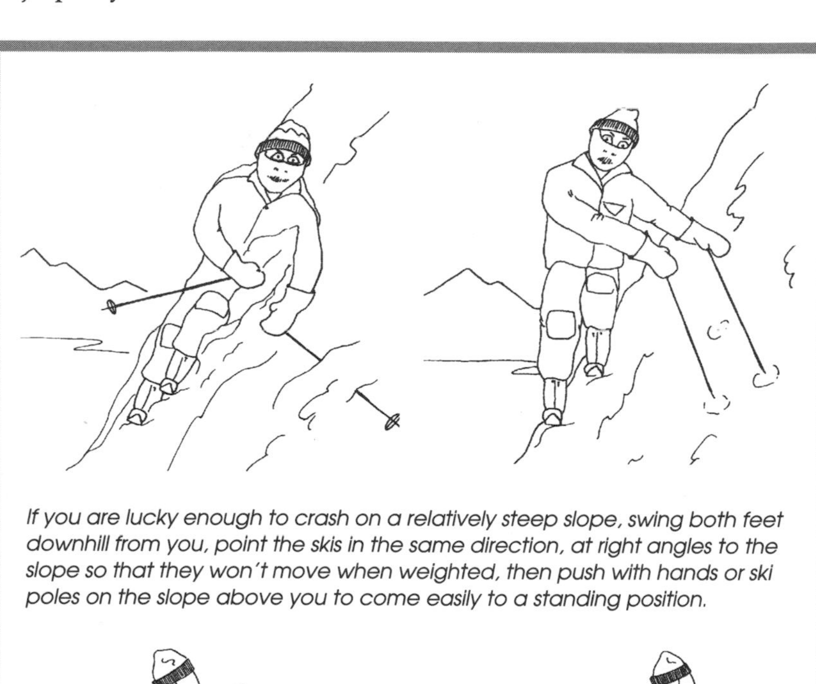

If you are lucky enough to crash on a relatively steep slope, swing both feet downhill from you, point the skis in the same direction, at right angles to the slope so that they won't move when weighted, then push with hands or ski poles on the slope above you to come easily to a standing position.

If you fall on flat terrain, try to roll onto your knees. Place one foot flat on the ground, and using your ski poles for support, stand on that foot. If you cannot get to your knees with the pack on, you will probably have to remove it.

PHOTOGRAPHY ALONG THE TRAIL

Elaborate photography with tripod and multiple lenses is seldom compatible with a group's objective of getting from point A to point B in time to set up camp. Although it is easy to take pictures at rest stops, remember that few trips consist entirely of people eating, drinking and sitting. To capture the adventure of your tour you want photos of people moving along the trail, exploring, or making turns and crash marks on powder slopes. Shots of your buddies from behind are fine in moderation, but you should also try to shoot people coming towards you or passing at right angles to you.

If you are very fit, you can step off the trail, take your photos and catch up to the group without difficulty. You can even rush ahead of your companions to catch them coming through a particularly scenic section. If you are slow you have to use strategy. One useful trick is to be the first on the trail after a rest stop. That will allow you to take at least a few pictures that don't feature the backs of people disappearing in the distance.

A small auto-everything camera that you can carry in a pocket and operate with one hand will allow you to take action shots with scarcely a stride missed. While you are still moving, plan your picture, take the camera from your pocket and remove one or both mitts. Then stop briefly, aim and shoot. With an SLR, which normally travels in a camera pack, you will have to step off the trail, but today's auto-focus program mode cameras do everything almost instantly for you except compose the picture. If you are using a manual camera, however, making all of the adjustments can be time-consuming, especially if your fingers are numb from cold.

How to make a manual camera behave like an automatic

Here's a trick I use on sunny days when there will be a lot of snow in most pictures. Use a fixed focal length lens, 35 mm or wider. Set the aperture to f11. Rotate the focusing ring of the lens until the infinity marker is set to the line representing f11 (if you will be mostly in the trees or the overall light is not sunny bright, set both the aperture and infinity marker to f8).

Scenes may now appear to be out of focus through the viewfinder, but trust me. Set the shutter speed according to the following chart:

Film speed (ISO)	Shutter speed
25	1/60
50 or 64	1/125
100	1/250

With the camera set in this way, you should be able to take shots for several hours (until the overall lighting changes) without adjusting the aperture or the focus. You need only adjust the shutter speed slightly (usually one speed up or down) for each scene so that the camera's light meter indicates that the preset exposure is correct. Allowing for the brightness compensation discussed in Chapter Eight, your light meter will give a correct reading when it indicates that you are overexposing by one to two stops. For unshaded scenes, you should not have to adjust the speed at all. Each time you remove the camera from its case, check to see that the infinity marker has not moved from f11 (or from f8, if you have set it there).

This type of shooting is called hyperfocal and is normally used to ensure good depth of field. Here the technique has been adapted to make a manual camera semi-automatic. Once you are comfortable with the procedure outlined above, you can play with it in different lighting conditions. You can achieve more precise exposure by leaving the shutter speed as set and adjusting the aperture, but you have to be a little more observant. For best results, keep the aperture between f8 and f16. The infinity marker should be set either to the f-stop you are shooting, or to the next lower number (f8 for an aperture of f11, f11 for an aperture of f16, etc.). If you err in the opposite direction, your picture will likely be out of focus.

DEALING WITH NATURAL HAZARDS

One of our favourite circuits in the Canadian Rockies is to ski up Healy Creek to Healy Pass, descend to the Egypt Lake shelter, and next day ski out to the highway via Pharoah and Red Earth creeks. The route down from Healy Pass is unmarked in winter and goes through steep forest. When you arrive at Pharoah Creek, it is difficult to know whether the shelter is to the right or left of your path through the trees. In a large party, if each person takes a separate route to the bottom you are guaranteed a late night as you try to round up everyone and guide them to the shelter. If someone has taken a bad spill in the trees, they may still be waiting for help hours later.

Descending steep forest requires careful group management. So do stream and lake crossings, glaciers and situations of zero visibility and bad weather. This section offers guidance in dealing with some major natural hazards. One particular hazard, avalanches, will be treated separately in Chapter Twelve.

Descending steep, treed slopes

Steep treed slopes should be descended in stages to prevent people from becoming separated. Accidents are more likely in the trees, and shouts for help may carry only a short distance. On short slopes with a clear meeting place at the bottom, the party can divide into small, independent groups (2 to 4 people). On more complicated descents, such as the Healy Pass to Pharoah Creek route, it is better to keep the whole party together. One or two people ski down a short distance and wait until everyone joins them. In a large group, count noses! Repeat the short descents until you reach the bottom. Whoever knows the correct route should lead the way. If no one is sure where to go, at least try to arrive together.

Crossing bodies of water

Small streams can be crossed on snow bridges if there aren't any of the man-made kind nearby. The strength of snow depends on a complex interplay of temperature and snowfall cycles making it impossible to specify a minimum thickness for bridges. Look for bridges of consolidated snow. A bridge with well-worn ski tracks across it is probably safe unless it shows actual signs of collapse, such as cracks, sagging or holes. If everything is covered by fresh snow, probe with a ski pole thoroughly before venturing forth over running water. If in doubt, cross one at a time (good policy in any case) and wait until everyone is safely across before proceeding.

Fallen trees can sometimes be used if the snow bridges are not safe. Remember that snow-covered trees are slippery. If you have instep or full crampons, they will provide the traction you need. Otherwise, you may want to straddle the tree and inch your way across. It's not very elegant, and hard on the seat of your pants, but it's effective.

A typical man-made bridge covered in deep snow.

The author, without her pack, testing a natural snow bridge across a fairly wide stream. Note that the water is not deep enough to be dangerous, but you could get very wet if the bridge failed.

If all else fails, you will have to wade. Never attempt to wade in winter water that is more than a few centimetres or inches deep. Carry your skis, because wet skis ice up the instant they hit snow. If you have to remove your boots to keep water from flowing over the tops, you have chosen a bad route. Keep your socks dry if you do remove your boots (a good argument for packing a spare pair) since you will have to deal with some very cold feet on the other side. One such experience will improve your route planning immeasurably.

Rivers and larger streams are best crossed on ice rather than snow bridges. Here, the consequences of falling in are so serious that extreme caution must be exercised. If you know that your route involves a major crossing, plan the trip for a time of year when the ice is usually dependable. A river that is treacherous in December may be safely frozen in March, or vice versa. Always try to verify ice conditions before the trip, then make your own visual inspection on the spot.

Rivers can freeze unevenly, with firm ice and open water in close proximity. The safest crossing, especially if the ice isn't very good, may be at the widest area where the water is normally more shallow and flows less rapidly. Ice can also form quite a thick pile on corners. If there is open water near your crossing, try to determine visually if the ice is thick enough to bear your weight.

If all is covered by fresh or deep snow, and you have no experience with this particular river in winter, you should re-evaluate your plans. Snow can cover running water, even if there is no ice or only thin ice beneath it.

Crossing a major river on ice just before spring breakup. Note the open water a short distance beyond the skier and signs of melting and cracking along the tracks. This much-used crossing was still safe the day the photo was taken, but would not have been for much longer.

If you decide to attempt a potentially hazardous crossing, one person should tie a rope around their chest, anchor the other end of the rope securely, make the crossing without a pack, and probe thoroughly with a ski pole before each step. The leader will get wet if the ice collapses but can possibly be rescued with the rope. If the crossing still appears to be hazardous and you must continue, the rope should be tied around the chest of each person in turn rather than fixed as a hand line (ropes have too much stretch for a hand line to offer safety under the pressure of broken ice and fast current). Undo the hip belt on your pack when you cross and slide one arm out of the shoulder straps. If you fall in you must be able to shed the pack instantly.

No matter how careful you are and how much help is available, anyone submerged in running water in the winter risks dying from drowning or near-instant hypothermia. As a guiding principle, if you are not 100% sure that the crossing is safe, you should not attempt it.

Lakes present a similar problem to rivers. They tend to freeze unevenly, and snow can mask weak spots in the ice. It is almost impossible to judge the safety of a snow-covered lake by visual inspection. Obtain reliable information about the ice before your trip. Unless you know that the lakes on your tour are safe, go around rather than over them.

Whiteout and storms

Until you have experienced a total whiteout, it is difficult to appreciate how deadly this phenomenon can be. A whiteout results from low cloud or falling or blowing snow which, combined with the snow on the ground, prevents you from seeing any reference points around you.

Four skiers in a total whiteout. The lead skier has no visual reference points and must be guided by signals from the stationary skier at the rear.

Lacking reference points, the human brain cannot control the direction of travel, and people automatically move in a circle. In extreme cases, it is scarcely possible to determine whether your skis are still sliding or you are standing still. Prairie farmers have died trying to find their way between buildings in a blizzard. Parties in the open, such as in fields, on glaciers or large lakes or above tree line, can become totally disoriented and unable to proceed. If wind has blown in the track behind them, they may also be incapable of retreat.

The primary defense against whiteout is to be competent with map and compass (see Chapter Thirteen). Although whiteout navigation is tedious and time consuming, the proper techniques will eventually get you to your destination. It is essential to keep the party together in a whiteout -- tie everyone into a rope if necessary. In hazardous terrain, keep a close eye on the weather and try to avoid being caught in an area where you absolutely require visibility.

If you know that you must retrace your steps, and whiteout is a possibility, you can mark your trail with glacier wands. These are nothing more than the bamboo tomato stakes sold by seed dealers in the spring. Some people like to put ties of fluorescent surveyor's tape on them. Dark red is better in bright whiteouts. I find the bare stakes to be as visible as flagged stakes, but many people feel that the flapping of the tape helps the eye to spot them. Even in the best of conditions they are hard to see. Place the wands at 30-metre (yard) intervals and at key junctures.

The final defense against whiteout is to stop where you are and make camp. If the whiteout is the result of a blizzard or violent storm, this may be the best alternative. In such situations, the ability to dig a snow cave can save your life.

Glaciers

Glaciers offer the best and very worst of winter touring. With a warm sun and deep powder, you have a good imitation of paradise. With a cold wind, no visibility and breakable crust over wet "cement," you have a skier's hell, especially if you are roped to three other people and are carrying a heavy pack. Regardless of conditions, the snow on a glacier covers crevasses into which the unwary can fall to their death. **If you have no training in the techniques of safe glacier travel, venture onto a snow-covered glacier only with a professional guide.** Most amateur mountaineering groups will take novices on easy glacier trips if they have a little basic training in crevasse rescue. If glaciers appeal to you, take the time to learn the necessary skills. Read about, or take a course on, the structure and characteristics of glaciers and take a mountaineering course which includes practice in crevasse rescue and roping techniques. Perfect your skiing technique as well. If you have to rope-up, incompetent skiing will exhaust both you and your rope mates.

BEING A PARTICIPANT ON A WINTER OUTING

A leader cannot be all things to the party. Each participant is ultimately responsible for his or her own well being. Sometimes a situation requires that we put aside our own discomfort for the good of our companions. This is true on a winter trip, but only up to a point. No one enjoys the person for whom nothing is ever right, who asks repeatedly "Will we ever get there?", who disagrees with group decisions and sulks, and whose every misstep is accompanied by profanity. Far better to put on a cheery face and accept that you are not the only one with aching shoulders. Nevertheless, if we are reluctant or embarrassed to admit that we are tired, cold, afraid or confused, we risk putting the whole party in peril.

When should we inform others that all is not well? It depends on the problem. If you are cold, take action immediately. Put on more clothing and make certain that the leader or some other responsible party member is aware of your condition. Hypothermia is so insidious that it can impair you mentally before you are even aware of it. Do not assume that your companions will notice that you are in trouble. If you are cold, squawk!

If you are tired, ask yourself if this is the result of a long, hard day (in which case everyone else in the party probably feels the same way), or are you having difficulty with actions that the others are performing easily? If the former, keep smiling unless you truly cannot continue. If the latter, speak up. For the good of the party, it may be necessary for others to take some of your gear, give you extra water or even change the itinerary.

Fear is crippling and exhausting. As you climb the mountain you may be terrified by the thought of having to ski back down it. Let the leader know how you feel. If the route is technical and perhaps beyond your abilities (a fact which should have been determined before you left home, but perhaps wasn't), the group may have to change plans. If the route is straightforward, the leader should reassure you that you will have plenty of help on the descent. This may involve skiing in front of you to show you the easiest route, taking some of the weight from your pack or giving you a quick technical lesson. No competent leader or group ever ridicules frightened participants or leaves them stranded to work out their own solution to a scary situation. If this happens, even once, to you or another member of the party, refuse to go on another trip with that leader or group.

Confusion and lack of knowledge should also be admitted freely by every participant, whether leading or following. Is it better to express doubt now, or later when the whole party is lost? If you are not certain that an avalanche slope is safe, don't plunge ahead to test it! Share your worries with others and seek their opinions. Most winter trips are not run by professional guides, but involve rather a group of friends each with strong and weak points. By pooling your knowledge and your ignorance, you stand the best chance of having a successful tour.

GOING ALONE

Going to the back country alone in the winter is dangerous. It should be attempted only by those who know how to keep the risk at the level of reasonable challenge rather than recklessness.

When I see how ill-prepared many day-trippers are, miles into the back country, with little gear and less knowledge, I hesitate even to mention the subject of solo travel. Yet nothing will be served by pretending that wilderness solitude does not attract some people. Indeed, some of the greatest ski tours in North America have been accomplished by parties of one. If you are thinking of going alone, however, at least consider carefully the harsh realities you will face. Even if you have no interest in solo winter camping, read on. What follows will show you how to become a better member of any group.

When you are alone, there is no one to help with decisions about whether to continue, stop or retreat, whether an avalanche slope is safe to cross, whether a bad storm is on the way, whether the correct route goes right or left, whether the ice or snow bridge will bear your weight. No one will be on hand to pick up the pieces if you are wrong. Do you have the knowledge to make these decisions on your own?

Every step should represent a conscious decision that it is safe to proceed. You must be constantly alert, observe the terrain, turn around frequently to see how the trail will look on the way back, take compass bearings, keep track of the time, look for telltale signs of avalanche hazard and changing weather.

You must be sensitive to the needs of your body. Keeping warm is your primary concern, and to do that you must pace yourself, drink and eat, avoid exhaustion. Once hypothermia progresses past the initial stages, you will be helpless.

You must assess your temperament dispassionately. Panic, of course, is deadly, but so is a tendency to be careless, to ignore details, to hope for the best and forge ahead blindly, to daydream when you should be alert. When you are alone, you should always err on the side of caution.

If you are injured or ill, you will have to provide shelter and first aid for yourself until help arrives (surely you told someone where you were going!). If equipment breaks down, you must repair it. Can you carry all of the gear you need?

With the exception of carrying excess gear, the behaviour and skills we have just described are no more than what a competent back-country tourer displays as a matter of course on any trip with any group. It is how **you** will behave in a few years if you find winter camping as exciting and rewarding as we think you will.

10.
Camp

There are two major considerations in deciding when to make camp. One is the time of sunset. You want to have everything set up and dinner well under way by the time it is dark. In January in northern latitudes, that may mean stopping by 2:00 or 3:00 in the afternoon. Allow yourself at least a two-hour window between the time you stop and the onset of darkness.

A second consideration is the condition of the party. Stop before people become exhausted and cold. If that means camping somewhat short of your intended destination, so be it. Late in the day, try to keep the party close together so that the lead skiers are aware of the status of people at the end of the line. Of course, if anyone begins to display signs of hypothermia, put up a tent on the spot or at the nearest safe location.

CAMPSITES

Sunlight strikes your tent, chasing away the chill of night. As the tent warms, you are coaxed from your sleeping bag and step out into a small meadow overlooking the wide valley that you ascended yesterday. You draw water from the creek by your tent and enjoy a leisurely breakfast, undisturbed by the morning breezes. This is winter camping at its finest.

Of course, you won't always find that perfect site — south-facing, sheltered, with running water and a view. Sometimes, weather and exhaustion force you to camp in places you hope never to see again. On balance, however, winter offers a wider choice of pleasant campsites than summer does. Mosquito bogs, ponds, debris-clogged forest floors and boulder fields become smooth expanses of snow.

Your first priority in site selection is safety. Do not camp in potential avalanche zones or on the middle of a lake that may not be completely frozen. In areas of high winds, you need a sheltered area, at least for tenting. Given a choice between running water and a view, I'll take the view anytime, but if your kitchen equipment is not geared to melting snow, stay by the water.

Once the general area is selected, plan your temporary village. Look for slopes or embankments for snow caves. Often a stream bed will provide good caving sites. Tents should be shielded from the wind, on a little rise or above a gulley that will act as a sink hole for cold air, and away from snow-laden trees. If you snore loudly, be considerate and locate your tent at some distance from the others. If you want a group kitchen, it should be centrally located. The biffy should be well away from streams or lakes, downwind from the tents, and as private as possible.

KITCHENS

I have never enjoyed squatting on my haunches to cook a meal. Dig a pit that is deep enough to allow you to stand while operating the stove. A few strokes of a shovel will give you a level platform and shelves for food, pots, dishes, water bottles, and anything else you want around you.

If you like, make a bench for sitting and cover it with a mattress. Orient the stove platform to provide maximum protection from the wind. If necessary, surround the stove with snow blocks on three sides. When the weather is really bady, I dig a deep pit and build a wall around it that will offer shelter to me as well as the stove. You will save yourself effort if you can face the kitchen into a hill or bank which will provide one wall.

Cooking in the tent

To cook or not to cook in the tent? My own answer is — don't! The risks and problems are too great — carbon monoxide poisoning from inadequate ventilation, setting the tent and most of your gear on fire, spilling a pot of water or stew on your sleeping bag, soaking the tent and its contents with condensation from steam. There are times when there is no choice. In my experience, these have been rare and have occurred only on mountaineering trips to windswept places like Mount Logan or the

A fair-weather kitchen. A few strokes of a shovel will give you a level platform and shelves.

A foul weather kitchen. A kitchen for extreme conditions on Mt. Logan.

Arctic. For the rest, I depend on a good winter stove and windproof clothing to see me through any weather.

IF YOU DECIDE TO COOK IN YOUR TENT

Many experienced and competent campers do cook in their tents on a regular basis. If you want to do the same, take the following precautions:

- **Learn to operate the stove in winter conditions and become thoroughly familiar with its behavior before you try to use it in a tent.**
- **Always prime and light the stove outside the tent, bringing it inside only when it has settled into a steady flame.**
- **If possible, cook right by the open door of the tent. You will have adequate ventilation and the stove can be tossed out into the snow if it develops a problem.**
- **Buy a tent with more than one exit, just in case.**
- **Keep your boots outside the tent while cooking. If you lose your sleeping bag in a fire you will still be able to ski out.**
- **If the weather is such that you must close the door, leave a wide segment open for ventilation and cook as close to it as possible. Better yet, have a cold meal.**
- **If other people are in the tent, they must stay alert. They should make no uncontrolled movement or become so engrossed in other tasks that they forget about the stove.**
- **Try to keep boiling and simmering to a minimum to reduce condensation.**
- **Collect all the water you need before you start to cook. If you are melting snow in the tent, fill a plastic garbage bag with snow and drag it to the entrance to ensure a ready supply. You won't have to leave the tent, and possibly upset the stove, just to refill a pot.**

SANITATION

Human waste is a serious pollutant, yet it is easy to assume that the next snowfall will hide all trace of your presence. It will—until next spring when all will be uncovered. Unfortunately you cannot dig a pit in the frozen earth to bury excrement as you do in summer. Winter calls for special and sometimes inconvenient measures.

Sanitary procedures and facilities must be adapted to the sort of site you are occupying. If you camp in an area that is used year round, there will probably be an outhouse. Shovel a path to it and use it. Excrement buried randomly in snow over the area will pose a serious health hazard to campers the following summer.

If you are not in a designated campsite, are well off a summer trail and there is no evidence that others regularly camp there, it is acceptable to dig a biffy in an out-of-the-way place where summer hikers are unlikely to stumble onto it. Stay well away from any water course and try to ensure that spring run-off will not pollute a stream or lake. Burn or carry out your toilet paper and carry out sanitary napkins and tampons in a plastic bag.

If you are in a high use area and do not have an outhouse, there is no responsible alternative to depositing solid waste in a heavy garbage bag and taking it out with you. This is not yet standard procedure among winter campers, but it should be. Be the one to set a good example. Take care where you urinate, too. Stay away from water courses and pick an area where other campers are not likely to collect snow for melting.

If you know that you will be camping in absolutely abominable conditions, you may want to pack a "pee bottle" for use in the tent. It saves excruciating trips in the middle of the night, and also discourages making yellow snow right outside the tent door. I have met only one woman who could use such a device without disaster, but for men the spare bottle can be invaluable.

On a glacier or high mountain, if you will be camping in one place for several days or have a large party, it is worthwhile to construct a sheltered biffy, surrounded by a wall of snow blocks. Biffy construction seems to inspire would-be architects even more than snow caves and kitchens. I have seen some with spiral staircases and elaborate thrones.

A well-protected biffy for an exposed location.

BEING COMFORTABLE IN CAMP

In camp, your first priority is maintaining a comfortable body temperature. You may start to feel cold the minute you take off your pack, partly because of the moisture in your clothing and partly from dehydration. Take the time, before doing anything else, to adjust your clothing, and continue adjusting it whenever you feel the least bit cold (or overheated).

If the weather is very cold you can easily spend as much time keeping warm as you do performing camp chores. Allow for this in your planning. At -30° C or F, it can take several times as long to set up camp and cook dinner as it does in the summer.

Mike and I plan our evening routine to keep us comfortable at all times. As soon as the tent platform is ready and we can put away our skis, we change from ski boots to down booties and overboots. If we have erred and allowed too much sweat to build up in our clothing, we remove the wet garments. As the evening progresses we add down pants, parka, hood—whatever is needed. While Mike arranges gear and fluffs out our sleeping bags in the tent, I build a kitchen and immediately serve hot drinks and soup. Dinner always warms us right down to the toes. If the weather is nice, we may go for an after-dinner ski, then return for more hot drinks before snuggling into our sleeping bags for the long winter night.

The ideal temperature range for a winter camping evening is -2° C (28° F) to -10° C (14° F). The snow will not be so warm that it melts on contact and your clothing will allow you to relax comfortably and enjoy

Down or fibre fill clothing, lots of liquid and hot food stave off the chill of a winter camp. You can be comfortable in camp in almost any conditions if you dress properly. The author on Mt. McKinley at 17,000 feet and -20° F.

a leisurely meal. This is the time for gourmet cooking. Most people will want to gather in the kitchen and socialize. The cook will not have frozen hands, and washing the dishes is not an impossible chore.

When the wind blows and the temperature plummets, however, people chill quickly from lack of activity, and hot food becomes more a necessity than a pleasure. Many people will prefer to retreat to the tent while the cooks persevere, clad head to toe in wind shells and down. In these circumstances, opt for a simple menu. If you have two stoves in the party, use the hottest one for continuous snow melting while food is prepared on the other. In this way, when dinner is over you will not still be faced with the task of filling the water bottles. Head for the tent and break out those games you packed.

TIPS FOR MELTING SNOW

Snow is more air than water. If you simply fill a pot and put it over high heat, all of the moisture will evaporate and your pot will burn. Always try to save a little liquid from the trail to start the melting process. If you have no liquid, then find the densest, wettest snow available and put it over very low heat until some liquid appears in the bottom of the pot.

You will have to fill the pot with snow several times in order to obtain a pot of water. Well-compacted snow which forms solid blocks or chunks is far more efficient for melting than loose surface snow. The snow disturbed when you built the kitchen will compact, so you may have only to reach out and grab a piece as you tend the pot. If you must dig elsewhere, brush aside the surface fluff to get to the solid snow underneath. You can increase snow density by shovelling it into a large garbage bag and letting it consolidate for several hours. If you make camp early in the day, leave the bag (which should be a dark colour) out in the sun while you go skiing. It will contain very wet chunks of snow when you return, and possibly some liquid.

Always cover the snow pot with a lid to conserve heat and save fuel. If you have a heat exchanger (see Chapter Seven), the process will be much faster. To keep your gloves dry, try to scoop wet snow into the pot with a cup or a shovel rather than your hands. Very cold snow will contain so little moisture that you can handle it without getting wet.

When pouring the melted snow into a bottle, set the bottle in another pot or a pot lid with sides, rather than holding it in one hand. You will keep your gloves dry, and the pot will capture any water spilled. Once a bottle is filled, it can be set on a kitchen shelf until needed if the temperature is moderate. In extreme cold, dry it carefully and put it in the inside pocket of your down parka or in the tent in a sleeping bag. Never replace the lid on an empty bottle. It will freeze shut and have to be dunked in warm water to thaw.

Melting snow consumes a lot of time. If possible, melt enough for breakfast while you are cleaning up from dinner. Fill all water bottles and put them where they won't freeze. If the temperature doesn't drop below -5° C (-23° F), the bottles will be okay in the tent if insulated from the snow. At colder temperatures, fill them with hot water and take them into your sleeping bag. Pots can be filled with water and buried at least 30 cm (12 inches) deep in snow. Be sure to mark the spot so you can find them next morning.

CLEAN-UP

In moderate temperatures, you can follow your standard clean-up procedures. If it is bitterly cold or you find yourself getting chilled, compromise is advisable, especially since the food stuck to the pots is frozen and won't spoil. The last thing you want to do is plunge your hands into water. Try to select a menu that does not leave the pot encrusted with burned sauce and food.

You can get dishes and pots reasonably clean by filling them with snow and scraping them with your spoon or a plastic pot scraper. Pour in a little boiling water to rinse, and they can be stored for the night. If you can't tolerate the remaining specks of food, or the pot is a hopeless mess, use boiling water and manipulate the pot scraper or dish-cloth with your spoon rather than fingers. Soap is really not necessary and is a pollutant. Empty the dishwater in a designated place away from the water supply. If you have a dog, let it drink the food-flavoured water.

Cover the stove and put it with the dishes and utensils in a corner of the kitchen, marked with a tall object in case there is a heavy snowfall overnight. Alternatively, bring everything into the vestibule of the tent.

PROTECTING YOUR FOOD FROM NATURE'S THIEVES

With most bears and rodents snug in their dens, you may think that you don't have to protect your food. Wrong! Winter has its own group of camp robbers. Fortunately, with the exception of polar bears, they are not likely to attack you, but they can make a mess of your camp and leave you hungry. The major culprits are martens and other weasels by night and birds by day.

All members of the weasel family are fearless, ill-tempered and intelligent. I have had martens come into my tent, waking on more than one morning to find two beady eyes and a black nose right in my face. Weasels will dig through snow for anything they can smell. I always bring food at least into the vestibule, and often into the tent, something one should never do in the summer in bear country. If using a bivy bag, I put the food right beside me and keep a flashlight handy.

The nastiest weasel is the wolverine. Although they are normally shy, if one should discover your camp and decide to stay in the neighbourhood, you may as well pack up and go home. It won't attack you but the minute your back is turned it will happily trash everything you own. Count yourself fortunate for having seen one — they are rare.

Most other winter predators seldom come into an occupied camp. We have never been bothered by foxes, wolves, coyotes or members of the cat family, although coyotes are certainly bold around humans. In the far north, polar bears are a concern. Your only defense, short of carrying a shotgun, is to avoid them. If you see signs, leave the area. Further south, it is not unknown for other bears to leave their dens far earlier than you might expect. Again, avoidance is the best tactic. A groggy, hungry bear is unlikely to be in a good mood.

The worst destruction I have seen inflicted on a winter camp was the work of ravens. In the north, especially on well-travelled routes, these intelligent birds consider you a prime source of food, see through the best camouflage and will tear anything apart to get at your supplies. When we left food caches on Baffin Island, we buried everything under a metre and a half of snow and were careful to leave no surface trace of our presence. Even then, we worried. In the south, winter birds are quite capable of stealing a sandwich out of your hand, but will seldom cause mass destruction.

You should never feed animals in the wild. Creatures that inhabit the winter landscape are adapted to their environment and fit into a cycle of life and death that may appear cruel to us but which seldom benefits from our intervention.

IN THE MORNING

Early starts are rare in winter, especially if you have a south-facing location. You will probably wait until the sun begins to warm the tent before venturing from your cozy nest. Metabolisms are at their most sluggish in the morning, and the required strip-down to attend to natural functions is not a warming experience.

A stove in the pit by the tent door can be used to make hot drinks before anyone stirs. Whoever is sleeping with head to the door rolls over and lights the stove, boils up a bottle of water and throws in tea or juice crystals. This is another good argument for keeping everything in or within reach of the tent.

In order to break camp efficiently, one person should prepare breakfast while the tent mate stuffs sleeping bags and packs gear. After breakfast, take down the tent, pack the kitchen, scrape frost from the skis and wax them or put on skins.

If you have a dog, let it carry the garbage and "poop bag". Otherwise, tie these securely to the outside of a pack, wrapped so that they will not be ruptured by tree branches or a fall. Shovel snow into the biffy and if the kitchen is in a location where someone could inadvertently ski into it, fill it in as well. If the camp area receives regular day use, cover any spill marks or yellow snow, clean up whatever the dog has done, and generally leave your site clean and white. I do this even in remote locations where I know that snow will fall before the next traveller passes through.

Putting on cold boots should be one of the last acts before departure. Of course, if you slept with your boots to keep them warm, and they are capable of keeping your feet warm while you break camp, you should put them on as soon as you get up.

Dress warmly while preparing to leave in the morning. Don't put on ski boots until the last moment.

11. Emergencies

Wilderness survival courses teach you such things as how to build a lean-to, light a wood fire, snare small game — how to survive if you are dumped in the middle of nowhere with almost no equipment. Most of what they teach has little to do with the sort of touring described here, is destructive of the environment, and is totally incompatible with the rules of national, provincial and state parks.

Recreational winter camping should never turn into a survival situation. Most emergencies are preventable with proper equipment, knowledge, procedures and common sense. Frostbite and hypothermia result from inattention to clothing, exhaustion and dehydration; equipment that is carefully selected for the purpose, scrupulously maintained and properly used should not break down; a well-managed party seldom has one of its members go astray; and common sense should keep you from skiing recklessly or setting fire to your tent.

Accidents happen, of course. You can break a leg falling on flat ground. Bad weather can keep you from moving or can exceed the design limitations of your gear. Whole parties sometimes take the wrong turn and get lost. People become ill. People get careless or attempt trips that are too ambitious for their skill and experience. This chapter will discuss some of the main hazards of winter travel; how to identify, prevent and treat them; what to do if an emergency occurs and how to send for help.

HYPOTHERMIA

In order to prevent and deal with hypothermia, it is necessary to understand the effects of chilling on the body. The behaviour and observable characteristics of the victim reflect changes going on inside the body, and treatment must be aimed at counteracting those changes. Hypothermia progresses through a number of stages from first symptoms to death. In terms of treatment in the field, however, hypothermia is best divided into two main categories: **early hypothermia**-defined as a body core temperature that is lower than normal (37° C or 98.6° F) but still above 32° C (90° F); and **profound hypothermia**-defined as a core temperature of 32° C (90° F) or lower.

Warning signs of early hypothermia

Shivering. This is the body's attempt to generate more heat through muscular activity. Shivering may not be apparent to others in the party.

Stiff and slightly uncoordinated muscles. The victim may be clumsy, have difficulty keeping up with the party, or fall frequently. Speech may be slurred simply from the stiffness of facial muscles.

Hands, feet and skin which feel cold to the touch. Blood vessels near the skin constrict and blood flow to the extremities is reduced, thus protecting the warmth of the body core by avoiding heat loss from the relatively large surface areas of the arms and legs. The victim may complain of cold hands or feet or of feeling cold all over.

Mild personality changes. Various internal changes increase the viscosity of the blood by drawing water from it, leading to dehydration. The blood delivers less oxygen to the tissues, with an immediate effect on the sensitive cells of the brain. The mind is still able to function, but more slowly than normal. The victim may be apathetic or short tempered, or exceptionally preoccupied with personal needs.

If recognized at the early stage (and if further cooling of the victim is prevented), hypothermia can usually be reversed in the field with little difficulty. Victims of early hypothermia are still able to generate heat, and they will not be harmed by rescuers' attempts to provide external warmth.

Warning signs of profound hypothermia

The most precise way to diagnose profound hypothermia—core temperature of 32° C (90° F) or lower—is to use a special hypothermia thermometer (the standard type registers only a few degrees below normal body temperature). It is usually more practical in the field, however, to be guided by the signs below.

- **Shivering stops**. The body has abandoned the effort to generate heat in this way.
- **Muscles lose coordination**. the victim may stagger, lose balance, be unable to perform the simplest tasks, faint.
- **The mind becomes confused, indecisive and functions illogically.** Sometimes the victim will appear willing and able to cooperate, yet will not do so. The profoundly hypothermic person may be unable to respond coherently when questioned.
- **The victim may lose interest in keeping warm** and may even begin to shed clothing.
- **Pulse rate falls.**
- **The breath may have a fruity odour.**
- **Speech is slurred** from decreased brain function.
- **Vision may be impaired.**
- **There may be loss of bladder control.**

In the final stages before death:

- **The victim lapses into a coma.**
- **The heartbeat becomes almost undetectable.** At this point the victim may appear dead, yet still be alive, with at least a small chance to live if he/she gets to a hospital. The hypothermic brain needs very little oxygen to survive. Dr. Cameron Bangs put it best: "No one should be considered cold and dead until he has been warm and dead!" (*Hypothermia, Frostbite and other Cold Injuries*, p. 53).

The progression from early to profound hypothermia is not always gradual and may bear little relationship to the length of time the victim has been exposed to the cold. The onset of profound hypothermia can be extremely rapid, especially if the victim has been immersed in icy water or buried in an avalanche. In such cases, I would automatically assume that hypothermia is profound and treat accordingly.

The signs of hypothermia can easily pass unnoticed in a party intent on reaching its destination or carrying out a task. On Mount McKinley, I was part of a large, inexperienced group ferrying loads to our first cache. One person had diarrhea, not uncommon on expeditions, and spent considerable time squatting, exposed to the cold, at some distance from the others. Because of the diarrhea, he lost a lot of fluid. He rejoined the group as we returned to camp, but we were all preoccupied with the thrill of starting the climb and being in this wondrous location. Back in camp, the victim sat down quietly by his tent and went unnoticed for some time. Someone finally spoke to him and realized that he was incoherent. By then, hypothermia had progressed to a serious stage and we were fortunate to be able to treat it successfully.

Treatment for any degree of hypothermia begins with the immediate prevention of further heat loss. Remove any wet clothing to prevent evaporative heat loss, provide shelter from the wind and insulate the person from conductive and radiative heat loss. Only if hypothermia is caught and reversed in its mildest stages will the victim be able to continue the trip.

Self treatment for the earliest stage of hypothermia

- Put on more clothing.
- Take fluids, to combat dehydration.
- Eat, to help the body generate heat.
- Make someone else aware of the situation.
- Move the large muscles to generate heat. If you are at a rest stop, get back on the trail. This is one occasion when you may want to ski for a few minutes in your down parka (be sure to remove excess clothing as soon as you begin to feel too warm).
- Although we have not yet tested it, the Canadian Cold Buster Bar (see Chapter Seven), which is designed to slow the onset of hypothermia, would seem to be appropriate at this point.

If the victim does not recognize the onset and the condition worsens, others in the party must take action at once, even if the victim protests. It is far better to overreact than to risk the development of profound hypothermia. A drop in core temperature of even 2° C (3.6° F) can have serious consequences.

Treating a victim of early hypothermia

- If a warm building or the trail-head is near, head for it, providing the person is still able to travel without difficulty. Otherwise, get the victim out of the wind at once.
- Remove any wet clothing.
- Have the person bundle up in warm clothing.
- Give food and water.

If rewarming is successful, the whole party should be able to continue after a brief rest, but if these measures do not bring rapid improvement:

- Put up a shelter and get the victim into a sleeping bag.
- Heat the interior of the shelter with a stove (be sure to provide adequate ventilation).
- Apply external heat from hot water bottles, chemical hot packs, a hot shower or bath, if available (**Warning**: Do not apply external heat, especially immersion in hot water, if you suspect profound hypothermia-see below.).
- If you have no other external heat sources, someone can get into the sleeping bag with the victim. Both should be lightly clad to speed transfer of body warmth.
- If the victim is able to drink easily, warm drinks, excluding alcohol, will give at least the illusion of providing warmth (the actual physical benefit of warm liquids-as opposed to cold ones-is debatable). Fluid intake is important to combat dehydration.
- Check carefully for frostbite, since circulation to the hands and feet may have been impaired.
- If the above measures were necessary, the victim may have suffered a significant drop in body core temperature. Even if all appears well after rewarming, it would be prudent to discontinue the trip and encourage the victim to see a doctor.

Treatment of profound hypothermia

Profound hypothermia is difficult to treat in the field. There is significant risk of a fatal outcome—just about anything you do, including external rewarming and any rough handling, can cause ventricular fibrillation, an uncoordinated heartbeat that is often irreversible. If you suspect profound hypothermia, consider that you have an emergency every bit as life threatening as a heart attack or severe head injury.

The victim of profound hypothermia is no longer able to generate heat and is unable to help himself either physically or mentally. Do not allow the victim to move in any way. Handle the person as gently as possible. Prevent further heat loss and remove any constricting garments. Make camp on the spot or move your established camp to the victim. If you must transport, use a stretcher arrangement and be gentle. If help is available, send someone out for it.

Put the victim in a snow cave or tent (a snow shelter is warmer but takes longer to produce), in a sleeping bag, and heat the inside of the shelter with a stove. Someone should get into the bag with the person, separated from him by as little clothing as possible. **If you can stabilize the victim so that body temperature is no longer dropping, the best medical advice seems to be, do nothing further.** The victim may slowly begin to recover on his own. Even if he doesn't, leave active rewarming to the hospital. If body temperature continues to fall, however, and rescue is unlikely or distant, there is little to be lost by gently applying very warm (but not burning) objects to the body, especially to the armpits and groin. People have made amazing recoveries in the worst circumstances and with the most primitive treatment.

You will not harm a victim of early hypothermia if you treat for profound hypothermia, but a profoundly hypothermic victim can die if treated inappropriately. Therefore, if you have any reason to suspect that hypothermia is profound, treat it as if it were: prevent further heat loss and be gentle, but DO NOT try to rewarm the victim rapidly.

Even when rewarmed, victims of any but the mildest hypothermia may suffer physical consequences. An immediate check for frostbite should be made because of the reduced flow of blood to hands and feet. If any of the signs of profound hypothermia were present, the victim should seek medical treatment as soon as possible.

Prevention

The best treatment for hypothermia is prevention. Take all steps necessary to maintain a comfortable body temperature. Dress properly, control heat loss, limit sweating, drink as much as possible, keep up your energy level with snacks, and avoid overexertion and fatigue, including that brought on by carrying too heavy a pack.

Be alert to signs of hypothermia in other members of the party. Note any changes in behaviour or attitude. The better you know your companions, the more likely you are to notice if they are acting strangely. Check anyone who is moving more slowly or awkwardly than usual or falling repeatedly, and those who appear not to be very fit. Pay particular attention to poor skiers, since their sloppy technique may exhaust them. Try to keep track of the amount people are drinking and eating at rest stops and encourage adequate consumption of liquids and carbohydrates. On really cold days, be prepared to abandon the trip immediately if anyone shows signs of fatigue or is having trouble keeping warm.

FROSTBITE

Frostbite is the freezing of tissue, usually of the hands, feet and face. Damage arises from the freezing itself, but even more so from the impairment of blood circulation to the affected area. If not recognized and treated promptly, frostbite requires a lengthy recovery period and possibly amputation of the affected tissue.

Causes of frostbite

- Any conditions which foster hypothermia can lead to frostbite. When the core temperature of the body is lowered, blood circulation to the extremities is reduced, leaving them vulnerable to frostbite. Even a slight drop in core temperature can endanger hands and feet.
- In extreme cold, any highly conductive object can freeze tissue almost instantly if you come into direct contact with it. Always wear gloves when handling a metal camera, pot, ski binding or repair tools. Don't put your tongue or lips on a cold metal spoon, cup or mattress valve.
- Rapid evaporative heat loss will cause severe frostbite. The fuel for your stove is highly dangerous because if you spill it on your skin it will evaporate almost instantly. Extremely cold alcoholic beverages, if gulped hastily, can do terrible (sometimes fatal) things to the mouth and throat.
- Convective heat loss causes freezing of exposed areas, usually the nose, cheeks and ears. Even a slight breeze at low temperatures can produce the telltale white patches.
- Anything that impairs circulation, including the nicotine in cigarettes, is a potential danger.
- Anything that impairs mental function, such as alcohol, high altitude, hypothermia or extreme fatigue, can result in poor judgement that leads either to frostbite or a to failure to recognize its onset.

Hands and feet

The hands and feet are especially at risk for a variety of reasons — they are far from the body core and subject to reduced circulation both from hypothermia and from constricting garments.

Blood vessels in, or leading to, the extremities must be protected from any external pressure which could reduce the flow of blood. If you lace your boots too tightly, wear too many socks, or have boots which don't fit properly, you risk frostbite. If you grip your ski poles too tightly or wear gloves or mitts which are too tight, you can restrict the blood supply to the surface tissues of the hands.

The blood vessels of the hands and feet are near the skin and they automatically constrict to reduce blood flow when subjected to cold. The feet are in close proximity to the cold ground surface most of the time and must be especially well insulated.

Hands often suffer conductive heat loss from gripping metal objects. As well, it is not unusual for your mitts to come off in a fall, exposing your hands to direct contact with the snow. This is another argument for wearing liner gloves, which are less likely to be lost.

If your feet or boots get wet, evaporative heat loss can contribute to the chill. On a warm spring day, wet snow may soak your boots. This isn't a problem as long as the sun is shining and you are active, but be careful when you stop to rest or the temperature drops. Gaiters which protect the entire upper boot should be worn whenever conditions are wet.

Wet gloves sometimes seem to be the norm when camping, especially for the cook, who must work with liquids and fill water bottles. To minimize evaporative chilling, carry spare dry gloves and make sure you have a garment with good hand-warmer pockets.

Long ski poles can raise the hands higher than the heart, making it more difficult for blood to reach them. When it's very cold and the pace is slow, you may have to ski for occasional short stretches with one or both hands by your side or in pockets in order to restore full circulation. Swinging the arms vigorously helps generate warmth.

Warning signs and treatment of mild frostbite

Frostbite on the face appears first as a white patch of skin, and is frequently not perceived by the victim. Party members should check each other for this early sign of frostbite. If you are heading into a cold wind, wear a face mask or other protection. If a white patch appears, warm it by skin-to-skin contact with your hands until it turns red, then keep it well protected. Minor patches of white skin on toes and fingertips can be treated in the same way.

Frostbite of hands, fingers, feet and toes is first signalled by pain, but if you are deeply involved in some activity, you may fail to notice it. Gloves and boots hide any skin discoloration from view. It is essential to try to detect frostbite at this early stage, however, because rewarming can take place with no damage to tissues.

Always be aware of the state of your hands and feet and of the sorts of heat loss they are subject to. Counteract frostbite at the first symptom. Put on more clothing, especially on your head. Move the large muscles leading to the extremities. If necessary, put your bare hands or feet in a buddy's bare armpit, between his thighs or on his stomach. Change to down booties for a while.

Severe frostbite

If not rewarmed in the early stage, the frostbitten part loses feeling. Since the pain stops, you may assume that the problem has gone away, when in fact it has worsened. If your judgement is impaired by other factors, you are likely to overlook this warning sign. When you next remove your boots or gloves, you will find pale or discoloured skin because of the reduced blood supply. At this stage, the tissues are usually hard and numb.

REWARMING A FROZEN EXTREMITY

Rewarming is best done when the victim is warm all over and can be kept that way. Thawing the foot or hand of a hypothermic person does little good because there will be inadequate blood supply to the extremity (in any event, the hypothermia needs treatment more urgently). A hut, tent or snow cave should be used.

Rewarming is done by suspending the frozen part in a large container of water with temperature carefully maintained between 38° C and 42° C (100° F to 108° F). Do not let the injured flesh touch the bottom or sides of the container. Check your thermometer constantly, because the frozen extremity will lower the temperature of the water. Maintain the temperature by adding hot water to the container. Be sure to remove the injured part from the water while this is done, and keep it out until you have stirred the container and verified the temperature. Continue soaking until the skin becomes flushed, or until there is no further improvement in colour.

You may need to give pain killers as feeling returns to the affected area (use only aspirin or equivalent).

One obvious problem with the above method is that few parties carry a pot large enough to rewarm a whole foot or have the capability to supply the gallons of hot water that will be needed.

Treatment depends on where you are and what you must do to get to safety. You want to restore circulation to the affected area as soon as possible. Once the extremity is rewarmed, however, it must not be subjected to refreezing or rough contact since even more damage will result. Hands and fingers should usually be thawed in the field if at all possible. If a foot or toes have been frozen, however, and the victim has to walk out, it is important to do so on frozen, not thawed, tissues. This can be a difficult call if thawing is likely to occur while the victim is walking. If it appears that the victim cannot be evacuated without the feet or toes slowly thawing and causing increased damage, you will have to rewarm them quickly in the field and then protect the injury by carrying the victim.

Once rewarming is complete, you must do everything possible to avoid irritation of the tissues and prevent infection. You cannot simply shove the thawed foot or hand back in a boot or mitten. Bandage it carefully and try to keep it from contacting whatever insulation you put around it, such as a sleeping bag. Sterile cotton or gauze may be put between fingers or toes. If blisters develop on the skin they must not be broken. Evacuate the victim as soon as possible.

Given the severity and permanence of the damage that may occur, prevention—for frostbite, as for hypothermia—is the best treatment.

OTHER INJURIES

It is late afternoon on a very cold day. You have been skiing the high country and are returning to camp down a steep, treed slope. Suddenly the lead skier, travelling a little too fast, catches a tip, somersaults and crashes heavily into a tree. She lies motionless for a moment, then begins to moan in pain. What you do in this situation is determined by how well you have prepared for it ahead of time.

Winter back-country emergencies are complicated by the environment in which they occur. First-aid training is a necessary but not sufficient prerequisite for dealing with them. The splint you apply to stabilize a fracture need only impair circulation slightly to cause frostbite. While you are trying to control bleeding, the victim may slip into hypothermia. While you are tending to the victim, the rest of the party may endanger themselves. You need two adjuncts to standard first aid: knowledge of how to apply it in a wilderness setting where medical facilities may be far away, and an awareness of how parties should behave in an emergency.

Wilderness first-aid courses are available, and a number of good books have appeared on the subject of wilderness medicine. In some cases you may have to go well beyond the limits of standard first aid. The more you know the more likely you will be to act in the victim's best interest. Follow the first rule of treatment — do no harm. Ideally, everyone in the party should be competent to deal with injuries and sudden illness. In my experience, relatively few back-country travellers have the necessary knowledge. Try to ensure that at least two people in your group are trained, and one of them should be **you.**

Group management in a crisis

Party management is important in a crisis. One victim is already too many — don't add others because of inattention to the basics of keeping warm and avoiding danger. The first consideration in any accident is the safety of the would-be rescuers. If the victim is lying in the middle of an avalanche slope where a slide is likely, you don't want 15 people milling around in the same spot. If cold and wind are at hazardous levels (and that is often the case in winter), make sure everyone dresses properly for a lengthy stop. If people must go for help, make sure they travel in pairs, are adequately equipped and know the route. If the main group must be sent out while a few people remain with the victim, make sure the group stays together, has a competent leader and knows where to go. If people are going to remain at the scene of the accident for hours, or perhaps overnight, give everyone something to do in establishing camp or assisting with the victim.

An accident scenario

Let's run through the scenario that opened this section. The injured person is the party leader and she is in no condition to give orders. Someone else will have to take over. Since the rest of the group is standing around uncertainly, you decide to act. What do you do? What decisions must be made? First, take a deep breath and compose yourself.

- **Take stock of the situation.** Your group consists of eight people of mixed abilities, but no one besides the leader is very experienced. Your camp is four hours from the road and not on an established trail. No other campers are in the area. It is about 30 minutes downhill through forest from the scene of the accident to camp but at least an hour and a half for an uphill return with heavy packs. The temperature is -25° C (-13° F), wind calm, and you have a little over an hour of daylight left.
- **Assess the danger to the rest of the party.** Is the victim in a location that poses any danger to rescuers? No. She is on a forested slope which is safe from avalanches. The group can approach her.
- **Try to establish how serious the accident is.** You approach the victim and see immediately that she has at least a broken leg and perhaps other injuries. You now have a major problem and need a co-leader. You designate a reliable individual and ask him or her to collect clothing and insulation for the victim and to make sure that everyone, including you, bundles up for a long stop.
- **Do an initial examination of the victim in order to identify and treat injuries that are immediately life threatening.** Your first priority is to deal with any life threatening conditions such as absence of breathing or heartbeat, or heavy bleeding. Because the victim is lying in the snow and is already very cold, however, your next urgent priority is to get some insulation under and over her.

As you examine the victim, you are calm, confident and reassuring. You tell her that everything is under control and that she will be all right. This is extremely important because the victim of a wilderness accident almost always fears that the injury is serious and that rescue will be long and difficult, or come too late. Most victims also feel guilty for inconveniencing the party.

- **Deal with injuries that are serious.** Your examination indicates that a broken leg is probably the only major injury. You follow first aid procedures to stabilize the leg and move the victim onto the insulation available. Once she is settled and warm, you hold a group conference. You have some hard decisions to make. Since the victim is coherent, you include her in the conference.

- **Consider your alternatives for dealing with both the victim and the rest of the party.** Carrying the injured person to the camp will obviously take too long, given the lateness of the hour. Furthermore, it is extremely difficult and dangerous to move an injured person very far. You would need a lot of strong, experienced people to descend the steep slope to camp.

It is possible that people can get to camp and return in the dark with a tent, but your group contains inexperienced campers who are already cold and nervous. You decide to send as many people as you can spare to the camp with instructions to return in the morning with a tent, sleeping bags, stove and extra clothing. Your co-leader or another level-headed person goes with this group. The departing people leave whatever water and food they have with you. (Note: You may not have made the best decision, but you have made a reasonable one under the circumstances. Don't waste time wondering if you did the right thing.)

- **Ensure that you have shelter for the victim and whomever remains with her.** Two fit, strong people stay with you and immediately begin digging a snow cave. They work quickly because cold is now the greatest enemy. You move the victim in as soon as you have a large enough area cleared, then continue digging until there is room for everyone. You are short on ground insulation so you put some pine boughs on the floor of the cave. With all of you plus a candle inside, warmth should be no problem.
- **As soon as you can, conduct a thorough examination of the victim.** Once the victim is settled in the cave you conduct a more thorough examination. You take careful notes of her condition and record any pain medication given. Everyone helps to keep up her morale and she participates in the discussion of what to do the next day.
- **Build a fire if you can do so safely.** One of your companions wants to build a fire outside the cave. There is no harm in it so long as he does not become too chilled or exhausted in the process (it is often very difficult to build a fire in the snow). The fire may not do much to warm you but it will raise spirits (and would have provided hot drinks if you had had the foresight to pack a pot).
- **Decide how best to evacuate the victim.** Your next consideration is how to evacuate the victim. Since you are not in a wild part of the far north, helicopter or snowmobile rescue will probably be available and will certainly be easier on everyone than trying to haul out a makeshift sled. At first light, you will send your two fit companions out to the cars. They will take with them the following information **in writing**:

  a) Exact location of the victim, preferably with the route marked on a map. You expect a helicopter rescue and you know that a clear area is close at hand, so you decide to move the victim to that spot for pick up. You indicate this in your message.

b) Nature of injury, measures taken, age and condition of injured person.
c) Description of type of terrain in which rescue must be made and any conditions which might affect rescue.
d) Number in party, their experience and resources. Plans of party: who is remaining with victim, who is skiing out.
e) Name and address of victim and yourself. Contact person and phone number for victim.

- **Carry out your evacuation plan**. When the rest of the group arrives in the morning, you use their muscle to set up a camp by the helicopter landing site and transport the victim there. You keep one other person with you so that you will have company skiing out, and send the others back to the cars. While waiting, you stamp out a landing pad for the helicopter. Both you and the victim are in good shape when help arrives, and the rest of the party emerges without damage.

Note that this scenario assumes that everyone is carrying extra clothing even on a day trip. Many parties routinely take a sleeping bag, mattress and bivy bag in terrain and climate such as described here. Flashlights and shovels should be standard gear. A stove and pot would be useful in an emergency, although these are less frequently carried. The ability to dig a snow cave is life saving. Rescue depends on knowing the exact location of the victim. Take repeated compass bearings during the day so that you always know where you are.

OFF ROUTE, BENIGHTED, ILLNESS, BAD WEATHER, EQUIPMENT BREAKDOWN

These problems should not create emergencies for well-equipped parties. Panic is the worst enemy. Ensure that everyone is sheltered, warm and hydrated while waiting for help or working through the problem.

BUILDING A FIRE

In 25 years of touring in difficult terrain, I have never built a fire in an emergency situation. Since a lot of our trips are above tree line, where the material for fires does not exist, we have learned to do without. Even in areas where wood is plentiful, a fire is of limited benefit unless you can concentrate its heat with a lean-to or similar shelter.

There are occasions where a fire can save your life, however. If you fall into water and soak your clothing, you must know how to light a fire to get things dry. In any unplanned bivouac, a cheery fire can boost the group's morale.

How to build a fire in the snow

- Stamp out a pit so that your fire will not melt into the snow. If the snow is so deep that your pit does not reach to the ground, cover the bottom with green boughs.
- Collect dry dead twigs and small branches for kindling — these should break with a snap. You can also use larger branches by removing any damp outer part and feathering them with your knife. Hairy lichens hanging from dead branches and trunks also make good kindling.
- In a separate pile, place larger dead branches for your fire, sorted by size.
- See what material you have available in your pack. Paper is good, a candle or some fire starter paste even better.
- Place the fire starter paste, if available, in the pit. Place paper on top, then a pile of the thinnest, driest materials you have.
- Light the kindling with the matches or butane lighter you always carry. If it burns well, gradually add larger pieces of wood until the fire is well established.
- If the kindling flares briefly and goes out, collect a lot more of whatever burned best and try again.
- You can also put a candle stub under stubborn kindling until it dries and blazes.

Building a winter fire is like building an igloo — many people fail the first few times. Practice making them in all kinds of conditions so that in an emergency you can proceed with confidence.

Unfortunately, most of the heat of an outdoor fire dissipates uselessly. You need a fairly high wall behind you to capture the heat and reflect it back. A well built lean-to is quite warm, but few ski tourers carry the tools for cutting large branches or have enough practice to make a useful shelter. A tent can sometimes capture a bit of the heat, but make sure you don't set your tent ablaze. If an embankment is near, place the fire near it to take advantage of a natural wall. A metallic space blanket draped over branches or skis behind you can reflect heat.

One danger of cold weather fires must be mentioned. Cold snow is very dry — your clothing can be covered with it and no harm will come to you. Melt that snow with a fire and you now have wet clothing. Be sure to brush off before approaching the fire.

12. *Avalanches*

Anyone who plans to tour the back country in the mountains, even if only on day trips, should take an avalanche awareness course from a qualified instructor, read as much as possible on the subject, and gain their first touring experience in the company of people who know what they are doing. Above all, do not listen to those who claim to have ski toured for years without taking such precautions. The vast majority of people in the back country probably fall into this category, and every year some of them encounter the fatal consequences of their ignorance.

An avalanche is the most destructive force the winter traveller will meet in the mountains. A small slab only a few inches deep can bury you in a terrain trap. A major avalanche can wipe out an entire slope of mature timber.

Most back-country victims trigger the slide that engulfs them. Avalanches occur on the slopes most favoured by skiers and climbers: steep,

Aftermath of an avalanche. This photo, taken in July, shows the residue of a spring avalanche that demolished a youth hostel and crossed the summer access road. Note the trees which were caught in the slide and carried down to the valley bottom.

Balu Pass in Glacier National Park, British Columbia. A beautiful place to ski but also prime avalanche country.

open, with a glorious view of the surrounding country. You can be relatively safe in such terrain if you know what you are doing, although avalanche forecasting remains an inexact science. Ignorance can not only kill you but will also endanger those who must venture into an area that is clearly hazardous in order to rescue you.

CONDITIONS NECESSARY FOR AN AVALANCHE TO OCCUR

All that is needed is a steep enough slope and some snow. Many slopes that are fun to ski are potentially dangerous, but danger can lurk even among the trees on a hillside, or in a valley floor. People tend to associate avalanches with the high mountains of the west, but they occur in the eastern mountains as well. Fill a steep gulley in the prairies with enough snow and you have the potential for a dangerous slide.

Snow holds to a slope by bonding to itself and to the terrain beneath it. Prediction of avalanche hazard involves determining just how well the snow is bonded relative to the steepness and type of slope it is on. After snow falls to the ground, the snow crystals begin slowly to change shape. Depending on how they change, the crystals may increase their bonding ability or lose it altogether. Snow is affected by temperature, wind, moisture and the weight and depth of the snow pack. The angle and shape of the slope also affect stability, as does the ground surface (for example, snow is more likely to slide from a grassy slope than from one covered with thick trees). Learning to judge the stability of a slope means learning how these factors work individually and together to affect the snow pack.

AVALANCHE HAZARD TERMINOLOGY

In the United States and Canada, public avalanche warning programs are common in heavily used areas such as the national parks. Although the details may differ, the terminology is relatively standardized. The definitions, and what they should mean in terms of your decision, as a novice, to tour, are given below.

- ***Low avalanche hazard.*** **Mostly stable snow. Avalanches are unlikely except in isolated pockets on steep, snow-covered open slopes and gullies.**
- ***Moderate avalanche hazard.*** **Areas of unstable snow. Avalanches are possible on steep, snow-covered open slopes and gullies.**
- ***High avalanche hazard.*** **Mostly unstable snow. Avalanches are probable on steep, snow-covered open slopes and gullies.**
- ***Extreme avalanche hazard.*** **Widespread areas of unstable snow. Avalanches are certain on steep, snow-covered open slopes and gullies. Large destructive avalanches are possible.**

Since temperature, wind and snowfall cycles vary considerably from region to region, the nature of the snow pack also varies. Mike and I do most of our touring on the eastern slopes of the Canadian Rockies, an area of bitterly cold temperatures and moderate to light snowfall. The snow is quite dry until the spring melt. Conditions are right for the formation of depth hoar, a faceted snow crystal with poor bonding ability that forms when the air temperature is very cold. Since it's beneath the surface (often far beneath), you can't see it, but it can be a very unstable layer which causes many of the avalanches in this region. In warm, wet regions like the Cascades, depth hoar is almost unknown. There, the wetness and amount of new snow are the prime causes of avalanches.

Begin your study of avalanches in the area you plan to tour. Because the subject is complex, seek the information that will be of most benefit to you. When I take novices out in the Rockies in January, I talk a lot about depth hoar and very little about wet snow.

Snow pack analysis is covered in avalanche awareness courses and goes beyond the limits of this chapter. Even those of us who have training in it, however, rely as much as possible on official hazard forecasts where they are available. Avalanche stations keep a record of snowfall amounts, temperature, wind and condition of the pack over the entire season. They are in a far better position to assess hazard than the occasional visitor who arrives with no knowledge of how the pack developed and must rely on a visual inspection of the slopes and digging a snow pit or two.

When avalanche hazard is **low**, back-country travel is safe. Nevertheless, novices should exercise caution and avoid steep, open slopes and gullies. Slopes of around 25° provide both enjoyable skiing and relative safety.

Novices can enjoy the mountains by selecting terrain that is not likely to avalanche. These gentle slopes in the Tonquin Valley of Jasper National Park, Alberta, provide excellent day touring and scenery.

When avalanche hazard is **moderate**, back-country travellers should use caution. Until you have some training, stick to designated trails and check with a park official, if possible, to be sure your intended route is safe. Don't linger in avalanche paths or other terrain that is obviously hazardous (see below).

When avalanche hazard is **high**, back-country travel is not recommended. Novices should stay out of the back country until they have the training to find safe routes.

When avalanche hazard is **extreme**, back-country travel should be avoided. With such a forecast, Mike and I head for a local park with rolling hills.

Checking and heeding the avalanche forecast should be as automatic as fastening the seat belt in your car or wearing a life jacket in a boat. If no public warning system is in operation where you tour, and the area is mountainous, then you **must** have an experienced leader with you until you acquire the necessary skills to select safe routes and evaluate hazards on your own.

RECOGNITION OF HAZARDOUS TERRAIN

Steep slopes

The steeper the snow-covered slope the more likely it is to avalanche. Consider any angle over 25° as steep enough to be dangerous. Slopes over 55°, however, may be safe much of the time simply because they avalanche soon after each snowfall. You won't be skiing such slopes until you know what you are doing, but your route may lead you below them.

Open slopes

Steep open slopes are obvious sites for avalanches. Slopes that are convex are more likely to avalanche than concave slopes, but both can slide. Downhill ski areas devote a lot of money and expertise to ensuring that their runs on open slopes are safe. In the back country you must make that judgement yourself. Since there are many slopes with an angle of 25° or less (an angle that is safe in most conditions), confine your skiing to them until you learn how to evaluate a snow pack. Just make sure that there are not steeper angled slopes above, where an avalanche could start.

Lee slopes

When wind blows on a slope it picks up snow from that slope and deposits it someplace else. Slopes which lie on the lee side of a mountain tend to collect a lot of snow from the action of the wind. These slopes will be loaded more than slopes which face in other directions, and are potentially more dangerous. Unfortunately, they also tend to have good powder snow, making them attractive to skiers.

You can often recognize a lee slope because of a cornice at the top (although some lee slopes have no cornice). Even a relatively short slope under a cornice can produce a big enough slide to cause injury.

Gullies

Wind also deposits snow in gullies. Gullies concentrate the force of an avalanche into a narrow channel. Stay out of them unless you're certain of snow stability.

Steep-sided valleys

Steep-walled valleys are usually marked by numerous avalanche tracks in the trees. These are open areas where earlier avalanches have swept down, levelling and pushing the trees around like matchsticks.

If you are on a forested trail in a valley and suddenly come into the open, look up. If you are in a narrow valley, look up on both sides. If you see only trees above you, especially mature trees, you are probably in a small meadow. If you can see far up the slope on **either** side of the valley, you may be in an avalanche track. It may look like a nice sunny spot for lunch, but don't linger here. Avalanches tend to follow the same paths year after year. If the hazard forecast is moderate or low, and you always move quickly across such tracks, however, your chances of ever being hit by an avalanche are minimal.

When you are in a steep-sided valley, always look for avalanche tracks. Many popular trails have several slide areas on them. Don't venture ahead without assessing the danger. Look up at the open tracks and any other high areas you can see.

Little Yoho Valley in British Columbia. Avalanches have swept down from the open slopes above, cutting a series of tracks through the trees. The valley is quite wide, however, and the avalanche tracks can be easily avoided.

Ask yourself the following:

- Are there signs of recent avalanches?
- Have you seen or heard any avalanches today?
- Has it been snowing heavily for a few hours?
- Has a strong wind been blowing for hours?
- Has a hot sun been baking the slopes?
- Has it been raining?

Portal Creek Valley in Jasper National Park, Alberta. The slopes are not as steep as in the preceding photo, but there are numerous tracks through the trees where avalanches have occurred. The valley is too narrow to allow you to avoid all danger, and should not be skied in times of high avalanche hazard.

Many avalanche tracks can be seen from mountain highways. It's a good idea to use binoculars to check conditions on them as you are driving to the trail-head, especially those facing the same direction as slopes that you expect to encounter. Look for cornices and for signs of recent avalanches.

If you answer yes to any of the above, extreme caution is advised. It doesn't matter what the hazard forecast was, this may not be a safe place for a novice. If you answer no to all questions, and the hazard forecast was low or moderate, it is probably safe to proceed, but move quickly across the avalanche tracks.

Steep, treed slopes

Even in the trees you may encounter danger. Although mature timber is an indication that no slide has come through there in many years, there is no guarantee that one won't happen in the future. Since you normally can't see much in heavy forest, use your map or inspect the valley from afar before you enter. If the valley has steep sides, especially if they rise above tree line, you may be at risk in times of high or extreme hazard. Know what kind of a valley you are in and what is above you.

WHAT KIND OF TERRAIN IS SAFE?

- **Slopes of 25° or less, so long as they are not below steeper ones. For very wet snow, I would lower the safe maximum to 20°.**
- **Forested and clear areas in the centre of wide valleys, so long as the clear area is not the run-out zone from an avalanche track.**
- **Mature timber in general, except when avalanche hazard is high or extreme.**
- **Most designated trails in times of low or moderate hazard (these same trails may be quite dangerous when hazard is high).**
- **Ridges or hill tops (these may pose other problems, but at least there is nothing above you to avalanche).**

Recognition of other factors contributing to hazard

Events that should cause you to abandon a trip at once if the terrain is at all steep include:

- avalanches seen or heard in the vicinity while you are touring;
- areas of snow settling under your feet with a "whump";
- cracks developing under your feet and radiating away as you cross a slope (flee for your life if this happens!).

Events that increase risk over a period of hours:

- heavy snowfall;
- high winds;
- major warming or thaw, hot sun;
- rain.

If these events are in the weather forecast you should not begin a long day-tour or any backpacking trip through avalanche terrain. If they happen during a trip, try to get back to the trail-head as quickly as possible. If they happen while you are camped (for example, heavy snow falls all night) and you must pass through hazardous terrain to return to the trail-head, then you must make a judgement call.

Clearings in the trees

A further problem in the trees can arise from small, steep meadows or clearings. If they exceed 25° they could avalanche and slam you into a tree at the bottom. Try to cross such clearings high, or at the bottom of the slope rather than making turns through the middle.

TRAVELLING IN HAZARDOUS CONDITIONS

Let's assume you have ignored the advice given here and find yourself in dangerous terrain and conditions. You have two choices: stay where you are until conditions improve or get out as safely as possible. The easiest choice involves hot afternoon sun that is triggering slides. Once the sun sets, the temperature will probably drop below freezing and stabilize the slopes. Wait till morning and pass through the dangerous terrain early in the day.

Heavy snowfall poses a more difficult problem because you don't know how long the storm will last. It is usually better to get out as soon as possible. In this case, if avalanche activity has not yet started, I would be inclined to make a run for it. If slides are thundering down all around, however, especially over the route you must follow, a long bivouac in a safe place is preferable to the fate that awaits if you proceed.

Factors that should not enter into your decision to wait or proceed include having to be at work on Monday morning and possible embarrassment if you have overestimated the danger.

- **Above the slope. Always safest in terms of avalanche danger, but may not be possible because of cliffs, narrow ridges, or other terrain hazards.**
- **Below the slope but well out of the run-out zone. Some avalanches travel farther than you would expect, and some valleys are too narrow to allow you to avoid the run-out.**
- **Right at the bottom of the slope. In times of high or extreme hazard, however, self-triggered slides are possible, and you could be unlucky.**
- **Above the convex area. You may trigger a slide, but you will be above most of the avalanche.**

How you travel in dangerous conditions depends on where you are and the route choices available to you. If you are in a valley floor, try to stay well out from any avalanche slopes. If you must cross the bottom of a track or slope, do so one at a time in order to limit risk. Those who are waiting should stay in a safe location, watch the person who is crossing and shout a warning if a slide starts. Before crossing, determine your point of no return so you know in which direction to run. Once safe on the other side, turn around and watch the next person cross. Each person across waits for the one behind, while the rest continue slowly ahead. If the slope is too wide for single crossings, keep at least 50 metres (yards) between people and have everyone wait in a safe place on the other side (well into heavy timber or on or at the bottom end of a ridge).

If your trail or route brings you to the middle of a track or steep slope, try to find a way either above or below it. Sometimes you can take your skis off and walk straight down the side of the avalanche track or slope. You are less likely to trigger a slide in this way and you may be able to escape to the side if necessary. If the slope is convex, try to find

The slope on which the skiers are travelling is not steep enough to be dangerous. People are spaced close together. If they proceed into the steeper terrain ahead, they should travel widely spaced.

The slope is steep enough to slide. The cornice shows it to be a lee slope. Even though conditions were judged to be very stable that day, the skiers maintain a wide spacing so that some may escape being caught if an avalanche occurs. A decision to traverse such a slope should be made only by someone well trained in avalanche hazard evaluation.

a line above the convex part. That way, the major part of an avalanche will be below you. If you must cross in the middle, try to pick a descending line that takes advantage of any safer spots along the way. Again cross one at a time, moving quickly and making no turns. If it is a wide slope, then keep at least 100 or 150 metres (yards) between people.

CROSSING A STEEP OPEN SLOPE OR AVALANCHE TRACK

- **Always cross one at a time, or at widely spaced intervals.**
- **Never assume that because one person has crossed safely the danger is past. A slope can avalanche under the first person, the last, or anyone in between.**
- **The rule for spacing people at wide intervals is often ignored, even when specific instructions are given by a leader. If necessary, someone should control departures, not letting the next person go until the person in front is far enough ahead. Fast travellers who persist in catching up to slower people should be dispatched first.**
- **People standing around in a group tend to get involved in conversations and let their attention wander from the person who is crossing. Make sure at least one person is doing nothing but watching.**
- **Prepare to shed pack, skis and poles instantly in case you are caught in a slide. Undo the belt and chest strap of the pack. Remove pole straps from hands. Set alpine bindings for easy release. Loosen cable and three-pin bindings as much as possible. Most 50 mm bindings are very tight, as are some three-pin bindings. If avalanche danger is obviously high and your bindings simply will not release under a strong pull, you can loosen the laces on your boots so that you will come out of them (this is a desperate measure — you may survive the avalanche but will almost certainly suffer frostbite).**
- **Should you be buried under the snow you will need as much protection as possible. Put on your shell parka, zip it up and tighten the hood over your head. Put on mittens. Check that your avalanche transceiver is securely attached to you underneath your clothing.**

Let me emphasize once more: **you should not be in a situation which requires the above measures**. Once you are safely home, review the events that led to the danger and determine what errors in route-finding, planning and judgement were made.

IF YOU ARE CAUGHT IN AN AVALANCHE

Back-country beginners who recognize the limits of their expertise and proceed with appropriate caution are seldom caught in slides. The whole point of this chapter is to alert you to the types of situations that you are not yet prepared to deal with and to urge you to avoid them. Ironically, people who have training and confidence in their ability to assess hazard are more likely than novices to enter dangerous terrain and trigger avalanches. Nevertheless, you should rehearse in your mind what you would do if caught in a slide.

Procedures to follow in the event of an avalanche

- Shout a warning to your companions. They may be unaware of the danger. They will also be your rescuers and must watch what happens to you.
- Try to get out of the way. You can't outrun the avalanche by skiing straight downhill, but you may be able to head for the side or some form of shelter.
- If caught, get rid of your pack and ski poles, and kick off your skis. They will drag you down when what you must do is stay near the surface.
- Grab at anything that presents itself. If the force of the slide is not too great, you may be able to hang on to a tree or a rock.
- Try to tread water with your feet and paddle with your arms or make swimming motions to stay on the surface. Fight as hard as you can.
- If you pop to the surface, try to ride out the slide in a sitting position, with your feet together in front of you.
- If you slip under the snow, keep your mouth shut. Snow can fill your mouth and throat and suffocate you.
- As you slow down, try to do several things: fight your way to the surface, fight to get at least a hand to the surface, and try to create an air space in front of your face with the other arm or hand. Spit out any snow in your mouth.
- When you stop, make a last effort to clear a breathing space. If at least one arm is above the surface, dig as quickly as possible to try to free your head. The snow will harden almost instantly, after which you won't be able to move it.
- Don't be surprised if the whole thing is over before you have time to do any of the above, but these actions have saved lives and should always be tried.
- If you find yourself buried, relax. Struggling will use up oxygen. Shouting is useless unless your rescuers are right above you because sound does not travel through snow. If you start to lose consciousness, don't fight it. An unconscious person consumes less oxygen.

EQUIPMENT FOR TRAVEL IN AVALANCHE TERRAIN

The equipment you carry is no protection against avalanches. It won't make slides any less likely or any less powerful. The only thing worse than a back-country tourer without avalanche gear is one who thinks that having gear eliminates the need to exercise caution and common sense.

Avalanche gear is carried precisely for that moment when knowledge, caution and common sense have failed and someone is caught in a slide. Chances of survival are almost nil if the victim is not recovered quickly.

Mountain travellers today carry the gear discussed in Chapter Eight: avalanche transceivers, shovels, probes or ski pole probes, and a group first aid kit.

I consider transceivers and shovels so essential that any participant failing to bring them is barred from the trip. Your shovel and probe should be carried in such a way that they can be ready to use in an instant. You shouldn't have to unload most of your pack or untie a bunch of knots to get at them.

The transceiver can be worn around your neck or under your clothing, but never kept in a pack or in the pocket of a jacket that may be taken off during the day. Turn it on at the start of the trip and leave it on until you are settled in camp for the night. Turn it on again first thing in the morning. If you start out with the transceiver in your pack or turned off because the first part of the trail is safe, you quickly fall into a guessing game as the terrain gets steeper. Should we turn it on now or wait just a little longer? Why run the risk of waiting too long? The transceiver is built to run for hours or days at a time, and one set of AA batteries will usually last a whole season unless you are out every day.

Checking your transceiver

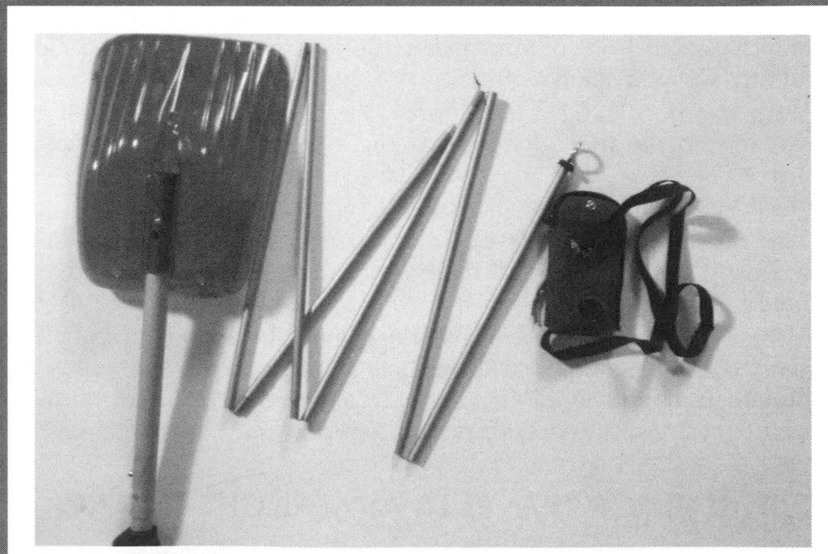

Equipment for travel in avalanche terrain: snow shovel, avalanche probe and transceiver.

Many transceivers have a device to indicate a weak battery. Check it every day, but do not depend on that alone. The transmitted signal should also be checked at the start of each day's tour. The best way to do this is for one person to put his or her transceiver on receive and stand some distance from the rest of the group, whose beacons are on transmit. The checker should be far enough away that the other transceivers cannot be heard. One by one the members of the party pass by the checker. Weak signals will become apparent from the fact that the weak transceiver must be brought much closer than the others before the signal is picked up. Replace the batteries and check again. Once the check is complete, everyone keeps the transceiver on transmit for the rest of the day.

HOW TO SEARCH WITH A TRANSCEIVER

Transceivers do not have a direction indicator. When you first pick up a signal, you have no idea where it is coming from. You can pinpoint the location of the signal, however, with a few quick manoeuvres. The technique given below should be practiced in fields, parking lots and other safe areas until you can consistently locate a buried transmitter in five minute or less. (Note: In a city, there is often too much electronic interference for transceiver practice.)

- While your back is turned, your partner buries a transceiver that is transmitting. Have your own beacon set to receive at the highest volume.
- Head quickly into the area while your partner serves as timekeeper.
- When you pick up the signal, mark the spot.
- Continue in a straight line until the signal is clearly decreasing.
- Return along your line to the point at which the signal is strongest.
- Now, turn the volume down until you can just hear the signal. **This is important.**
- Pick a line 90° from your original track; it doesn't matter which direction. Proceed in a straight line.
- If the signal fades, turn around immediately and go in the opposite direction. The signal should increase, then begin to fade.
- Again return to the point of strongest reception and **turn down the volume as low as possible**.
- Proceed at 90° from your last track, using increase or fading of signal to guide you.
- At the point of strongest reception on this third line you should be very close to the transmitter.
- Turn the volume to its lowest setting and hold the transceiver right at snow level.

- Continue the pattern of straight line searching at 90° angles with the transceiver at snow level. You should be able to pinpoint the exact location of the strongest signal and dig out the transmitter with your hands.

A common problem for beginners is forgetting to turn down the volume each time they locate the point on a line where the signal is strongest. The buried transmitter should be wrapped in plastic to protect it. Keep your own transceiver around your neck; In a real rescue you could be caught by a second avalanche and will want the beacon attached to you. The neck strap should be adjustable for length to facilitate this. When searching, try to keep the transceiver oriented in the same direction. If you wave it around you may get conflicting indications of signal strength. If you are using a visual receiver you must learn to distinguish sudden spikes signal from true increases in strength — the former will be brief, the latter steady.

RESCUE

Rescue may seem an advanced skill, beyond the needs of beginning tourers. In fact, anyone travelling in the mountains may encounter an avalanche, perhaps involving another party, or your own leader could be buried. It is important to know what to do.

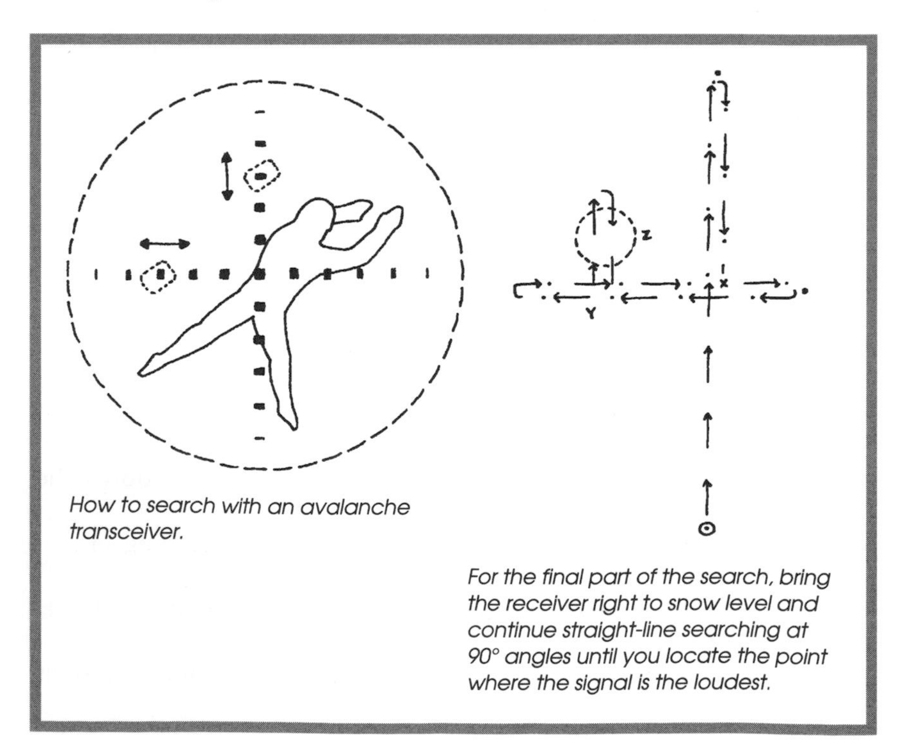

How to search with an avalanche transceiver.

For the final part of the search, bring the receiver right to snow level and continue straight-line searching at 90° angles until you locate the point where the signal is the loudest.

A person buried in an avalanche depends on the people already on the scene for rescue. There is no time to go for help. An effective search results from organization, not from everyone rushing madly onto the scene. Assuming you have followed proper procedures, only one person will be caught in the avalanche.

Procedures to follow in case of an avalanche.

1. Watch the victim. You will search downhill from the point where he or she disappears.
2. If you don't have a leader, designate one immediately. This should be the most knowledgeable person. The procedures they use may differ somewhat from the ones recommended here. If you are all about equal, the person most adept at leadership will usually take control. This is no time for a fight. Unless the person giving orders is clearly making grave errors, keep quiet and obey.
3. Check for avalanche danger. If the whole slope has slid from the top, it is probably safe now. If large amounts of snow are still in a position to come down, assign someone to keep watch and shout a warning. Establish the best lines of escape in case a second slide occurs, and make sure that everyone is aware of them.
4. Take off skis and ram them upright into the snow in a safe location. Avalanche debris is firm enough to walk on and almost impossible to ski. Also, if people must go for help later, you don't want to risk losing the skis. Most packs should also be left with the skis so that searchers can move more quickly.
5. Mark the point at which the victim disappeared, then do a quick surface search below that point. Pay particular attention to obstacles like trees or boulders that might have caught the victim. The victim may be partly on the surface. Pull at mittens, poles or skis to see if a hand or foot is attached. Victims have died because rescuers failed to use their eyes or made incorrect assumptions about objects on the surface.
6. Gather everyone together. Leader orders everyone to turn transceivers to receive at maximum volume and checks each person to make sure that they have done so. The only signal you want out there is the one from the victim. From this point on, no one talks but the leader.
7. Locate the signal. If you can hear the victim's signal from where the group is gathered, the most competent person should conduct the search, using the procedure already described. Otherwise, form people into a line with no more than 30 metres (yards) between searchers and no more than 15 metres (yards) from the side of the avalanche to the first searcher. Unless it is a truly massive avalanche on a wide slope, and you have no idea what part of the slope the victim was on when caught, you should be able to cover the prime search area with the people available (the technique for

one or two searchers is given below). It doesn't matter if you proceed up from the bottom of the slope, down from the point of disappearance, or across, so pick the one you can set up most quickly or with the best coverage.

- **There are two ways to proceed from this point**. The easiest to set up but hardest to control has the line move steadily forward, maintaining its alignment, until someone picks up the signal. That person then conducts the final search. It is difficult to keep the line straight, however, and there is a risk of missing the victim if people wander off course. Also, the signal may be masked by the noise of people tramping over the snow.
- **If the leader can control the group, the following procedure is faster and more foolproof:**

  a) Once the line is formed, leader asks anyone who can hear a signal to raise a hand. If one or two people respond, go to step ***d.***

  b) If no one responds, the leader orders line to move forward five metres (yards), maintaining the alignment. The line stops. The leader asks again if anyone can hear a signal.

  c) Keep moving forward in five metre (yard) increments until the signal is picked up.

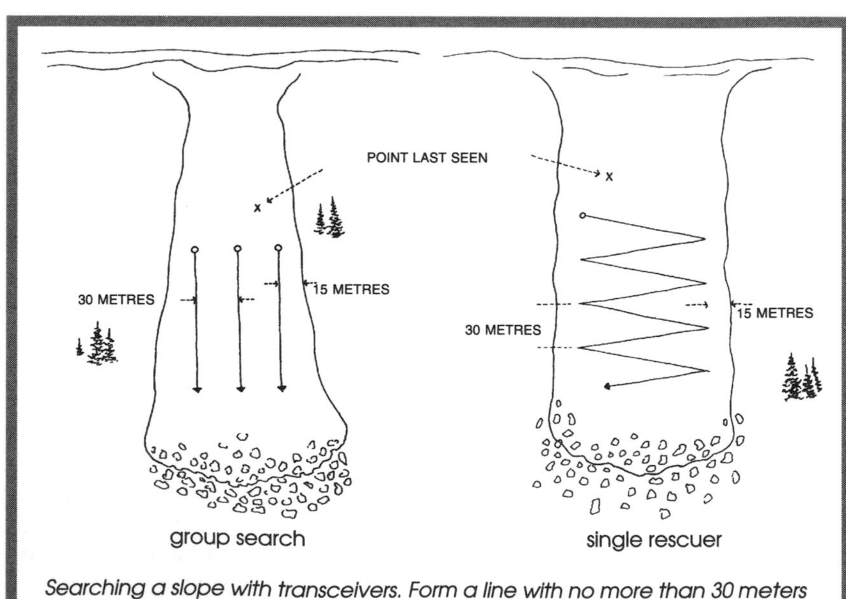

Searching a slope with transceivers. Form a line with no more than 30 meters between people and no more than 15 meters from the side of the avalanche to the first searcher. Because the signal travels in a circle from the victim's transmitter, it will initially be picked up by only one or two searchers. As the line moves closer, those receiving the strongest signal will be directly in line with the victim.

d) When the signal is first received, the leader orders the line to advance another five metres (yards). The leader then asks who hears a **strong** signal. The victim is probably located in a triangular area in front of those people. The leader orders searchers to turn volume down one step.

e) The line advances another five metres (yards). Transceiver volume is turned down one more step. The leader asks who has a strong signal. If the searchers are closely spaced, you may have to turn the volume down again until only two or three people hear it. By now the person(s) still receiving the signal should be very close to the victim.

f) Locate the victim. The person(s) receiving the strongest signal will conduct the final search. Everyone else should hurry to their packs to get shovels, probes and first aid equipment. The final search is done by the method you have practiced with your transceiver, utilizing straight lines at 90° angles to determine the point of greatest signal strength. Since the victim may be buried much deeper than a practice transceiver, the area of maximum signal strength may be fairly large. To avoid a major and time-consuming excavation, use the probes first to try to establish the exact location of the victim. Don't worry about harming the victim with the probes — fast recovery is more important. Once the victim is located, shovel with the help of all the adrenalin your system can produce. Every minute under the snow lessens the chances for survival. Exercise caution, however, when you get near the suspected area of the victim's face, so that you do not inflict serious injury with a shovel blade.

8. If there are multiple victims, follow the above procedure until you have the first victim pretty well located. Check to make sure that you are not receiving a strong double signal. Sometimes two victims end up in the same place. While some people complete the first rescue, the rest of the search line re-forms and continues to work the slope. Turn the first victim's transceiver to receive as soon as you uncover it.
9. If you are the lone rescuer, or if there are only two of you to search a large area, work the slide in a zigzag pattern, being careful to pass within 15 metres (yards) of every point on the slope.

   If the slide is not massive and you know the general area to search, no more than ten minutes should elapse between the avalanche and recovery of a victim buried at a shallow depth. Don't give up until you have searched the whole slope thoroughly, however. Victims have survived for hours or even days.

Treating an avalanche victim

Few scenes are more traumatic than the aftermath of an avalanche. The rescuers themselves may not be in very good shape after the frenzy of digging and the emotional stress of the search. Whoever will treat the victim should make a concerted effort to calm down and review mentally the steps that must be taken while the recovery is still in progress. Even if you are the least experienced member of the party and are just following orders, by remaining collected and alert you will be a valuable participant.

Uncover the victim's head as soon as possible. First priority must go to clearing the mouth and throat of snow and establishing a clear airway. Start mouth-to-mouth breathing at once if the victim is not breathing. Assume that there is a neck or spinal injury and take the necessary precautions (as indicated in Chapter Eleven, it is your responsibility to be properly trained in first aid and CPR).

As soon as possible, move the victim very gently to a firm surface. Hypothermia may be profound by now, so handle the victim accordingly (see Chapter Eleven). The question of whether to start CPR is difficult. The pulse in profound hypothermia may be almost undetectable. CPR is a rough procedure that could turn a slow but life-sustaining heartbe at into ventricular fibrillation. On the other hand, if the heart has stopped, you want to try to start it. Check very, very carefully for a pulse before starting CPR.

There may well be other injuries from the avalanche, so as soon as the victim is breathing, check for these and treat them. Remember that hypothermia and shock are probably present and frostbite will result quickly from carelessly splinted limbs.

Transport the person gently to the nearest safe place where shelter can be provided. Put up a tent or dig a snow cave and prevent any further heat loss from the victim. Keep careful notes of the patient's condition, any changes that occur and any treatment administered. The hospital will need this information.

Follow the emergency procedures described in Chapter Eleven. Make sure the rescuers are safe and warm. They will suffer an emotional let-down in any case, and if the victim is a friend or spouse, they may not look after themselves very well. Run through your options, which include: evacuating the victim, especially if he or she is able to walk (snow conditions permitting) or assist in the process; sending for help if there is time for the messengers to get out before dark; spending the night.

If you cannot locate the victim

When you have made a thorough search of the avalanche without success, it is time to bring in outside help. There is still a remote chance that the victim is alive, so send the two fastest people out while the rest of the group continues the search.

Those going for help should take the following information **in writing**:

1. Exact location of the slide, preferably with map reference and route marked on a map. The messengers should be prepared to guide the rescue party to the scene.
2. Time of the avalanche, size, type (slab, loose snow, etc. if you know), and general avalanche and travelling conditions in the area.
3. Name of victim, with contact phone number, if known.
4. People on scene: number, experience, equipment, plans, ability to spend night at location.
5. Leader's name and qualifications.

If you are the sole rescuer, do not abandon the search until you are certain that you cannot locate the signal, or until concern for your own safety forces you to leave.

Searching with avalanche probes

There is no excuse for venturing into avalanche terrain without a transceiver. Probe searches by small or even large parties are unlikely to find the victim in time unless you know almost exactly where to look. Work the area or areas of probable location in a close formation, probing at every step. If you don't find the victim and hope for live recovery has passed, send for reinforcements while the rest of the group continues the search.

13.
Map and Compass

TOPOGRAPHICAL MAPS

A map is a drawing that represents selected features of an area, such as highways, bus routes or mineral deposits. The type of map most used for back-country touring is a topographical map, which represents natural surface features (mountains, lakes, swamps, glaciers), some man-made objects, and also indicates the approximate elevation of everything shown.

One of your first tasks is learning to associate terrain features as you see them with their representation on a map. For features such as cabins, bridges, railway tracks, lakes or swamps, you need only learn the specific

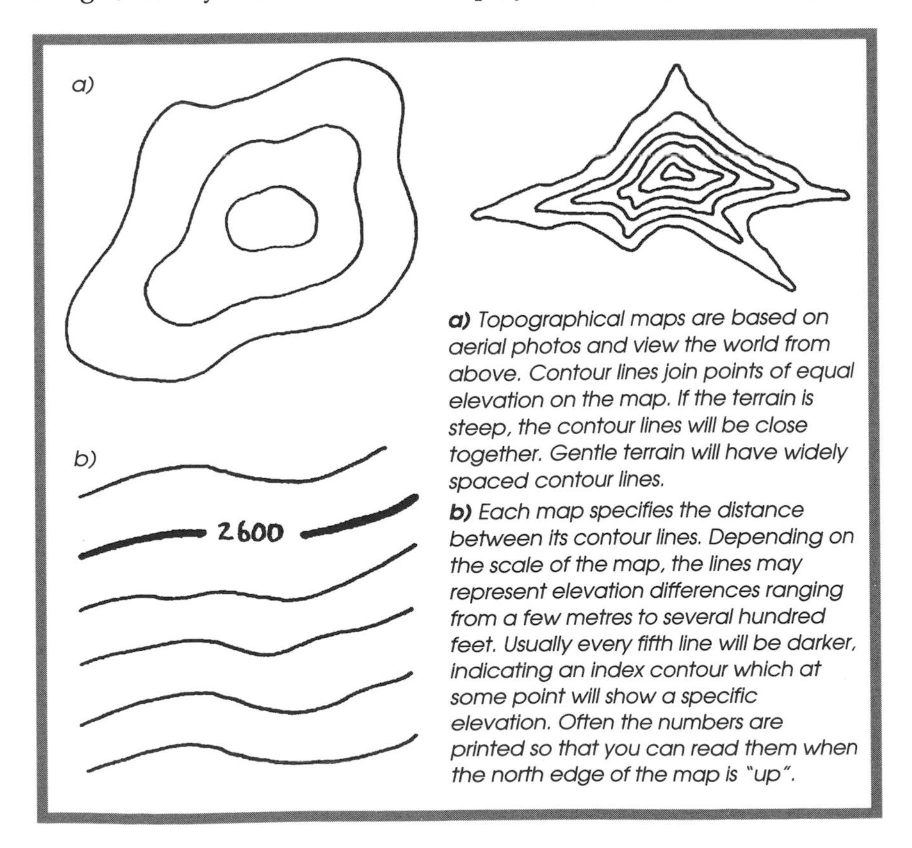

a) *Topographical maps are based on aerial photos and view the world from above. Contour lines join points of equal elevation on the map. If the terrain is steep, the contour lines will be close together. Gentle terrain will have widely spaced contour lines.*

b) *Each map specifies the distance between its contour lines. Depending on the scale of the map, the lines may represent elevation differences ranging from a few metres to several hundred feet. Usually every fifth line will be darker, indicating an index contour which at some point will show a specific elevation. Often the numbers are printed so that you can read them when the north edge of the map is "up".*

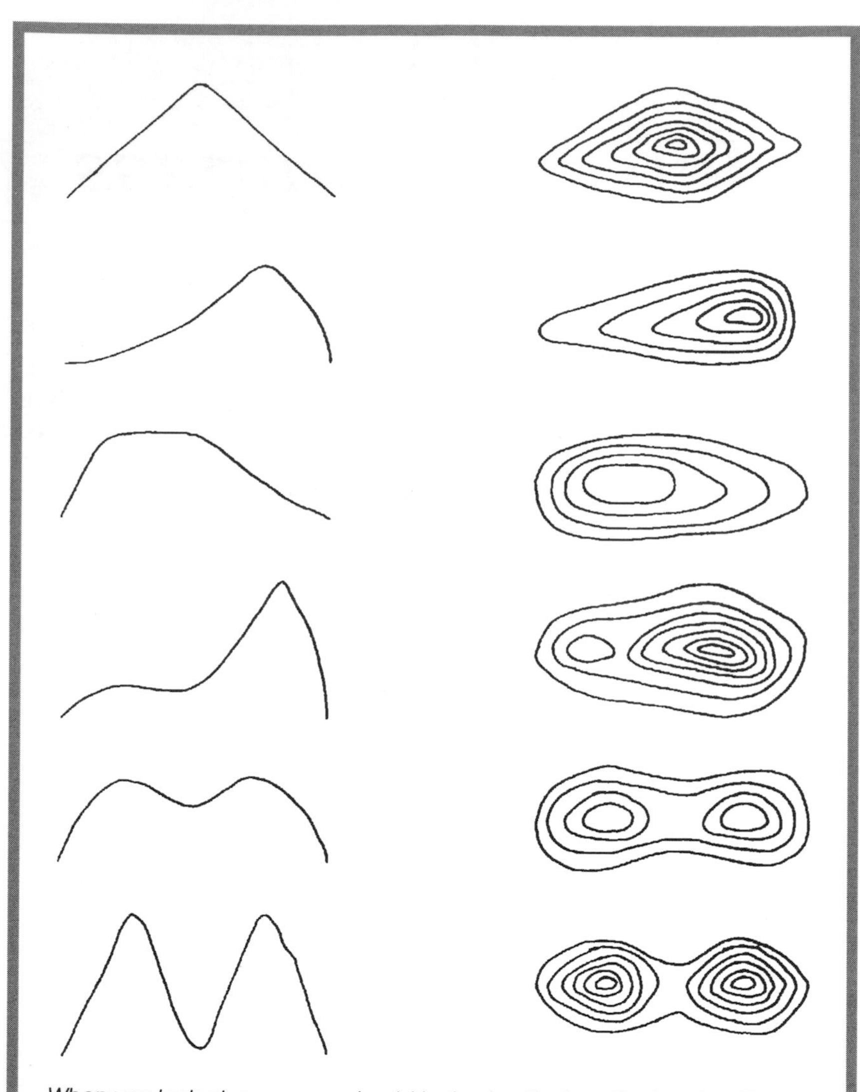

When you look at a map you should try to visualize how the terrain will actually look. This takes considerable practice, but what you already know about the terrain will help. Indeed, the best place to practice map reading is in an area you know well. Major features like mountains and lakes are easily identified. Remember that streams and rivers run in valleys, never along ridge tops. This drawing shows some important vertical terrain features are as they appear on a map and as they would look to the traveller.

symbols and conventions used to depict them. These symbols are standardized, so that once you learn them you can use any map. Thus water features such as lakes, rivers, glaciers and permanent snow fields are usually depicted in blue, although glaciers may be indicated in white. Man-made features such as trails or huts are black (occasionally red). Vegetation features, especially forests, are green. Vertical features are brown on land, blue on glaciers. A white background with brown lines indicates a non-forested slope, while with blue lines it indicates a glacier. Most maps also contain a key to the symbols used, in case you forget.

Map Scale

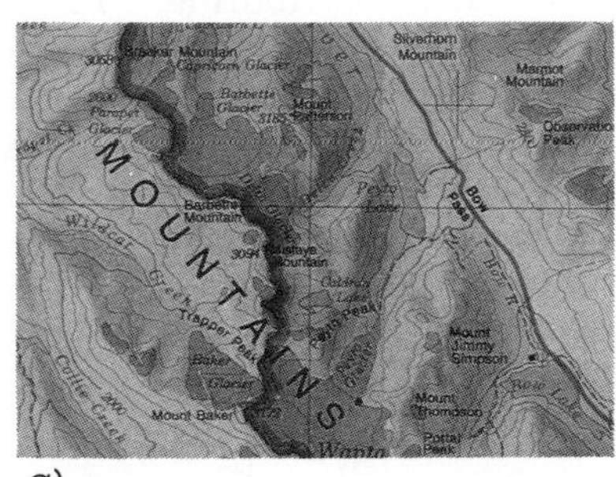

a)

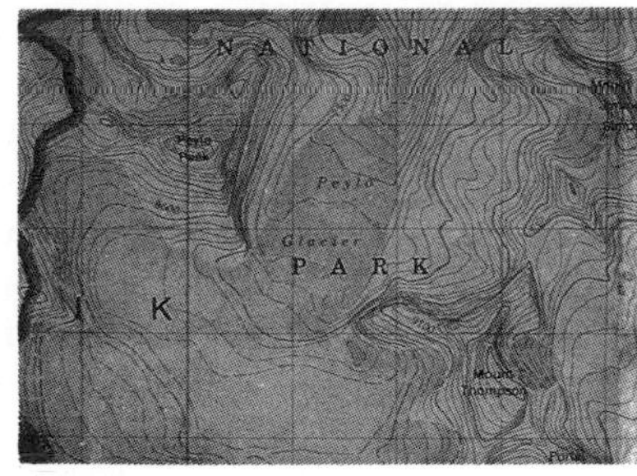

b)

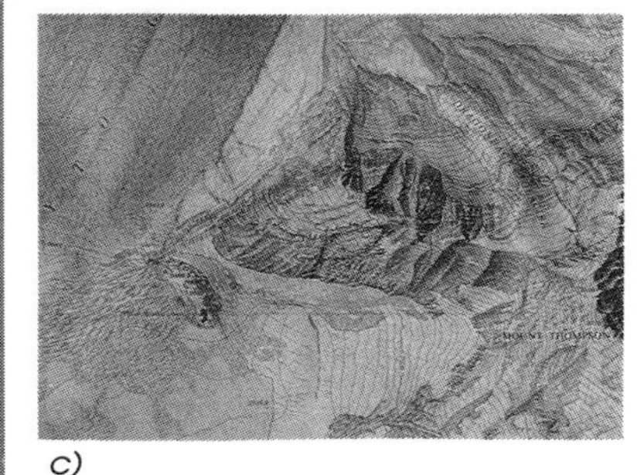

c)

a) *The Peyto Glacier area in Banff National Park shown in a scale of 1:200,000. Since the contour lines are 200 metres (650 feet) apart, it is impossible to tell much about the steepness of the terrain. The only clue that the glacier is accessible on foot is the hut symbol at the base of Mount Thompson. The entire Peyto Glacier is a small part of the approximately 30 km x 20 km (18.6 by 12.4 mile) area in the photo.*

b) *The Peyto Glacier shown in a scale of 1:50,000. The contour interval is 100 feet. Where the contour lines are close together, on Mount Thompson and Peyto Peak, the terrain is very steep, but the Peyto Glacier itself is relatively flat.*

c) *The Peyto Glacier shown in a scale of 1:10,000, with a contour interval of 10 metres (30 feet). Virtually every feature of the land is visible, including the crevassed parts of the glacier. You could ski from the letter "P" at the bottom left of this photo to the letter "A" at the top in a few minutes, or in the reverse direction, coming uphill, in about one hour. I have used this map in the hut to plot a safe course for whiteout navigation, but it is too big to unfurl out on the glacier, where I use the 1:50,000 instead.*

Topographical maps provide an accurate representation of terrain because they are drawn to scale. Horizontal distance is calculated from the map by taking any unit of measurement, such as an inch, and multiplying it by the scale of the map. On a 1:250,000 (read, one to two hundred fifty thousand) scale map, for example, one inch represents 250,000 inches, or about four miles. On a 1:50,000 map, one inch represents 50,000 inches, or eight tenths of a mile. Metric distances are easier to calculate since you need only move the decimal point: to convert centimetres to kilometres, move the decimal point five places to the left. On a 1:250,000 map, one centimetre would equal two and a half kilometres, while on a 1:50,000 map, it would represent half a kilometre.

Scale determines the detail as well as the amount of terrain that can usefully be portrayed on a map of a given size. For ski touring, a 1:24,000 map (the 7.5 minute series in the United States) gives enough information about the terrain to determine whether or not a route is skiable (as opposed to requiring technical climbing), and how susceptible the terrain is generally to avalanches. Because it covers a relatively small area (six by nine miles), however, you may need to carry several maps with you to show all of your route. The 1:50,000 scale, standard in Canada, and 1:62,500 in the U.S. do not show as much detail (for example, the 100-foot contour lines on Canadian maps can hide a 90-foot cliff band), but have a more manageable format.

Using a Map to plan your trip

Maps should be an integral part of your trip planning. They will show you the length of your proposed trip, the nature of the terrain, any elevation gain or loss, potential avalanche areas (for example, steep-sided narrow valleys), major landmarks that you can use for reference while travelling, probable areas of difficult travel and probable travelling time. If there is no trail, the map will help you plan the best route. If you know the prevailing wind direction in the area, you can identify probable lee slopes, which you will want to avoid. You can determine whether obstacles should be tackled head on or bypassed. You can plot a course to take advantage of contour lines, rather than gaining and losing elevation constantly.

To facilitate discussion of map locations you need to know about grid references. Many maps have grid lines that run south/north and west/east and divide the entire map into squares. Each line is numbered on the sides of the map. Each square is identified by the number of the line that forms its left side followed by the number of the line that forms its lower edge.

The scale on the map is 1:50,000, with contour lines every 100 feet (30 metres). On a map of this scale, each square has sides of 2 cm and represents one kilometre (.62 miles). Note first the general character of the terrain: mountainous, much of it above the tree line, with extensive glaciation. Elevation ranges from 5,300 feet on the Yoho Valley Trail (3409) to over 10,000 feet on the summit of the President (304051).

Let's assume that you want to go to the Alpine Club cabin (303082) from the Yoho Valley Trail, using the Little Yoho Valley Trail. How far will you ski, how much elevation will you gain and how steep is the trail? You will traverse four squares, so the distance is approximately four kilometres (2.5 miles). You cross fourteen contour lines, each higher than the last, so you will gain 1,400 feet (425 metres). Most of that elevation, however, (900 feet) is gained in squares 3308 and 3408, in just a little over a kilometre. The first part of the trip will involve fairly strenuous climbing, after which the trail becomes relatively flat.

How long will the trip take? Here you must consider the fitness of the party, the weight of their packs and the snow conditions (will you, for example, have to break trail?). If you are fit, not too overloaded and have a good track, figure six km (four miles) per hour on skis, plus one

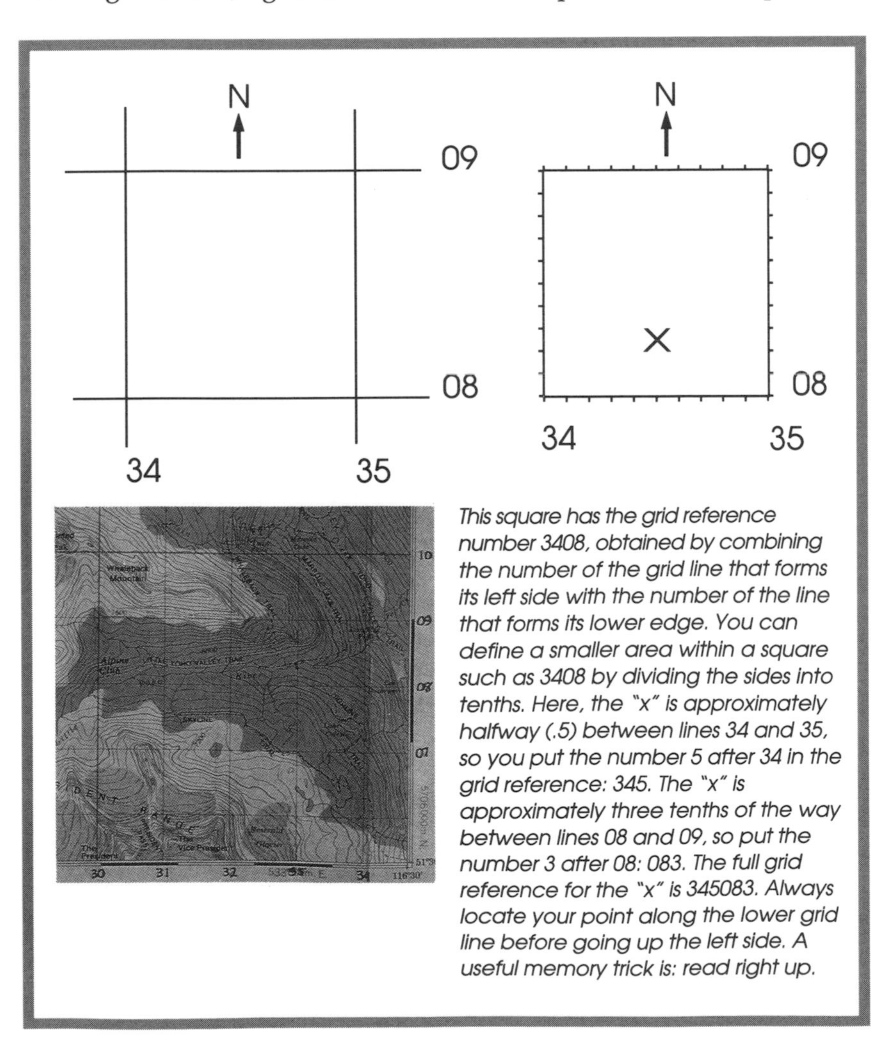

This square has the grid reference number 3408, obtained by combining the number of the grid line that forms its left side with the number of the line that forms its lower edge. You can define a smaller area within a square such as 3408 by dividing the sides into tenths. Here, the "x" is approximately halfway (.5) between lines 34 and 35, so you put the number 5 after 34 in the grid reference: 345. The "x" is approximately three tenths of the way between lines 08 and 09, so put the number 3 after 08: 083. The full grid reference for the "x" is 345083. Always locate your point along the lower grid line before going up the left side. A useful memory trick is: read right up.

hour for every 1,000 feet (300 metre) change in elevation, or six minutes for every 100 feet (30 metres). Unless everyone is a good skier, a party with heavy packs will not descend trails any faster than they go up them. Using the above rule, you should reach the cabin in about two hours. Until you know your party and the area, allow at least half that amount for extra time, making the total estimate three hours.

Is there any avalanche danger on this trail? The first part is up a forested slope that is well below the tree line. No danger likely here. Once in the Little Yoho Valley, you are surrounded by steep mountains that rise above the tree line. Obviously there will be avalanche hazard on these slopes, but the valley floor is very wide, and the trail runs through the middle of it. The trip to the cabin should be safe, but you will need to exercise great caution if you do any day touring in the area.

Using a map in the field

Once you learn to visualize terrain from the map, you can keep track of your general location simply by looking around you and noting major landmarks. This is easiest to do in the mountains, where the valleys typically have steep sides and few exit points, and higher summits are visible from a great distance. Even in relatively flat terrain, unless you are in dense forest, you can learn to observe the landscape carefully and relate it to the map. Turn around as you travel and note landmarks for the return trip. Most people prefer to orient the map so that the top always points north.

WORKING WITH A COMPASS

Precise navigation requires the use of a compass. As indicated in Chapter Eight, the most useful type of compass for ski touring is a Silva with a

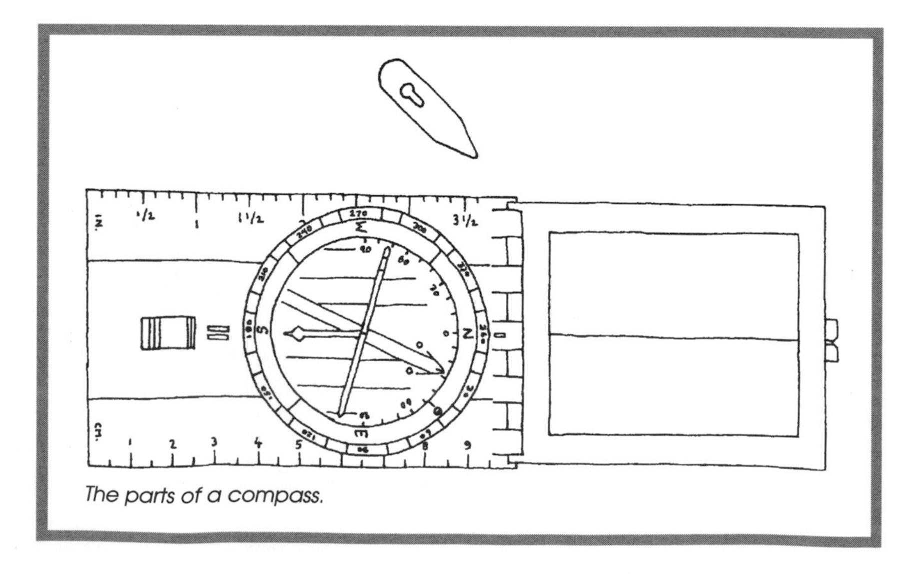

The parts of a compass.

large transparent base plate, floating magnetic needle, adjustable declination, mirror and, for the mountains, a clinometer.

Adjusting for declination and taking bearings

A compass will give you a true reading in only a small part of Canada and the United States. That is because the compass needle responds to

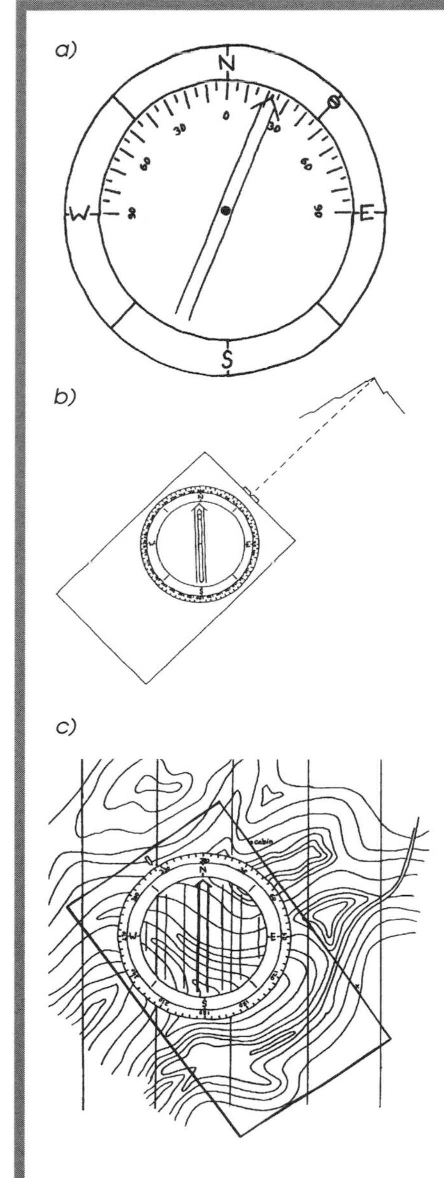

a) *Each map indicates the declination for the area it covers, as of the date the map was published, and indicates the amount of shift in magnetic north for each year. The declination for the centre of the map of Yoho National Park, which we used above, is 22°07' east as of 1979 (that means, Yoho is 22°07'* ***west*** *of magnetic north). The declination decreases annually by 5.35. Using the tool that comes with your compass, turn the declination screw in the housing until the orienting arrow in the base is 22° to the right (east) of zero.*

b) *To take a bearing from the landscape with your compass, face the object you are sighting and hold the compass steady and level in front of you with one hand, aiming it at the object. If you have a sighting notch in the mirrored lid, look at the object through this. With the other hand, adjust the mirror, if you have one, until you can see the dial in it, then rotate the housing to line up the orienting arrow with the north end of the magnetic needle. Now read the degree number at the index marker. This is the direction in which you must travel to reach the object.*

c) *To take a bearing from the map, set your compass on the map so that one edge of the base plate passes through or aligns with both your present location and the object you want to reach. Now rotate the housing until the lines on the transparent base align parallel to the north/south grid lines on the map.*

magnetic north, a slowly shifting point hundreds of miles south of the geographic North Pole. Most of North America lies either west or east of magnetic north. Maps, however, are drawn to true, geographic north. A compass which has adjustable declination can be set so that it compensates for the difference between true north (the direction indicated by the grid lines of the map) and magnetic north. If you fail to compensate for declination, you can wander far off course. A 15° error, for example, will cause you to be one quarter mile off for each mile you travel. Large parts of North America have a declination greater than 15°.

If you do not have a compass with adjustable declination, then you must add or subtract the declination each time you take a compass reading, or reset the compass after each reading. For example, if you are 22° **west** of magnetic north and your bearing reads 180°, you must **subtract** 22° from 180°. Either do the arithmetic in your head or reset the compass to 158°. If you always travel in this zone, you could also mark a spot on the base 22° east of the index mark line up the magnetic needle with this new mark. If you are in a part of the continent which is **east** of magnetic north, however, you must remember to **add** rather than subtract the declination. Obviously, it is much easier to work with a compass which is already adjusted for declination, especially when you are tired or facing an emergency.

Travelling by compass

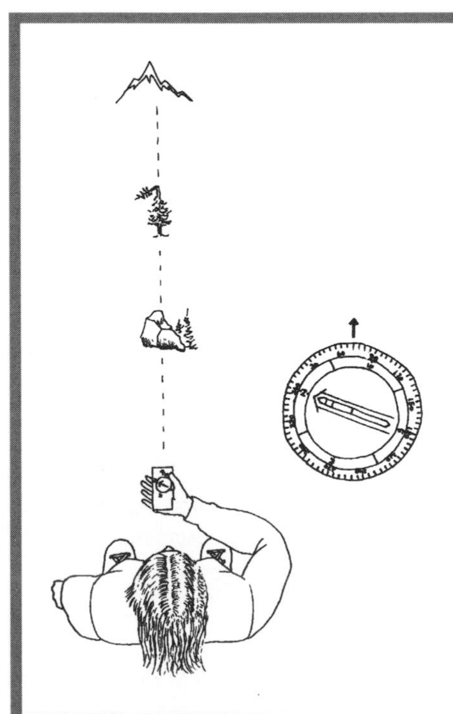

To travel on a bearing, rotate the housing until the bearing is set to the index marker. Now, hold the compass in your hand and turn your whole body until the orienting arrow aligns with the north end of the magnetic needle. As you move forward, keep this alignment. Since it is difficult to ski with your eyes glued to a compass, the normal procedure is to identify some landmark that lies in your direct line of travel and head for it. Once you reach that object, find another one that lies in the same line, and so on until you reach your destination.

Whiteout navigation

In a whiteout, without visible land features to take a bearing from, a member of the party must serve as a landmark to allow travel on a bearing. One person with a compass remains stationary while another person, on vocal directions or hand signals from the first, travels in the correct line for as long as he or she can be seen, then stops. This lead person then takes a bearing back towards the stationary person to counteract any error in the original compass reading. Once both compass users are satisfied that the lead person is on the correct bearing, the rest of the party moves up to the human landmark and the process is repeated. Whiteout navigation is time consuming but, if done carefully, will maintain an exact course.

In some types of terrain, you can use natural barriers as a guide for whiteout navigation. For example, I have ski toured many times to Mount Columbia on the Columbia Icefields. The normal approach is up the Athabasca Glacier through a narrow ramp in the middle of a large icefall that leads onto the icefields. From there it is several miles to the mountain, too far to conveniently mark the route with glacier wands (bamboo stakes left at regular intervals along a route). In a whiteout, you would have to be very precise in your navigation to find the small ramp on the return, and if you missed it, you could come to grief in the icefall. Fortunately, there is another exit from Mount Columbia: the wide, gentle Saskatchewan Glacier that is bounded on both sides by high mountains. Here you have a target that is more than a kilometre wide, and little chance of missing it if you are within 20° or 30° of the proper course because the mountains serve as a funnel. Knowing this, you can ski out fairly quickly, making only quick checks with the compass to ensure that you are not travelling in a circle.

Shortcuts to navigation

There are many tricks to travelling by compass. For example, if a small object is located near a prominent landmark such as a mountain or lake, it is best to aim for the landmark and from there find the small object. If you must find something which is not easily seen and which is located along a linear feature such as a valley or bottom of a cliff band, you can aim to arrive some distance to the right or left of the object so that you know which way to turn when you reach the linear feature.

People who regularly travel in featureless back country tend to become more expert with a compass than those who have prominent land features to guide them. Visually prominent features can also lead to careless navigation. I have been in several parties that went over the wrong pass simply because no one bothered to take a compass bearing. All of this can be innocent fun (I have seen some wonderful scenery while off route), but if you are caught by a whiteout or have an emergency, you had better know exactly where you are and how to reach safety. Back-country travellers should practice with map and compass at every opportunity and do some reading on route-finding as well.

HOW TO DETERMINE YOUR LOCATION WITH MAP AND COMPASS

If you are standing on a lakeshore or mountain top, you probably don't need a compass to know where you are (although it is not unknown for people to climb the wrong mountain!) While you are travelling, however, you should try to establish your exact location frequently. If you wander off course, you will have to use your map and compass to try to reorient yourself.

Triangulation

The method used for determining a location is triangulation. Take a bearing from two, or preferably three, recognizable landmarks and transfer those bearings to the map, drawing lines along each bearing until they intersect. Your location is where the lines meet. Let's see how this works. Suppose that you are in a valley with three major landmarks: Mount Ugly, Mount Hideous and Mount Fatigue.

Take a bearing on Mount Ugly. Leave the compass set on this bearing and place it on the map with one corner of the base on Mount Ugly. Now rotate the housing until the grid lines of the compass align with the north/south lines of the map (be sure to keep north and south straight).

Now take a bearing on Mount Hideous and transfer it to the map. The line from Mount Hideous will intersect the line from Mount Ugly at some point near your location. Finally, take a bearing on Mount Fatigue and transfer it to the map. It will cross the other lines and probably form a small triangle between the junctions. If all has gone well, you are within that triangle.

With the bearing set for Mount Ugly and the compass aligned with the grid lines on the map, draw a line from Mount Ugly along the edge of the compass base, extending the line if necessary to reach the area in which you think you are. You are located somewhere along or close to this line.

But maybe your triangulation shows you to be on the west side of a valley when you know that you are well up on the east side of it. What could have gone wrong? You may not have taken accurate bearings. Try again. The true summit of one or more of the peaks may be blocked from view by a lower but nearer summit. Recheck the map for that intervening summit. You may have misidentified one or more of the peaks (perhaps you took a bearing on Mount Insignificant). Again, check that you have correctly matched terrain with map. The peaks you selected may not be far enough apart. Ideally, there should be 90° between any two points from which you are taking a bearing. Select one or more other landmarks and take a bearing. The compass may be affected by magnetic forces in the environment or even your equipment. Remove all metal objects from the vicinity. Move to a different location. Perhaps you are north of the Arctic Circle. Compasses are notoriously unreliable there, and you may have to take repeated bearings. The map may be wrong (rarely with government issue maps). Finally, you may not be where you think you are. Assuming that you are not three days off course, and hence beyond the terrain covered by your maps, examine other valleys on your map or maps to see if you could have taken a wrong turn.

If you can recognize only one prominent object in the vicinity, then take a bearing on it and use whatever other information is available to determine your position on the line from that landmark. Perhaps you are near a stream or a gulley. Perhaps you are in the only large flat area in the valley. Perhaps you are at tree line.

Altimeters

One very useful tool for determining location is an altimeter. With an altimeter you can place yourself relative to the contour lines of the map. The combination of one compass bearing and one contour line is often sufficient to determine location. As well, in a whiteout it can often show how far you have travelled. Since the altimeter reads barometric pressure, and thus is sensitive to changes in the weather, you must remember to reset it every time you come to a point of known elevation, such as a lake, pass or summit. Try to triangulate the location of your campsite as accurately as possible so that you can start out each morning with the correct altimeter reading. In places of wildly fluctuating weather, however, the altimeter is of limited usefulness in navigation. On Baffin Island, we frequently witnessed changes of 150 metres in half an hour, corresponding to alternating blizzards and sunny breaks.

WHEN YOU DON'T KNOW WHERE YOU ARE

Being lost is a state of mind, akin to panic and just as deadly. If you can keep your wits about you, you will never be lost, only more or less confused as to where you are. Parties that stick together seldom come to serious harm no matter how badly they bungle their navigation. Someone in the group will retain the power to reason and suggest appropriate action. It is the lone individual who is most likely to press on blindly and minimize the chances for rescue or survival.

The first rule for the confused navigator is to stop and assess the situation. Mark where you are with something visible and try going off a short way in several directions to find the route, returning always to the starting point. If that fails, ask yourself where you went off course? When did you last know where you were? If you can return fairly quickly to a known point, do so, even if it means slogging up a miserable slope that you have just descended with difficulty. If you know your approximate location, but also know that a return to a previous known point will be long or hazardous, carry on cautiously and look for a landmark. If the hour is late or the party is exhausted, bivouac. Everyone will benefit from a good rest and your navigational skills will probably be sharper in the morning.

If you have a compass and a map or some idea of the area, you probably know what direction will eventually lead you to a main trail, highway or other avenue of salvation, no matter where you are. Unless the terrain is too hazardous or difficult, it is usually better for a group to try to get out on its own. If you decide you must wait for rescue, make yourself as conspicuous as possible. Snow caves make wonderful bivouacs, but a rescue party can pass within a few feet of you without either of you being aware of the other's presence. Place visible markers around the cave for ground rescuers and try to devise a signal that can be seen from the air. If possible, move your bivouac to an open location. Keep a fire going. Shout and whistle from time to time.

A confused party of one must be especially cautious. Even when you have won the mental battle against fear, any move you make is inherently more hazardous than it would be for a group. Don't attempt to get out over dangerous terrain. By staying warm, dry and conspicuous in one place, you increase your chances of being found and of suffering no more than embarrassment.

Conclusion

One midnight in May, a few years ago, I stood with two other women atop a previously unclimbed mountain on Baffin Island, well north of the Arctic Circle. On all sides lay a primeval world of ice and rock, scoured by wind and bathed red in the glow of an alien sun scuttling along the horizon. We had skied many hours from our tent, were further still from base camp and our companions, while more than forty trackless, blizzard-swept miles separated us from the nearest Inuit settlement. It was the bleakest place that I have ever seen, yet even as we fought to keep our balance against the gale, I knew that the moment was precious and unforgettable.

Expeditions to the Arctic lie at the outer extreme of winter camping and touring. The objective dangers, physical hardship and unrelenting loneliness demand rigorous preparation and training. Even so, the northern part of our continent is one of the few truly wild places left on earth, and in spite of the challenge it presents, it remains accessible to ordinary mortals who are willing to make the effort. Indeed, the satisfaction of travelling in such a wilderness is as great for me as the conquest of Himalayan summits is for the best climbers.

Most winter camping is carried out in gentler regions. If it weren't, there would be few enthusiasts. For the most part, snow camping is a logical extension of summer backpacking. The winter environment enhances the feeling of comradeship among party members as you work together to make your trip successful. Summer backpacking shows you part of the natural cycle of the wilderness while winter camping offers a way to enjoy nature in all seasons. As in summer, you alone decide if you want your tour to provide a challenge or simply be a relaxing escape from the daily grind.

If you live where snow falls, you probably won't have to travel far to find a place where you can put up your tent and begin to explore the winter world. The best place for your first trips is in terrain you already know from summer hikes. Contact whatever organization has jurisdiction over the area to learn what facilities are available and what regulations apply. Often, there are differences between winter and summer.

As you assemble the required equipment, don't forget to pack your sense of humour. Almost inevitably, some things will go wrong on a trip no matter how well you plan and prepare. If human beings and the natural world were entirely predictable, there would be little point in leaving the comforts of home in order to carry a ridiculously heavy pack to a remote snowbank just to set up housekeeping. The tales of experienced backpackers and mountaineers feature more mishaps than heroism. Indeed, many of the anecdotes in this book arose from my own foibles and those of my friends. So when you get to the campsite and discover that you left the tent poles in the car, remember that trips where everything goes right don't make very good storytelling. Training, planning, preparation and common sense can help you keep problems to a manageable level, but they don't guarantee a perfectly smooth journey.

As you gain experience, you may want to tour outside your local area. Where do you get the information you need to plan such trips? No comprehensive guide to ski touring exists for North America as a whole, and although regional guides have been written for many areas, they tend to be marketed in the regions they apply to, rather than nationally or continent-wide.

In Canada, the Alpine Club of Canada and Parks Canada (the national parks service) can direct you to sources of information on all parts of the country. The Alpine Club of Canada operates a number of huts in the mountain regions and has local sections across the country. Both the main club and its sections organize winter camping and ski trips. In the United States, the Forest Service and the administrations of the various parks are good sources of information. Major outdoor clubs include: the Adirondack and Appalachian Mountain Clubs in the east, the Mountaineers in the northwest and the Sierra Club (international in terms of conservation but more limited in terms of organized trips).

Useful information can be obtained from articles written by people who have done interesting tours. Consult current and back issues of major backpacking, skiing and climbing magazines, as well as journals of clubs such as the Alpine Club of Canada. Many magazines have an occasional article on ski touring: *Canadian Geographic* recently ran an account of a ski traverse of Ellesmere Island, and *Arizona Highways* carried an article on a ski tour and traverse of the Grand Canyon. Most books on winter outdoor skills and ski touring include helpful bibliographies. Finally, don't be afraid to get on the phone and speak directly to people who publish in the field of outdoor winter recreation or who are recognized experts. Most of them are more than willing to offer advice and information.

I couldn't begin to list all of the great and good winter camping areas in North America. To even try would be unfair to the many places that would be omitted. I have my own list of favourites, of course, but it is heavily weighted towards glaciated mountains and the Arctic, terrain which may not appeal to everybody. Besides, my list changes every time I explore a new region. Winter touring is, in any event, whatever **you** want it to be. The best advice I can offer is, go and explore! With knowledge, good judgement and a sense of adventure, you will soon discover your own favourite destinations.

Index

A

B

C

D

E • F

G • H

I • K • L

M • N

O • P • Q

R • S

T • U

V • W

Y • Z

Recommended Readings

Armstrong, B., and K. William. *The Avalanche Book*, Fulcrum, Inc., Golden, CO, 1986.

Daffern, Tony. *Avalanche Safety for Skiers and Climbers*, Rocky Mountain Books, Calgary, AB, 1983.

Fredston, Jill A. & Doug Fesler. *Snow Sense, A Guide to Evaluating Snow*, Alaska Mountain Safety Center, Anchorage, Alaska, 1988.

Perla, R.I. and M. Martinelli, Jr. *Avalanche Handbook*, Revised Ed. U.S. Department of Agriculture Handbook 489, U.S. Government Printing Office, Washington, D.C., 1978.

Dunn, John M. *Winterwise A Backpakcker's Guide*, The Adirondack Mountain Club, Inc., Lake George, NY, 1988.

Maning, Harvey. *Backpacking One Step at a Time*, New updated edition, Recreational Equipment, Inc., Seattle, 1986.

Peters, Ed (ed). *Mountaineering: The Freedom of the Hills*, Fourth Edition,The Mountaineers, Seattle, 1982.

Randall, Glenn. *Cold Comfort: Keeping warm in the Out-doors*, Nick Lyons Books, New York, 1987.

Watters, Ron. *Ski Camping*, Douglas & McIntyre Ltd., Vancouver, 1979.

Wilkerson, James A. (ed), Cameron C. Bangs and John S. Hayward. *Hypothermia, Frostbite and other Cold Injuries*, The Mountaineers, Seattle, WA, 1986.

Tejada-Flores, Lito. *Backcountry Skiing*, Sierra Club Books, San Francisco, 1981.

Osgood, William and Leslie Hurley. *The Showshoe Book*, Third Edition, Stephen Greene Press, Lexington, MA, 1983.

Prater, Gene. Snow-Shoeing, Third Edition, The Mountaineers, Seattle, WA, 1988.

ABOUT THE AUTHOR

When her academic career led her to Edmonton and the Canadian Rockies in 1966, Jo Ann Creore's idea of wilderness exploration was to drive her car through a national park; she had never backpacked or skied and was afraid of heights. Nevertheless, a friend persuaded her to take a climbing course from the Alpine Club of Canada and thus kindled a love for the mountains and outdoor adventure that has never flagged. Since then, Jo Ann has climbed three of the highest peaks in the Western Hemisphere — Mounts McKinley, Logan and Huascaran; made two ski touring expeditions to Baffin Island, climbed in Nepal and climbed and ski toured extensively in Europe. The mountains of western Canada and the Arctic remain her favourite areas, however, where she and her husband, Mike Sweet, spend every spare moment and most holidays. She has taught courses in winter camping, mountaineering and CPR for the Edmonton Section of the Alpine Club of Canada and served as an amateur climbing leader and camp manager at General Mountaineering Camps of the Alpine Club of Canada. She is also a member of the Canadian Wildlife Federation. After 26 years as a professor at the University of Alberta (10 as Chair of the Department of Romance Languages), Jo Ann is now devoting her full time to a second career as a writer and photographer.